One Year

Devotional
Prayer Book

One Year

Devotional Prayer Book

THOMAS NELSON
Since 1798

NASHVILLE   DALLAS   MEXICO CITY   RIO DE JANEIRO   BEIJING

Published in Nashville, Tennessee, by Thomas Nelson. Thomas Nelson is a registered trademark of Thomas Nelson, Inc.

Thomas Nelson, Inc. titles may be purchased in bulk for educational, business, fundraising, or sales promotional use. For information, please email NelsonMinistryServices@ThomasNelson.com.

All Scripture references are from THE NEW KING JAMES VERSION® (NKJV) © 1982 Thomas Nelson, Inc. Used by permission. All rights reserved.

Cover and interior designed by Kristy Morell, Smyrna, TN.

ISBN-13: 978-1-4041-8955-3

ISBN-13: 978-1-4041-1418-0

Printed in China

Introduction

I was thrilled when Jack Countryman of Thomas Nelson Publishers contacted me about doing this project. It so compliments two of my greatest passions—prayer and devotions. In today's culture it is necessary that we set aside a time during our busy schedules to spend valuable time alone with God. Sometimes we allow our daily activities to interfere with what should be our most important time of the day.

I pray this beautiful devotional prayer book will be an important resource for each of us. To some, it will be a starting point in their daily time with the Lord. To others, it will be a challenge to refocus these disciplines that should be the most relevant things done on any given day.

I have chosen men of God to join me each week to encourage the importance of prayer and devotions. Some writer's names you will recognize and some you may not. Rest assured, these are men who love God, who practice what they preach, and who are serving Him with all their hearts.

I trust the Lord Jesus will use this devotional prayer book to minister to you and to those with whom you wish to share its contents.

Johnny M. Hunt

Dr. Johnny M. Hunt
President, Southern Baptist Convention

Contents

One Year

Devotional
Prayer Book

Week 1, Monday

My dear heavenly Father, it is my desire to be a man of integrity. Realizing that I am what I am by the grace of God, please so work in my heart this day that the tongue in my mouth and the tongue in my shoe are going in the same direction. I realize that if I am to affect others for Your cause, You will have to do it through me. I surrender to Your control now and ask You to be in me, no longer me but You. Resurrection power, fill me this hour, Jesus be Jesus in me. In Jesus' name, Amen.

"Blessed are the undefiled in the way, who walk in the law of the LORD!"
PSALM 119:1

The Bible does not call us to be sinless, but it does call for blamelessness. The word *undefiled* speaks of those who are blameless, referring to integrity. Integrity is the opposite of duplicity and hypocrisy, which is the pretense to be something we are not. The most difficult life to attempt to live is the one you are not. Yet the most blessed and least difficult to live is the life you have been given; be who you are! Job was a man in the early writings of the Bible who was described as blameless (Job 1:1). His life was described as one who walked in consistency in every area of his life. *Blameless* means to be complete, whole, and truthful. When Jesus cried, "It is finished!" (John 19:30), He used the Greek word *Teleios,* which later His half brother James used in James 1:4. Remember, He has not called us to a life of sinless perfection, but rather to a lifestyle that is growing and conforming to His Word. The person who desires to be blameless will indeed be a blessed person. Happiness will be the overflow of His joy. He always weds happiness to holiness.

EVENING

My Father, as this day comes to a close, anything good that has been imparted through my life is simply a gift from You through me for Your greater glory. I am grateful that You answer prayer and that You have chosen to work through Your servants. Please help me to be consistent in the area of a blameless life, and please keep me close and clean. Your presence has been real and affirming today, and for that I am grateful. May even the thoughts and dreams of this night be Christ-centered and wake me to a new day of service that will know even greater opportunities of making You known. In Jesus' name, Amen.

Lord, as I begin this new day, thank You for the gift of a good night's sleep as well as the opportunity of a new day. I want to simply say that I love You this morning and I praise You for the way You love me unconditionally. Help me to love You more today than yesterday, and even more than ever before. May my heart be fully focused on You today and may I love as a fully devoted follower that unashamedly bears Your witness. In Jesus' name, Amen.

"Blessed are those who keep His testimonies, who seek Him with the whole heart!"
PSALM 119:2

How many of us know that a divided heart will kill a relationship? Half-hearted Christianity has done its share of damage to the church as it pertains to meeting the needs of a lost and dying world. When Jesus was asked to declare the greatest commandment in the Word of God, He gave us Matthew 22:37, 38: "Jesus said to him, '"You shall love the LORD your God with *all* your heart, with all your soul, and with all your mind." This is the first and great commandment.'" To the believer, nothing is more important than loving Jesus with all your heart. How each of us needs an undivided heart that is guarded by the testimonies of our Lord, meaning the things that God witnesses. A whole-hearted commitment to the Lord and His Word will put our lives together.

Psalm 127:1 says, "Unless the LORD builds the house, they labor in vain who build it; unless the LORD guards the city, the watchman stays awake in vain."

Listen to the truth of Jeremiah 24:7: "Then I will give them a heart to know Me, that I am the LORD; and they shall be My people, and I will be their God, for they shall return to Me with their whole heart."

EVENING

Lord, it is clear to me that I often allow my heart to be divided in its loyalties. Please keep me focused and fully devoted in heart to the lordship of Jesus Christ. I realize that if I am to love others, I must first love You supremely. Goodnight, Jesus—I love You. In Jesus' name, Amen.

Lord, may my heart be desperate for a deeper, loving relationship with You. Oh God, help me to never take You for granted, and may I never place my ultimate dependence on anyone but You. Thank You for Your forbearance with me when I allow my mind to drift to all of the "what-ifs." Please draw me close to You and never let me go. I desire to finish well and to live in such a way that You will be glorified in and, yes, through my life. Jesus, I crown You King of my heart this morning. In Jesus' name, Amen.

"How can a young man cleanse his way? By taking heed according to Your word. With my whole heart I have sought You; oh, let me not wander from Your commandments!"
PSALM 119:9, 10

The Bible often mentions the need to consider and reconsider the great need of moral purity. I have often said that this is probably one of the greatest qualities and characteristics in the Christian life in the 21st century. When Paul was preparing his young mentee, Timothy, for spiritual fortification in order to lead the church of Ephesus following his approaching death, he called Timothy to this priority in his private life in 2 Timothy 2:22: "Flee also youthful lusts; but pursue righteousness, faith, love, peace with those who call on the Lord out of a pure heart." The psalmist knew as well as the apostle Paul that it takes obedience to God's Word to keep his moral life clean before the Lord. I have prayed for years that the Lord would keep me *close* and *clean.* It is in my closeness to Jesus and in obedience to His Word that my purity becomes a reality. It is my prayer, as with the psalmist, that I not wander from His Word. And once again, the secret lies in being whole-hearted.

EVENING

Lord, I am reminded that it is not my promises to You, but Your promises to me that make the difference in my life. Lord, help me to live my life with eternity in view. May I forever be reminded of the judgment seat of Christ and be inspired to live a life that will receive Your approval. May I do now that which I will be grateful for then. In Jesus' name, Amen.

Lord, I desire to be taught by You today that I may know and obey. Too often I seem to be a hearer but not a doer. Please work in my heart that I would be overwhelmed with delight in doing Your will. Thank You for the privilege of serving You, and most of all for the unbelievable opportunity of knowing You. Please choose to use me today to be one that would decrease in living out my desires and increase in living out Your life. In Jesus' name, Amen.

"Teach me, O Lord, the way of Your statutes, and I shall keep it to the end."
PSALM 119:33

There are three words you find over and over again in the psalms: *knowledge, understanding,* and *wisdom. Knowledge* is that which is gained by our education and what we are taught. *Understanding* speaks more of discerning, which enables us to see the sense in what we have been taught. We need inner illumination to discover what the teaching means to our lives. What we learn with our minds and apprehend with our hearts must motivate the will to do what God commands. *Wisdom,* on the other hand, is a gift from God. The apostle James referred to wisdom as coming from above (James 3:17). The psalmist made it clear that he desired to know God's will in order to do God's will. He was both teachable and had a desire to learn. We hear both a tone of humility and dependence come through. He was not filled with just intellectual curiosity but also a desire to comprehend God's truth in order to use this truth in a life of obedience to God. He sensed the truth of the hymn, "Trust and Obey," for there's no other way to be happy in Jesus. May this be our desire today.

EVENING

Dear Lord, may the words of this text and the words of this hymn be the desire of my heart until I see You face to face. Help me to read Your Word with the thoughts of learning in order to obey. Help me not to be a hearer only, but also a doer of Your truth. Remind me often that it is not the truth I know but the truth I obey that makes the difference in my walk with You. Thank You for Your dear Word. In Jesus' name, Amen.

Lord, there are times I feel useless, yet I am trying to learn to always hope in Your Word. Even as the psalmist sensed his need for a new beginning, my heart so identifies with his. Would You please reach down this morning and grant me a fresh start at the start of this new day? Please stabilize my faith, and may I find my purest delight in You. Give me the desires of my heart that are in keeping with Your perfect will. Thank You that You are my hope. In Jesus' name, Amen.

"For I have become like a wineskin in smoke, yet I do not forget Your statutes."
PSALM 119:83

Have you ever felt that you were losing, or had lost, whatever influence you have known in this life? The psalmist felt that everyone and everything was working against him. It is as though he was reminding himself that the only thing worth holding on to was that which he must never forget: "I do not forget Your statues." Charles Spurgeon once said, "Never question in the dark what God showed you in the light." It really is true that we learn far more in the valleys than on the mountaintops; however, thank God for the mountains. Have you ever felt like a "wineskin in smoke"? The psalmist was referring to containers used for water, wine, and milk that were made out of animal skins. These containers, due to smoke and fire, often dried up and shriveled. As a result, they became useless. Talk about a dry spell—the psalmist felt parched in his spiritual life! His request was for a word from God that he believed had the power and potential to bring transforming power to his life. Today, maybe this is your need. Ask Him to revive you as His servant.

EVENING

My heavenly Father, I cannot count the times that I have felt useless. As I study Your Word, I am made aware that I am not alone. Help me to learn the lessons of those who have gone before me, and help me to leave a faithful trail that would speak of Your faithfulness to the next generations. Lord, when I feel that I do not have the strength to come to You, please come to where I am and breathe Your transforming breath into me. You are my only hope to stand in this world with all of its distractions and temptations. I look to You alone now. In Jesus' name, Amen.

MORNING

My dear heavenly Father, help me to walk in Your path today. Remind me of the joy that has always been mine when I have chosen to follow You. Let me never forget the heartache, pain, and disillusionment that come from my disobedience. Thank You for Your patience and love for me. Lord, I praise You that Your mercies are new with each new day. I am reminded this morning of Your promise that if I will delight myself in You, You will give me the desires of my heart (Ps. 37:4, 5). With a thankful heart, I love and praise You for who You are. In Jesus' name, Amen.

"Make me walk in the path of Your commandments, for I delight in it."
PSALM 119:35

There are some scriptures in the Bible that seem to be paradoxical. Why would someone ask the Lord to make him do what he delights in? The psalmist knew all too well that the Christian life is not a playground but a battlefield. Maybe he also knew that the Christian life is not about what we do for Him but about what He does in and through us. Our obedience is certainly the result of His power working within our yielded hearts. Paul understood this truth and spoke of it in Galatians. There is a war going on in the souls of all of us, and the real victory is in Christ alone. "Make me walk" is a request that I pray regularly in my own prayer time. Romans 7:14–25 clearly describes our need for God's intervention in our Christian walk. Grace really is the power to obey. I cannot and do not obey by my own power, but by His sufficient grace that empowers me to walk in His path. Today, my victory is dependent on His grace and my submission to Him. Psalm 37:23 says, "The steps of a good man are ordered by the LORD, and He delights in his way." Thank God that He can change our "want-tos."

EVENING

Dear Lord, as I come to the close of another day, I come with praise for Your sufficiency. I rest in the assurance that Your grace is enough. Make me walk in the path of Your Word, and may it always be my delight. Thank You that as I awake tomorrow, I have Your Word to direct me and teach me Your ways. Until You call me home, may it serve as a light to my path (Ps. 119:105). I love Your Word, dear Lord, and thank You for it. Please allow nothing to come between Your Word and me, for Jesus' sake. In Jesus' name, Amen.

Week 2, Monday

Lord, this morning I wait with eager anticipation to see what You have in store for this day. Help me to find my hope in You and in Your Word. Teach me to wait for Your perfect will to be done. Thank You for waking me this morning with another opportunity to live for You. Amen.

> *"I wait for the LORD, my soul waits, and in His word I do hope.*
> *My soul waits for the Lord more than those who watch for*
> *the morning—yes, more than those who watch for the morning."*
> PSALM 130:5, 6

Hopefully, you will notice that each devotional this week will be related in some way to the Word of God. In a day when so many things we trust may fail us, we can still stand confidently on the truth of God's Word. In our verse for today, the psalmist instructs us to put our *hope* in God's Word.

The psalmist paints a word picture of a watchman in the night, a night guard, who is waiting anxiously for the daybreak so he can leave his post. Perhaps God has you in His waiting room. Be patient. Waiting on God is never wasted time. He hears you! As you wait, your hope is in His Word.

It is often said that God answers our prayers in one of three ways: yes, no, and wait. The important thing is that God hears and answers every one of our prayers for our good and for His glory. We are living in difficult and dark days. For the Christian, it is becoming gloriously dark. I am waiting and watching, "more than those who watch for the morning," for any faint light in the eastern sky—looking for the bright and morning star, the Lord Jesus, when He comes for His own. "Even so, come, Lord Jesus!" (Rev. 22:20).

EVENING

Lord, as I go to sleep tonight, may I be reminded of the night guard who watches for the first ray of morning light. May I be just as vigilant as I watch and wait for Your glory to be revealed here on earth and for Your ultimate return to take me home with You. Thank You that my every hope is found in You, the author and perfecter of my faith. Amen.

MORNING

Father, thank You for Your Word that lives forever. Thank You that through Your Word I have received the supernatural gift of a new life in You. Through Your love, help me to love others as You do. As I spend time with You reading Your love letter to me, help me to put what I read into practice in everything I do today. Amen.

"Since you have purified your souls in obeying the truth through the Spirit in sincere love of the brethren, love one another fervently with a pure heart, having been born again, not of corruptible seed but incorruptible, through the word of God which lives and abides forever."

I PETER 1:22, 23

When we obey God's truth, we will see positive changes in our lives. Two benefits that result from our obedience are mentioned in these verses: a purified life and a sincere love for fellow believers. These results actually have a cause and effect relationship. A changed, purified life will positively affect our relationship with other believers. We will have a deeper, heartfelt love for our brothers and sisters in Christ. This love Peter is talking about here is an unselfish, unconditional, "all-out" love.

How is this purified life and no-holds-barred love possible? Peter says it is through the supernatural experience of our new birth in Christ. Through Him we are now able to obey the truth of God and purify our lives. This change, brought about by God's imperishable Word, will last forever. We are made safe by the blood of Christ, strong by the Holy Spirit, and, according to the Bible, eternally secure. God thought of everything we will need.

Peter closes this chapter a verse later by quoting Isaiah 40:8: "The grass withers, and its flower falls away, but the word of the LORD endures forever." Not only does this verse from the Old Testament attest to what Peter was saying about God's Word, but his ability to remember and put into practice Bible verses speaks to the power and importance of hiding God's words in our hearts (Ps. 119:11).

EVENING

Father, make Your words alive and active in my life. Give me a fervent love for my brothers and sisters in this spiritual family of believers. Thank You for giving me everything I will ever need to live for You. Amen.

FRED LOWERY, BOSSIER CITY, LA

Week 2, Wednesday

Father, You are mighty to save and worthy of all praise. This morning, as I prepare for battle, help me to choose the right weapons: the helmet of salvation; the sword of the Spirit, which is Your Word; the breastplate of righteousness; the shoes of the gospel of peace; and the shield of faith. Thank You that You go before me in this war and have prepared the way for victory. Amen.

"For the weapons of our warfare are not carnal but mighty in God for pulling down strongholds."
2 CORINTHIANS 10:4

P aul had to wage warfare, but he did "not war according to the flesh" (2 Cor. 10:3). Paul was not contrasting his weapons with physical ammunition like spears, knives, guns, or missiles, but with the conventional weapons his opponents were using to promote their own agendas.

These "false apostles" were apparently Jewish Christians in the church who challenged Paul's God-given authority and were trying to establish "strongholds" of power for themselves in the Corinthian church. While they used tools like manipulation and intimidation, Paul's weapons of choice were prayer and the proclamation of the gospel. Both of his weapons contain supernatural powers. As believers, the weapons we fight with are "mighty in God for pulling down strongholds."

Christians do not live by conventional wisdom, and we do not fight our battles with conventional weapons. The cause of Christ is never advanced by carnal actions or methods. Our spiritual weapons, weak by the world's standards, are more than sufficient to see us through and to defeat the Enemy. Living according to God's Word is the way of inner peace, continuous joy, and spiritual victory.

EVENING

Thank You for being the strength that got me through this day. Thank You for supplying everything I needed for my fight against a dark and dying world. Remind me when I am tempted to fight like the world does that the weapons You have provided for me are far superior to theirs. Help me to rest in You as I prepare to get up and go back into battle tomorrow. Amen.

Week 2, Thursday

Thank You for showing me how desperately I need a Savior, and thank You for saving me from my sin. Thank You that, like Abraham's trust in You, my faith will be counted as righteousness in Your eyes. Help me to remember that in my own strength I cannot live the life You have called me to live, but I can do all things through Christ who gives me strength. Help me to walk in that strength today. In Jesus' name, Amen.

*"But the Scripture has confined all under sin, that the promise
by faith in Jesus Christ might be given to those who believe."*
GALATIANS 3:22

Paul sees Scripture (the law) as a declaration that all people everywhere are prisoners of sin. The law is like an MRI that shows us the darkness and dirt hidden in our hearts that separates us from God. The law is a teacher that shows us our need for Christ. Without a sense that we need to be saved, we have no way of knowing how desperately we need a Savior. The law prepared the way of salvation for those who believed by faith in the promise of Jesus. The promise of Jesus preceded the law and was dependent on God's Word alone.

Therefore, salvation did not come through the law. The promise of Jesus was given to those, who, like Abraham, believed by faith. God provided Abraham a way of salvation over four hundred years before the law was even given.

Old Testament believers and New Testament believers were saved by grace through faith and not by the law. Does that mean we no longer have to obey God's commandments? Not at all. In fact, only now in Christ do we have the ability to obey God's laws at all. We could not follow them in our own strength, but through Christ, full obedience is finally possible. The result of the gospel far exceeds that of the law.

EVENING

God, thank You for giving me guidance in Your Word for how I am to live. Help me to live, not as one who is held in bondage by rules, but as one who is free to obey and live an abundant life through the power of Jesus. Thank You for being with me today and for giving me the strength I needed for this day. Amen.

Dear Jesus, You are perfect and true. Thank You for giving me the best example of how to live on this earth. When I am tempted today, help me to resist the devil as You did. Bring to my mind Your Word that I have hidden in my heart so that I will know what to do. Thank You for making a way out of every temptation for me. Amen.

"But Jesus answered him, saying, 'It is written,
"Man shall not live by bread alone, but by every word of God."'"
LUKE 4:4

The Spirit led Jesus into the wilderness where He was tempted by the devil. From Scripture, we know that the reason for these temptations was so Jesus, the God-Man, could personally experience what we go through. Now we know it is possible to overcome the devil by relying on the Spirit of God and His Word.

Jesus was really God and really man, and His temptations were real. In this verse, Jesus had fasted for forty days and was very hungry. The devil often attacks us at the point where we are the weakest. After all, a man has to eat, and it had been over a month since Jesus had eaten anything!

Satan tempted Jesus to devise a human plan to provide His own food by turning stones into bread. Jesus could have used His divine power to turn stones into steak if He wanted, but He did not. Why not? Jesus was God-driven, not need-driven. God had led Him into the wilderness and told Him to fast. Jesus was comfortable with waiting on God to provide food rather than jumping ahead of God and meeting His own needs. Jesus had a one-point plan: do what God says and wait on Him!

How did Jesus answer the devil when He was tempted? He quoted God's Word and acknowledged His dependence on His heavenly Father. How can we answer the devil when we are tempted? The exact same way.

EVENING

Thank You for providing everything I needed to get through this day. Please forgive me for the ways I failed You today. Thank You that Your forgiveness is complete and Your mercies are new every morning. I look forward to a fresh chance to live for You tomorrow. In Jesus' name, Amen.

MORNING

Thank You for being my Father. Help me to be Your obedient child today. As I read Your Word, open my ears to hear what You are telling me, and then help me to do what You have told me to do. May my relationship with You take priority over every other relationship. I know that when I put You first, I am better equipped to love others. Remind me today that no one should ever take the place that rightly belongs to You. Amen.

"And it was told Him by some, who said, 'Your mother and Your brothers are standing outside, desiring to see You.' But He answered and said to them, 'My mother and My brothers are these who hear the word of God and do it.'"
LUKE 8:20, 21

Jesus never missed an opportunity for a teaching moment. He used a visit from His earthly family as an object lesson to explain what it means to be a member of His spiritual family. Jesus was not disrespecting His mother and brothers; He was making a statement about His primary allegiance to His heavenly Father. Jesus said that those who listen to God's Word and then do what it says are His family. Making God's will our will is what shows the world that we are truly kin to Jesus.

The message Jesus was sending His mother and brothers was, "I love you and you are important to Me, but what God wants Me to do has to come before anything you want Me to do. I have a greater loyalty and a higher calling that determines what I do and where I go."

Jesus was demonstrating what He requires of us: to love God supremely and obey Him completely. Once we become Christians our relationship with God is primary and all other relationships are secondary. An added benefit is that our earthly relationships are greatly enhanced by our spiritual intimacy with God as the first and most important thing in our lives.

EVENING

Lord, thank You for giving me clear instructions in Your Word. Thank You for allowing me to be a part of Your forever family. Help me to continue to make my relationship with You my top priority. Thank You that as I grow closer to You, I also grow closer to the people You have placed in my life. Amen.

Week 3, Monday

Good morning, Lord! I thank You for the richness of your Word today. Thank You for the treasure it is in calling me to repentance and holy living every time I read it. Your thoughts are infinitely higher than my thoughts. I would never find Your will for my life without the clear direction of Your Holy Scriptures. I praise You for Your guidance. You are the great God of the universe. Your majesty is awesome, and I am undeserving of Your love. Even though I do not understand why You would choose to love on me, I humbly accept Your love today. Amen.

"The law of the LORD is perfect, converting the soul;
the testimony of the Lord is sure, making wise the simple."
PSALM 19:7

The law of the Lord and the testimony of the Lord are synonyms describing the Word of God. In this psalm, David declared the dynamic power and effectiveness of the Word of God. God's Word transforms and brings us back to God. God's Word opposes all of this world's imperfect theories with an authoritative word that says, "Walk in My ways" (see Jer. 6:16). It cuts directly to the center of the soul. The unconverted person rambles down various religious, philosophical, and ideological blind alleys, but once God's Holy Spirit convicts through the truth of God's Word, our notions about sin, self, and salvation change. God's Word has the power to challenge every thought. It convicts and draws us back to the point of divine truth. God's Word makes wise the simple. It replaces our foolishness, our simple ways, with His wisdom. True wisdom only comes from God.

EVENING

Lord, thank You for Your precious Word. Thank You that Your Word is truth. It continually brings joy to my heart; Your pure commandments enlighten my eyes. By Your Word, I am warned from error; in keeping it there is great reward. I cannot fully understand my own ways and my errors. I ask You to cleanse me from my secret faults. Dear Father, let the words of my mouth and the meditation of my heart be acceptable in Your sight. Thank You, Lord, for Your love letter to us. Amen.

MORNING

Lord Jesus, You existed before the beginning of time. I come to You this morning thanking You for being the God of understanding and wisdom, leading me in the way I should go. Thank You for the Bible and that You point out my sins through Your Word. May the words of my mouth and the meditation of my heart be acceptable in Your sight. Oh Lord, my strength and my Redeemer, bless me today; keep me in Your Word. Amen.

"In the beginning was the Word,
and the Word was with God, and the Word was God."

JOHN 1:1

John's opening verse in his Gospel shows us the eternal significance of God's Word, as well as the power and personality of God's Word conveyed to us through His Son Jesus Christ. In this introduction, an equality between two terms is expressed, "the Word" and "God." We know from Genesis that God was in the beginning. Here we see that "the Word" was also in the beginning. A few verses later in John 1:14, we are told that the pre-existent Word became flesh: "The Word became flesh and dwelt among us." We begin to see a glimpse of what John is telling us. We can unravel the mystery of the identity of this Word as we let Scripture explain itself. In John 17:5, Jesus teaches that He was with God before the world was created: "And now, O Father, glorify Me together with Yourself, with the glory which I had with You before the world was." There it is! Jesus is the Word! The writers of the New Testament repeatedly show Jesus as the one and only Son of God and confirm that He coexisted with the Father before time began. The phrase "was with God" in John 1:1 conveys both friendship and intimacy with God the Father. John takes it a step further and states, "the Word was God." He affirms Jesus the Son was equal with God the Father.

EVENING

Thank You, Father, for sharing Your Son with me. He existed with You before time began, yet You sent Him in human form so we could experience and know You through Him. Open my eyes to comprehend Your Word, Your revelation of Yourself, Your one and only Son, Jesus Christ! Amen.

Almighty God, as I begin this day, I commit my mind, soul, body, possessions, and relationships to Your care. Incline my heart to fully obey You. Mold me wholly to the image of Jesus as a potter forms the clay.

"And those who heard it said, 'Who then can be saved?' But He said, 'The things which are impossible with men are possible with God.'"
LUKE 18:26, 27

A young, rich ruler came to Jesus but went away unsatisfied. This was a man who had business sense and great wealth. He came to Jesus, as the good teacher, because he wanted something that he couldn't buy. He came to ask how he could obtain eternal life. Jesus' reply is puzzling. He gave the man two answers. First, Jesus said to obey the commandments. The man claimed he had kept the commandments of God since childhood. Since all of us are imperfect, it's doubtful that this man had completely kept the commandments according to Jesus' standard. However, instead of arguing or correcting him, Jesus gave a second revealing requirement. Jesus asked the young ruler to sell all of his possessions, give the money to the poor, and follow Him. Sadly, the young man turned away, unwilling to make a commitment he wouldn't keep. Jesus used this encounter to explain to His disciples how difficult it was for a rich man to enter heaven. This was completely contrary to their way of thinking. Many in their culture saw riches as proof of God's blessing. They thought the rich had a spiritual advantage. But according to Jesus, financial status makes no difference. The only way to receive eternal life is through Jesus. His requirement is to exchange your life for His, transferring ownership of your life to His ownership. Jesus doesn't want part of your life; He wants to be your life.

EVENING

I'm Yours, Lord, completely. I yield myself to You. You are my only desire. Help me to be willing to give up anything that stands in the way of my commitment to You. Show me those possessions that seek to control my attention, my time, and my soul. Turn my heart toward You so I can answer Your call to "Follow Me." Amen.

MORNING

Lord, thank You for another day to meditate on Your Word. Help me to understand Your truth. I long to know You better. Your Word is my comfort in affliction; it gives me life. I will not turn aside from Your Word as I remember Your judgments of old. I will use Your Word to guide and direct my steps. Help me today to apply Your principles to my daily life and make Your paths my paths, to make Your priorities my priorities.

"The law of Your mouth is better to me than thousands of coins of gold and silver."
PSALM 119:72

Where do I most want to succeed? Whose approval do I seek? Am I working to please God or to succeed by this world's standards? Jesus said in Matthew 6:24 that "no one can serve two masters." If success in God's eyes is to be achieved we must "seek first the kingdom of God and His righteousness, and all these things shall be added to you" (Matt. 6:33). The psalmist knew that obeying God's Word yielded a greater treasure than all the gold and silver in the world. Proverbs 2:4, 5 teaches that if we seek God's wisdom as silver and search for it as hidden treasures, we will find understanding. Rather than waiting for wisdom, we are to pursue it through God's Word. We are to study as if we are searching for valuable buried treasure. "Be diligent to present yourself approved to God, a worker who does not need to be ashamed, rightly dividing the word of truth" (2 Tim. 2:15). I must realize God's Word is infinitely more valuable than any reward this world has to offer. My goal must be to succeed in the ways that count for eternity. Gold and silver are valuable resources, but the Word of God is worth far more!

EVENING

Lord, thank You for Your gracious riches. Your Word is a treasure. Nothing compares to it. Nothing lasts like it. Nothing gives reward like it. I long to remember Your Word through the night and keep Your law each moment. I am a companion of all who fear You and those who keep Your precepts. The earth is full of Your mercy. God, thank You for the eternal treasure I have in You. I praise Your holy name. Amen.

Lord, I humbly come to You this morning to bless Your name. Your praise will continually be on my lips. I will magnify and exalt Your holy name in all I do today. Whether I eat or drink or whatever I do, I want to do it all for Your glory. I ask You to deliver me from all of my fears. Do not let me be ashamed when I have opportunities to exalt Your name and be Your witness. Give me opportunities to be a living testimony for You.

"All Scripture is given by inspiration of God, and is profitable for doctrine, for reproof, for correction, for instruction in righteousness."

2 Timothy 3:16

This verse is the golden text on the inspiration of God's Word. At the time these words were written, some of the New Testament books had not yet been written, so "all Scripture" refers largely to the Old Testament. The original Greek translated "inspiration of God" is from one word that literally means "God-breathed." God spoke, or breathed, His Word and men wrote what He said.

The writers of Scripture were controlled and moved by the power of the Holy Spirit, as the apostle Peter revealed: "For prophecy never came by the will of man, but holy men of God spoke as they were moved by the Holy Spirit" (2 Pet. 1:21). Four profitable uses of Scripture are listed in 2 Timothy 3:16: *doctrine*—teaching a correct understanding of the truth and reception of salvation; *reproof*—conviction of sin bringing confession and repentance; *correction*—restoration to an upright position; and *instruction*—training in righteousness as it gives God's view concerning life's priorities. Simply put, God's Word teaches us what's right (doctrine), what's not right (reproof), how to get right (correction), and how to stay right (instruction)!

Evening

Lord, thank You for your precious Word, how it instructs and guides, how it never returns void. It gives instruction, disciplines, convicts, and corrects. Thank You for the joy Your Word brings as You speak. Please guard my heart and mind through your Word. Your eyes are over the righteous, and your ears are open to my prayers. Thank You for answering my prayers according to Your Word. Amen.

MORNING

Thank you, Lord, for your Word. You have promised to teach me in the way I should live and guide me in the paths of righteousness. I ask You to keep my eyes focused on You and open to Your truths. Give me eyes to see, ears to hear, and a heart to receive what You will have for me today. I commit myself to follow You as you lead me by Your Word.

"For the word of God is living and powerful, and sharper than any two-edged sword,
piercing even to the division of soul and spirit, and of joints and marrow,
and is a discerner of the thoughts and intents of the heart."
HEBREWS 4:12

The Word is alive, powerful, active, and effective in our lives. No other book has power in itself to open the human heart—only the Bible! It is "sharper than any two-edged sword" because it penetrates deeper than the physical body. It reaches into all the hidden parts of an individual and makes judgments about our inner thoughts, secrets, and motives. It reaches our conscience, into the deep areas where others cannot see. God's Word always hits the bull's eye of our heart, detecting hidden hypocrisy. It reveals our true heart, nature, and mind so there can be no escape from true guilt.

God's Truth has the power to show us who we are, whether it is preached, read, or communicated in conversation. God's Word is alive with an unbelievable vitality and dynamic that breathes, speaks, pleads, and conquers. It includes an energy that produces results. Whether we admit it outwardly or not, we cannot deny the accuracy of God's opinion of our hidden self. He knows us better than we know ourselves. As we see the truth, we have the opportunity to move toward God in repentance and thankfulness. He never pierces us to wound us, but like a surgeon, He touches the place of disease or infection so we can be healed.

EVENING

Lord, give me the courage and humility to respond to the truth of Your Word when it convicts of sin. Let your Word have its full effect in my life to make me more like Jesus each day. May Your Word be the effective scalpel that brings healing and wholeness to my soul. Amen.

DANNY LOVETT, CHATTANOOGA, TN

Thank You, Lord, for Your living Word, Jesus Christ, and Your written Word, the Holy Bible! You are awesome, oh God, and I praise You today, for You have not left me to wander in darkness—You have given me the light of revelation in Your Word. Speak to me as I read Your Word and empower me I pray by Your Spirit to live by Your laws and precepts. Help me to remember You throughout this day and meditate continually upon Your revealed Word. Amen.

"I will meditate on Your precepts, and contemplate Your ways.
I will delight myself in Your statutes; I will not forget Your word."
PSALM 119:15, 16

David said he would meditate, contemplate, ruminate, and allow God's Word to dominate his thinking. No wonder the Bible refers to him twice as a man after God's own heart (1 Sam. 13:14; Acts 13:22). David was after the heart of God, not the crown of Saul or any other worldly possession. He knew God and continually feasted upon the Word of God. Acts 13:36 says that David "served his own generation by the will of God." And the key to his victorious living and effective service was living under the shelter of God's Word. When David removed himself from that protective umbrella, he got into serious trouble. Let us take notice! Here is something practical you can do that will enable you to meditate, contemplate, and ruminate on Scripture so God's Word dominates your thought life. Today, read God's Word, and then throughout the day pray back to God the very words of Scripture that you read this morning. It will change your life!

EVENING

Dear heavenly Father, I love You and thank You for the treasure of the Word of God. Help me to ponder and never forget it. Help me to hide Your Word deep within my heart so that I may not sin against You. Amen.

MORNING

Father, thank You for being the sovereign Lord of the universe, the one true God who is, was, and always will be. I praise You, for You are God and You do not change. You make promises to Your children, and You always keep them. Help me this day to read the promises in Your Word and be confident and at peace that You will accomplish all You desire to accomplish in my life. Thank You, Lord! Amen.

"So shall My word be that goes forth from My mouth;
it shall not return to Me void, but it shall accomplish what I please,
and it shall prosper in the thing for which I sent it."

ISAIAH 55:11

God called Bill Wallace to be a medical missionary when he was a senior in high school. He earned an M.D. degree from the University Medical School in Memphis. He served as a medical missionary in Wuchow, South China for fifteen years. Wallace was in China as a witness to the Word of God first and a medical doctor second. He often stuttered when he spoke the gospel, but God richly blessed. Dr. Wallace stayed in China during the Communist takeover. He said on one occasion, "We'll do what God wants us to do. It doesn't make any difference what happens to us. The only important thing is that when it does happen, we be found doing the will of God."

On December 19, 1950, Communists arrested and accused him of being an American spy. For weeks he was imprisoned, persecuted, and tortured. And on February 10, 1951, Bill Wallace went home to be with Jesus. Was his life a waste? Hardly! God's Word accomplished all He intended to accomplish through Wallace's life. The life and ministry of Bill Wallace has inspired many to serve as missionaries to the nations. The Baptist Student Union at the University of Tennessee is named after him, and there is the Wallace Memorial Baptist Church, a vibrant growing church in Knoxville, that is named in his honor and memory.[1]

EVENING

God, You reign! Help me to persevere today through whatever hardship I will face and empower me, Lord, to trust that You will indeed accomplish all You desire to accomplish as I live for You and share Your Word. Amen.

DANNY FORSHEE, LAVACA, AR

Week 4, Wednesday

Week 4, Wednesday

MORNING

Father, I love You, and I lay my life before You. Take me and use me for Your glory and Your purposes. Forgive me when I complain and do not see all the wonderful things You do for me, things I take for granted like being able to wake up today and see the beginning of another day. Give me strength to worship You, encourage Your people, and speak Your name to a lost world. Amen.

"Let the word of Christ dwell in you richly in all wisdom, teaching and admonishing one another in psalms and hymns and spiritual songs, singing with grace in your hearts to the Lord."
COLOSSIANS 3:16

There are two types of people in the world. One type loves and seeks the best while the other drains and complains and seeks the worst. With some people, you look for a place to hide when you see them coming because you know there will be plenty of criticism and complaints. But then there are others who, when you hear their name or better yet see them, your spirit is immediately lifted because you know they are such a blessing and encouragement to be around.

There is a guy in the Bible that was such a constant source of encouragement that the apostles gave him the name Mr. Encouragement! Yes, his name was Joseph, but the disciples of Jesus changed it to Barnabas, which means, "Son of Encouragement" (Acts 4:36). Wow, what a way to be known! When you read about him throughout the Book of Acts you see him loving, encouraging, building up, and blessing many. Anybody can be a complainer, but it takes effort to be an encourager. Let God's Word soak deeply within your soul. God will give you the grace and wisdom to encourage others, and He will put a contagious song in your heart.

EVENING

Dear God, it is so easy for me to complain and bring others down. Please help me today to focus on Your Word and encourage everyone with whom I come into contact. Place a song of joy and contentment within me that spills over in others' lives so that I demonstrate the grace of God to them. Forgive me when I am negative. Help me today to love unconditionally and encourage. Thank You, Jesus. Amen.

22   ONE YEAR DEVOTIONAL PRAYER BOOK

Week 4, Thursday

Thank You, Lord, that You promise to be with me no matter what comes my way. May Your Word abide in me throughout today, and please enable me to be strong and live for You. Guide my thoughts, speech, and behavior. Grant to me victory over the Evil One as he tries to distract me from serving You. Amen.

"I have written to you, fathers, because you have known Him who is from the beginning. I have written to you, young men, because you are strong, and the word of God abides in you, and you have overcome the wicked one."

1 JOHN 2:14

Josh Hamilton, the all-star outfielder for the Texas Rangers professional baseball team, is a strong young man within whom the Word of God abides. Hamilton was the first player selected in the 1999 baseball draft by the Tampa Bay Rays. As an eighteen-year-old, he could hit the ball five hundred feet, throw the baseball ninety-six miles an hour, and from the outfield wall, he could hurl a baseball all the way to home plate on the fly. But while in the minor leagues he was injured, started using drugs, and his life spiraled downward for the next three years. He lost fifty pounds and did not play baseball for those three years. He tried to kill himself five times and went to rehab eight times, but it was not until October 6, 2005, when everything changed.

Today Josh Hamilton is the all-star center fielder for the Texas Rangers and led the American League in RBIs in 2008 with 130. Hamilton said, "I was out of baseball a year-and-a-half ago. I didn't have my family back, my wife was going to leave me, and I was doing drug[s]. People think there are coincidences in life. There are no coincidences when God's got a plan. It's nothing I did except try to make the right choices and let God take over from there. There's one solid and permanent way out of it, and that's finding the Lord Jesus Christ and accepting Him."[2]

EVENING

Dear God, help me to make wise decisions today. Help me to be strong, and may Your Word be on my mind and come out of my mouth. Thank You for the strength to overcome Satan. You are my shield and my strength. Amen.

DANNY FORSHEE, LAVACA, AR

Thank You, Lord, for saving me and setting me apart to live for You. Should You allow some trial or difficulty to come my way, please help me not to complain or become bitter; rather, please enable me to praise You through the storm. Use me to praise You in the hard times so others see You in my life. Amen.

"For every creature of God is good, and nothing is to be refused if it is received with thanksgiving; for it is sanctified by the word of God and prayer."
1 TIMOTHY 4:4, 5

Corrie ten Boom experienced suffering and persecution firsthand. She was a remarkable lady who led a girls' club in her homeland of Holland from 1921–1940. Boom provided recreation like gymnastics, camping, and music for the girls, and she also led them in Bible devotions. But in 1940, the Nazis captured Holland after only five days of fighting. Boom and her family loved the Jewish people and hid them, thus the name of the famous book and movie, *The Hiding Place.*

The Boom family suffered horribly for their assistance to the Jews. Corrie and her sister Betsie were taken to the Ravensbruck Concentration Camp in Germany in September 1944, where the living conditions were deplorable. The fleas were so bad that the guards would not check on the prisoners, thus allowing them to study God's Word together. Corrie even thanked God for the fleas! Betsie died at Ravensbruck, but Corrie was "accidentally" released on December 31, 1944. All the women her age were killed a week later. Corrie traveled all over the world telling her story until she died at the age of ninety-one on April 15, 1983. She said, "When we are obedient, God guides our steps and our stops." And she also said, "Do not hold tightly your possessions; hold them loosely, that way when God takes them out of your hand it will not be so painful."[3]

EVENING

Thank You, God—even for the "fleas" in my life. Thank You for the Word of God and prayer. Help me to trust You during those hard times when I do not understand what You are doing. You are amazing, oh God. Your ways are so much higher and holier than my ways. Amen.

MORNING

God, I ask You to help me tell someone about You today. Holy Spirit, please empty me so I can be filled with You. Guide me to someone who needs You, Lord, and give me the boldness I need to tell him or her how awesome You are. Amen.

"And when they had prayed, the place where they were assembled together was shaken; and they were all filled with the Holy Spirit, and they spoke the word of God with boldness."

ACTS 4:31

Eight out of ten unchurched Americans would respond favorably to an invitation to attend church if they were invited. It is ironic and sad, really, that during a time of unprecedented interest in Jesus, those who know Jesus are not talking about Him. We have this amazing Good News called the gospel, but we keep it to ourselves. The disciples in the Book of Acts spoke the Word of God with boldness, and they turned their world upside down (Acts 17:6). Would it not be a wonderful compliment to you and your church if the local citizens in your city said the same thing? But in order to share Christ, we first must know Him and be filled with the Holy Spirit. When Jesus is in our hearts and on our minds, He always comes out of our mouths.

I spoke with a man recently who was a retired Vietnam veteran. When he was told I was a pastor, he began to use curse words so I would be sure to hear him. I walked close to him, looked up at him, invited him to our church, and gave him a gospel tract. I was not sure what he would do after that, but he received the witness and invitation. Was that a successful evangelistic encounter? According to the late Bill Bright it was. Bright said, "Witnessing is sharing the gospel in the power of the Holy Spirit and leaving the results to God." Go tell someone about Jesus today!

EVENING

Lord, I **recognize** that I need to be filled with Your Holy Spirit. I **repent** of my sins of not caring and sharing with others as I should. I **request** that You fill me with Your Holy Spirit so that I have Your love, power, and compassion for a lost world. I **receive** Your filling and go gladly to tell the world that Jesus loves them. Amen.

DANNY FORSHEE, LAVACA, AR

Father, thank You for coming into my world as a person so that I can experience Your love. Thank You for loving me the way I am. Your love is my security and confidence. Thank You for your kindnesses to me. Thank You for allowing me to be a part of Your perfect plan for this world. I know that because of You, love is the music of the universe. My prayer is that love will be the song that I am singing today. Amen.

"Love suffers long and is kind; love does not envy; love does not parade itself, is not puffed up; does not behave rudely, does not seek its own, is not provoked, thinks no evil."

1 CORINTHIANS 13:4, 5

I confess that I often live my life in general terms. General sermons on love generally produce general love. Generally nothing changes. Love is specific and 1 Corinthians 13 teaches us the specifics. Love is broken into portions for us to understand God's love. History is His story. Replace "Jesus" for "love." Jesus suffers long and is kind. Jesus does not envy. Jesus does not parade Himself. I am stunned at how great a lover Jesus is.

Applying that in my own life is difficult. To exchange my name with love and to say that I suffer long and am kind is a powerful reminder of the responsibility I have as a follower of Christ. For example, the phrase "love does not parade itself" is personal to me. When I replace love with my name, I am uneasy on a platform before I speak. I prefer to sit down front and then speak. Love "is not puffed up," though, and if that is protocol where I am speaking, I sit on the platform. These verses in 1 Corinthians help me consider God's amazing love in my everyday life and remind me of the standard I'm striving for.

EVENING

Lord, thank You that Your Word is given to us not just to instruct us but also to change us. Help me to understand that the only cure for my self-centeredness is to center my attention on the well-being of others. My prayer is that love would flow from my heart the way it flows from Your heart. My hope is that the love that I feel from You will reproduce itself in my everyday world. Amen.

MORNING

Lord, may I begin today with love as my guide and my partner. Forgive me for not demonstrating Your love to others. When I am at the end of my patience, help me depend on your limitless reserves. Give me a new way of seeing people. Help me understand that love's divine purpose is to redeem, restore, and renew. May my whole life be a winsome witness to Your eternal message of love. Amen.

"And now abide faith, hope, love, these three; but the greatest of these is love."
1 CORINTHIANS 13:13

Scripture teaches us the importance of faith and hope. Walking the way of love demands faith and hope. They are essential components in the process of love, but they will have no purpose in heaven. Love is inherently greater because it lasts. It is the one lasting connection we have with an eternal God. Love is the greatest because it is the most Godlike quality. Christians are referred to as people of faith, but based on 1 Corinthians 13:13, we should be known as people of love.

At the heart of the divine nature is a love that flows out in compassion for all. Even at Calvary when God could have blasted humankind, He chose to bless us. With outstretched hands on a cruel Cross, He said, "It is finished!" (John 19:30). He finished the business of loving us and has given us the business of loving others. Management guru Peter Drucker said to find out what your company's business is and then ask, "How's business?" God made it clear that His business is the greatest business. It is the business of not only proclaiming but also practicing His eternal message of love. The question for us is, "How's business?"

EVENING

Lord, help me give my life to the greatest thing, the love of God. Forgive me for living under pressure rather than priority. Too often I dwell on distractions and not Your direction. Keep me from wasting my life on small, petty things. I pray that Your love will be displayed in my life. May I be known as a person of love. May my family be known as a family of love, and may my church be known as a church of love. I pray that I will be a partner in the God and Son Love business. Amen.

CHARLES LOWERY, LINDALE, TX

Week 5, Wednesday

Father, thank You that You not only command me to love, but You also provide the power to make it gloriously possible. In these times when we learn selfishness over sharing, teach me Your way of forbearing, forgiving, and ever loving. Teach me to think "we" instead of "me." Help me to see that the disorder, discouragement, and dysfunction in this world is a cry for love. May I be Your love ambassador to this beautiful, broken world. My prayer is that those damaged by the destructive love of this world will be delivered by the divine love of Your world. Amen.

"With all lowliness and gentleness, with longsuffering,
bearing with one another in love."
EPHESIANS 4:2

Love is longsuffering. Every demonstration of God's patient longsuffering is extended to us through Scripture. We can become an extension of His patient longsuffering. Practically, you don't know if you have longsuffering until you have been long bothered. The test of this quality in our lives usually happens in our homes. Raising teenagers comes to mind when I think of long bothered. Each aspect of love is tested in the home. Home is where we are the most natural and comfortable. Therefore it is the hardest place to act supernaturally. We try to have our own way rather than loving God's way.

A lady told her husband that the pastor dropped by to see them. He asked if she had told him how much money they gave to the church, how involved their kids were, and that they had not missed a Sunday in weeks. His wife told him that she didn't tell him all of those things because the only question he had asked was if Jesus lived in their home. She then said, "I told him no." If the Lord of love, Jesus, is at home in your house, you will experience supernatural love in all of your relationships outside your house.

EVENING

Lord, move through our home with Your supernatural love. As I love You and You love me, prepare me to love the ones in my life who are difficult. May the fruit of Your Spirit grow in me, even longsuffering. Do what You need in my life to make me lovable. Give me the strength to love even those who I think are my enemies. Allow our home to be Your home where love is supreme. Amen.

MORNING

Father, thank You that Your love is changeless and that Your covenant love never ends. Help me to remember that when I lose my grip, You are holding on to me. Give me the confidence to know that I will not be separated from You, because Christ's love that He demonstrated on the Cross cancelled all of my past and future sin. I thank You that Christ willingly came so that I can trust His holy, humble, forever love. Amen.

> *"For I am persuaded that neither death nor life, nor angels nor principalities nor powers, nor things present nor things to come, nor height nor depth, nor any other created thing, shall be able to separate us from the love of God which is in Christ Jesus our Lord."*
> ROMANS 8:38, 39

This Scripture is the high point of the Roman letter. It tells us that nothing changes the eternal purpose of God and nothing can stop the divine love of Christ. When my daughter was young, she injured her chin and needed stitches. When I arrived home, she felt better and did not understand her need for stitches. It is impossible to reason with a four-year-old. Why hurt her chin again when it didn't hurt? I asked her if she knew that I loved her and if she knew she could trust me. We decided a prize would help the situation, and she decided she wanted the prize first! She cried, the doctor cried, and I cried during the procedure. I thought she would have nothing to do with me for a long time, but I felt her little hand in mine. She thanked me for not letting go.

God never said we would not have pain and death, but nothing separates us from the love of God. Not even death. Today's scripture closes with the reason why. Nothing can separate us from God because of the love of Jesus. Death cannot separate us from the love of God, because Jesus conquered death and has the scars to prove it.

EVENING

Father, thank You that even in death You never let go. Help me to forget the scars of this world and remember what my Savior did for me. Thank You, Jesus, for coming back from death and giving me resurrection power that allows me to come back from whatever knocks me down. In my time of pain, help me to never forget that one day You will take me home and give me my prize. Amen.

CHARLES LOWERY, LINDALE, TX

Week 5, Friday

Father, my prayer today is that my devotion to You will overrule the emotion of my flesh and that I will love others the way You have loved me. Help me to understand that Your Scriptures take me down the path that love walks. May Your Word give me the courage and confidence to love Your way even if it calls for restricting or limiting my own plans. Lord, I have so much to learn from You; teach me to be a lover. Amen.

"But whoever keeps His word, truly the love of God is perfected in him. By this we know that we are in Him."

1 JOHN 2:5

Our passage today teaches that God's love keeps His Word. This love is not a mere unregulated impulse. It is disciplined love. The love of God is like the banks of a river channeling His love in the right direction. This love doesn't do whatever it wants when it wants. This love is lived in connection with the wisdom of Scripture. It does not act on emotions that might harm others. This love is based on devotion to God, believing by faith that His will is best for all. This is the love of faith, not fear, believing God's timetable is perfect.

Today's scripture teaches that right living and righteous loving combine to form real love. God's Word guides this love. It does not demand my way, but seeks God's way. Divine love accepts Scripture as the supreme authority over the decisions of life instead of insisting that I am the authority. This allows me to stretch my love muscles and move beyond my selfish emotions and truly love God's way.

EVENING

Father, thank You for Your Word. Help me to understand that it is Your love directed toward me and that Jesus is the fulfillment of the living Word. I know that because of Jesus, real love demands obedience and sacrifice. Thank You that Your love is secure, dependable, and available. Help me to learn from You. I want to be submissive to the Scriptures and that still, small voice. Teach me to love Your way. Amen.

MORNING

Lord, today keep me in Your love. Thank You for Your love, and I know how much it cost for You to love me. Help me to love others no matter the cost. Help me to realize that every person I meet today was made in Your image. I know there is someone I will meet today that may be in pain. Allow me to be an instrument of Your healing love. May Your loving-kindness revealed in me win an unbeliever to Christ. Amen.

"Keep yourselves in the love of God, looking for the mercy of our Lord Jesus Christ unto eternal life."
JUDE 21

A pastor asked a children's Bible study class why they loved God. One little boy said, "I guess it just runs in the family." Today's scripture teaches that God's love runs in His family and that this divine love leads to eternal life. A couple that was adopting a child at an orphanage was attracted to one little boy. They told him of all the things they would give him—clothes, toys, and a nice house. Nothing seemed to appeal to him. Finally they asked what he really wanted most of all. The little fellow replied that he just wanted someone to love him. That is what our world wants and needs. A physician once said after many years of practice that the best medicine he could prescribe was love. When asked if that didn't work, he replied that we should double the dose. The Great Physician tells us that the prescription for the world is to love others as He has loved us.

EVENING

Lord, build me up in Your love so that I can build others up. Allow Your love to make me tactful as well as truthful. May I value people over projects. When I am tempted to aim at fame and fortune, give me the courage to aim for love. Move through Your world today with Your healing love. For the one that thinks no one cares, may I be the one to show that You care. May each reader know of Your secure eternal love. Let our lives speak of Your divine love. Amen.

Week 6, Monday

Father, Your love is clearly seen in the Lord Jesus. Thank You for convicting me of sin and changing my heart through the gospel. As I start a new week, I pray that You will open my eyes to see people who need to know Your love. Show Your love through me today. I seek Your face in Jesus' name. Amen.

"He who does not love does not know God, for God is love.
In this the love of God was manifested toward us, that God has sent
His only begotten Son into the world, that we might live through Him."
1 JOHN 4:8, 9

God is love! God is the source of love—love is from God (1 John 4:7). But love is not just something that God does. Love always has been and always will be an integral part of who He is—His very essence. The sending of His Son was not about the worth of man, but the nature of God. The point is not that we were intrinsically worth dying for, but that God's nature is intrinsically loving. It was His nature that moved Him to the Cross.

Without God, we would never know love. He manifested, disclosed, and brought love to light in the sending of His only begotten (unique, one-of-a-kind) Son. The infinite God-Man, Jesus the Messiah—He is love incarnate. Through the Cross we come to know God and His love. Looking at the Cross, our hearts shout with Paul, "God loved me and gave Himself for me!" (see Gal. 2:20). Love moved Christ to give His life. Now, through the Cross and resurrection, we have a whole new kind of life. Since we know Him, we love. The distinguishing mark of this new life is the love that we know and the love that we show.

EVENING

Lord God, as the day comes to a close, I thank You that I can close my eyes convinced of Your love. I find refuge and rest in Your unchanging love. I praise You for the confidence I have when I think about Your love sending Christ Jesus, my Lord, and it is in His name that I pray. Amen.

MORNING

Father, I praise You. You are the all-powerful, all-knowing God of the universe. Nothing I encounter today will come as a surprise to You. And no matter what I face today, I know that You are for me and are working all things together for good. I praise You as the source of all good things, and I thank You for Your incredible commitment to provide everything I need to do Your will. Nothing I encounter today will be too hard for You! Finding my life in the gospel, I walk into another day. In Jesus' name, Amen.

"He who did not spare His own Son, but delivered Him up for us all,
how shall He not with Him also freely give us all things?"
ROMANS 8:32

God is for us! Wow! This almost leaves us speechless—it did Paul. When Paul considered what God has done for us in sending Christ to die for our sins, he asked, "What then shall we say to these things?" (Rom. 8:31). Although it defies description and transcends comprehension, it does lead us to a very certain conclusion: God is for us!

Every day there are many things that we cannot control or figure out. There are times when emotions and circumstances seem to tell us that things will not work out—that life is against us. How do you respond? What do you think when things get a little foggy? Are you like a little girl picking flower petals and saying, "He loves me; He loves me not"? If that is how you are approaching your relationship with God, you are ignoring what He has done and what He has said about His continued commitment to His children.

The demonstration of His love at Calvary proved that God is for us, not against us! Since we have come to know Him through the glorious gospel of His dear Son, we can confidently know that He will provide everything we need to do His will.

EVENING

Lord, You have been my Rock, my Shield, and my Fortress. You have gone before me, and now I entrust my life to You as the day ends. As You give rest to my body, I pray You will give deep, abiding rest to my soul. In Jesus' name, Amen.

Father, heaven is Your throne, and the earth is Your footstool. You said You could never be contained in a building made with hands, yet amazingly, You have chosen to live in me. Today, I pray that You will live the life and love of Jesus through me. In Christ I abide, Amen.

"And we have known and believed the love that God has for us.
God is love, and he who abides in love abides in God, and God in him."

1 JOHN 4:16

God abides in us! Before Jesus went to the Cross, He promised His disciples that the Spirit of God would come to live in them. Later, John declared that this had indeed happened, not only to them but to us as well!

Those who have come to know God through the love of Christ know that God is alive in them. Think about that a minute: God is alive in us! Does the Spirit of God really live in you? When God arrested our hearts with His love, He confronted our sinfulness and convinced us of His forgiveness in Christ. By the work of His Spirit, we confessed Christ as Lord and came to know His love by responding to His Word. Because of this, the Spirit Himself took up residency in our hearts and gave us a new life and a new love.

The fruit of the Spirit is love. It's not optional. This new life from the Spirit is evidenced in a new kind of love and a new kind of lifestyle. Why? Because that is who God is, and God is abiding in us! How differently would we think, feel, and act if we truly recognized this divine love living in us?

When Augustine was asked, "How do you know you have the Spirit?" he replied, "Ask your heart; if it is full of love, you have the Spirit."

EVENING

You have sent the Spirit of Your Son into my heart, crying, "Abba, Father." I praise You for giving me new life and new love, and I close my eyes resting in Your indwelling Spirit and Your abiding love. Amen.

Week 6, Thursday

Father, open my eyes to see others through grace. Sensitize my heart to notice those who are overwhelmed by sin and desperate for mercy and grace. Deliver me from selfishness and lead me, Lord! Amen.

"For I know that You are a gracious and merciful God, slow to anger and abundant in lovingkindness, One who relents from doing harm."

JONAH 4:2

God is gracious and merciful! How did Jonah know this about God? Perhaps Jonah remembered other incidents when people deserved judgment but God gave mercy. Maybe Jonah recalled the children of Israel's sin in worshiping the golden calf—they deserved judgment, but God gave them mercy.

Or maybe Jonah recalled when the children of Israel responded in fear to the spies' report on the Promised Land. Even as God pronounced severe judgment on them, He did not turn His back on them completely. The reason? He is a gracious and merciful God who is ready to forgive (Num. 14:18). Jonah was angry and wanted God to judge the Ninevites, but Jonah knew that God was ready to forgive. There are many times that we are just like Jonah. We think we are being righteous when we are really being selfish and even bigoted.

What do we really know about God and His grace? Do we understand that He is ready to forgive? Grace and mercy sent Jesus to the Cross to provide forgiveness for those who repent and believe in Him—those who are near and those who are far off! God alone is able to keep judgment and mercy in tandem. We will never understand how His love and judgment come together until we look at the Cross. Holiness and justice demanded payment for sin. Love provided the payment through Jesus' death. Now, the Spirit of God pours out His grace and mercy on us—the ones who really deserved to die.

EVENING

Lord, as the work of this day ends, may I come to the end of my human works that can never satisfy Your righteousness. I praise You for the righteousness that You have given me in Christ, and I find my rest in Your grace and mercy. In Jesus' name, Amen.

Week 6, Friday

Oh God, You are my God. My heart seeks Your face as You pour out Your grace on another day. Because of Christ, my heart delights in Your Word, and I want to know Your ways. In Jesus' name, Amen.

"For this is the love of God, that we keep His commandments.
And His commandments are not burdensome."

1 JOHN 5:3

God's love turns duty into delight. Loving God is so much more than external obedience! Overtaken by the love of God, gratefully responding to the gospel, the hungry soul finds delight in the outworking of His love. His commandments are impossible to keep in the strength of the flesh. The commandments reveal sin and weigh heavy on the heart that is lost. The only way to keep His commandments is to be changed by the gospel.

When God changes our hearts, He gives us new desires. Because of this new love for God, the changed heart now desires to do His will and finds clear direction from His commandments. Obedience is not fleshly diligence to perform a duty. It is a Spirit-empowered delight to fulfill the direction that God's Word has provided.

If obedience becomes a burden to the believer, it proves that something in the heart is out of line. The walk with God is a life of faith, the flow of faith is love, and the flow of love is delight in living out His commandments. If obedience is a struggle, don't ignore the shouting of your soul. Your heart is telling you that something is seeking to undermine your faith. The indwelling life of God makes obedience possible. The indwelling love of God makes obedience delightful. Has duty become your dread? Back it up a step. Delight in His love and discover how He changes the desires of your heart.

EVENING

Father, my inner man agrees with the psalmist: "I delight to do Your will, O my God, and Your law is within my heart" (Ps. 40:8). Remove the clutter in my head and heart and let Your eternal ways be my delight. Like the little children who came to Jesus, I put all of my life in Your loving arms. Amen.

MORNING

Father, Your love is amazing! There are no words to describe what You have done in forgiving my sin through the blood of Christ. I praise You for the indescribable gift of eternal life that You have freely given me in Christ. Amen.

"To know the love of Christ which passes knowledge;
that you may be filled with all the fullness of God."
EPHESIANS 3:19

Christ's love is not something we can achieve—it is something we receive. God in His wisdom determined that we would not figure Him out or come to know Him through earthly intelligence. Instead, He determined to use the message of His love on a Cross to bring us into a relationship with Him. His love purchased our salvation and secured our eternity. Love that does that can do anything!

God's love is enough! Nothing is lacking. His love is full, complete. There is nothing we can add to His love; there is nothing we can take away. There is no way to make Him love us less, and there is no need to make Him love us more. The love He has shown through Christ is complete.

When we examine His love, we discover that it is inexhaustible, unfathomable, and beyond human description. His love is wider than anything we will ever have to cross, longer than any distance we will ever have to go, higher than we will ever have to climb, and deeper than we could ever sink or fall. His love goes beyond anything we have ever known, but it is love that we know because we know Christ!

When we know the love of Christ, we know that nothing can ever change it. There is no circumstance, problem, or need that can ever change God's love or what His love has done. His amazing love fills the longing of the soul, and it is enough—more than enough!

EVENING

Lord, today You are reminding me that I am more than a conqueror through Christ who loved me. My soul overflows with the overcoming song that nothing can separate me from Your love! Because of Jesus, I rest in Your love. Amen!

Father God, I worship You for the truth that weeping endures for a night, but joy comes in the morning. May this morning bring me word of Your unfailing love, for I place my trust in You. In Jesus' name, Amen!

"Though He causes grief, yet He will show compassion according to the multitude of His mercies. For He does not afflict willingly, nor grieve the children of men."
LAMENTATIONS 3:32, 33

God's love is evident to His children in grief. There is goodness in the midst of our grief as Christ followers. Goodness in grief is one of the spiritual paradoxes of our faith, just like the following: we die to ourselves that we might live; we are crucified with Christ to live spiritually; we humble ourselves to be exalted; the last shall be first, and the first shall be last; greatest is the least among you.

There is goodness in the midst of our grief, for the Lord manifests in trials the greatness of His love to us. Grief means to bear a heavy burden, and God uses seasons of sorrow to manifest the depths of His grace to His children. There are some important and eternal things that we can only learn in times of sorrow and suffering. C.S. Lewis said, "God whispers to us in our pleasures, speaks to us in our conscience, but shouts in our pains: It is His megaphone to rouse a deaf world."

EVENING

O God, I pray that You would shout to me in the midst of my pain. Speak to me, Lord, for Your servant listens. May times of difficulty drive me closer to You and not drive me from You. May You teach me what it means to walk by faith and not my feelings. Regardless of what heavy burdens I experience in life, I will still praise You. In Jesus' name I come to You, Amen.

Father God, as I awaken this day, I confess that Jesus Christ is Lord of all, over all my life and my physical existence. My life is in Your hands, and I pray for Your healing grace over all my physical weaknesses. May Your grace abound in my weaknesses, and may my inward person be renewed today. In Jesus' name I pray, Amen.

*"Heal me, O LORD, and I shall be healed; save me,
and I shall be saved, for You are my praise."*
JEREMIAH 17:14

In this passage, the prophet Jeremiah was experiencing physical illness in a time of testing when he was falling prey to his opponents. He cried out to the Lord in utter dependence for His power and grace. Yet in his personal storm, the prophet still praised the Lord.

Suffering and sickness are normal experiences for the believer, and they are to be expected. Will you still praise Him—not only when the Lord gives you health but also when He takes away health and personal comfort? In times of sickness and distress, the Lord so desires for you to look to Him for healing and comfort.

Tribulations are God's divine design to make us better, never bitter. God's purpose in suffering is that we are conformed to the likeness of His Son. Healing and salvation come alone from the Lord, and be assured that God's mercy is sufficient to meet the deepest needs in life. Jesus is the Savior who can move the mountains in life; He is mighty to save as you cry out to Him!

EVENING

Lord Jesus, I do cry out to You, for this day is a gift from You. May my successes and my sufferings praise You, for You are the reigning Lord in my life. May my health and my illnesses bring glory to Your name. No matter whether You give or take away, I will worship You. Teach me Your ways. Accomplish Your purposes in my life. In Jesus' name I pray, Amen.

Abba Father, I praise you for Your eternal love that has redeemed me by the blood of Your Son. Your love has forever adopted me as Your child, and it sustains me through all my days. I acknowledge the truth that You will never love me more than You do right now, and You will never love me any less than you do at this moment. Open my eyes to see the vast dimensions of Your love. I pray in Jesus' wonderful name, Amen!

"Who shall separate us from the love of Christ? Shall tribulation, or distress, or persecution, or famine, or nakedness, or peril, or sword? As it is written: 'For Your sake we are killed all day long; we are accounted as sheep for the slaughter.'"
ROMANS 8:35, 36

The apostle Paul asks a very good question: "Who or what circumstance can separate you as God's child from His love?" Notice the list of seven tragedies that might befall you, which are things people mistakenly believe signal divine disfavor: tribulation, distress, persecution, famine, nakedness, peril, and sword. These difficulties are things that make one think, "God does not love me." Yet Paul's answer to his question is, "No! None of these circumstances can separate us from the love of God in Christ Jesus our Lord!"

Painful circumstances may separate you from health and wealth, from family and friends, from comfort and ease, but they cannot separate you from Christ!

EVENING

Father God, thank You for the simplest, most elemental truth of Your Word: You love me! This is amazing to me! I can understand how You might ignore me because of my failures; I can understand how You might reject me because of my sinfulness; I can understand how You might condemn me because of my transgressions. But why and how You should love me by the delivering up of Your Son on the Cross for my sin is amazing! I give You my heart and all my worship in Jesus' name. Amen!

MORNING

Heavenly Father, captivate my heart with Your love this day. I desire for my mind, will, and emotions to be surrounded by Your faithful mercy. May Your love burn as a holy fire through my life to share the message of my Savior with every person I meet today. Set my heart on fire, Lord! Set me on fire! Make my life a witness of Your saving power today. In Jesus' saving name I pray, Amen!

"For the love of Christ compels us, because we judge thus:
that if One died for all, then all died."
2 CORINTHIANS 5:14

What motivates you? A gold medal motivates Olympic athletes to strive and put in long hours of physical discipline and endurance to reach the prize. What is it that moves you to get out of bed and actually share the love of Christ with others by your life and through your lips? It is "the call from within" your heart—the love of Christ—that compels and motivates you to share the Good News of Christ with others. It is the reality that Christ died for all people, because all people are spiritually dead and need the life that only He as the risen Lord can give to them.

The opposite of love is not hate; it is indifference. Being indifferent to those who are lost and perishing without Christ is a form of resistance to the persuading call of Christ's love that moves us to go and tell.

EVENING

Father God, I rejoice in Your Son, the Lord Jesus Christ, who is my reason to live. Thank You for the opportunities that You have given me to share the love of Christ with others. May Your love continually motivate and compel me to share every day of my life the greatest message in the entire world that Christ died for our sins, that He was buried, and that He rose again. In the resurrected name of Jesus I pray, Amen!

Week 7, Friday

Heavenly Father, this is the day that You have made, and I will rejoice and be glad in it. I am so grateful that I woke up this morning and I am not in hell. You have not given me what I do deserve, commendation and hell, and You have given me everything I do not deserve, the gift of eternal life through Jesus Your Son. Open my heart to experience the fullness of Your love. In Jesus' wonderful name I pray, Amen!

"The LORD is merciful and gracious . . . He has not dealt with us according to our sins, nor punished us according to our iniquities."
PSALM 103:8, 10A

Psalm 103 is a sterling example of a life overflowing with thanksgiving. In this one psalm, there is not one complaint, not one mention of bitterness nor harbor of hate; it is filled with joy and thanksgiving. After counting many of God's blessings in life, the psalmist considers the greatest blessing in life, the Lord's grace and mercy in salvation. Mercy can be defined as God not giving to us what we do deserve; grace can be defined as God giving to us everything we do not deserve. Through the Cross of Christ, God has extended to us mercy and grace.

The reality of life is that a happy heart is a thankful heart, but a sad heart is a grumpy, complaining heart. Anything short of hell is grace; therefore, all of our life as a believer should be one of deep gratitude to God. Thanksgiving affects every area of life—it affects our worship, for God is alone worthy of thanksgiving; it affects our witness, for people are drawn to positively thankful people; it affects our worth, for it makes everything about our body, mind, and spirit feel so much better.

Are you a thankful person? Do you exhibit a daily attitude of gratitude?

EVENING

Abba Father, I bless You with all my soul for all the benefits of Your steadfast, faithful love. Blessed are You, O Lord, for blessing me with every spiritual blessing in Christ, for choosing me in Christ, for redeeming through Your Son's blood, and for sealing me eternally by the Holy Spirit. In Jesus' name I worship You. Amen!

Morning

Father God, I rejoice in the gift of Your Holy Spirit who indwells me. May Your Spirit fill my life and pour out Your amazing love in my heart. Open up heaven over my life as I obey You, and pour out your Spirit in my life. In Jesus' name I pray, Amen.

"Now hope does not disappoint, because the love of God has been poured out in our hearts by the Holy Spirit who was given to us."
Romans 5:5

Christ's love in your heart is an abundant overflowing experience of His Spirit living in your innermost being. Have you ever watched a large water fountain in a park or mall overflowing continually? This is a picture of the Spirit's work in our hearts.

The moment you trust in Christ, you receive the Holy Spirit (Rom. 8:9), who constantly encourages you in your hope in God. The context of this amazing promise of the overflowing love of God is in the midst of difficulties. Are you facing any difficulties in a relationship, sickness, death, or life disappointment?

As a follower of Christ, you have a blessed hope in the midst of heartache and trouble. A good definition of hope can be found by using the word as an acrostic—**H**aving **O**nly **P**ositive **E**xpectations. Faith (Rom. 5:1), hope (v. 2), and love (v. 5) all combine to give the believer patience in the trials of life.

Evening

Heavenly Father, I bless You for the promise of Your Son who said, "He who believes in Me . . . out of his heart will flow rivers of living water" (John 7:38). May the refreshing waters of Your Spirit and love flow through my life and grant me abiding hope in the promise of Your return. In the name of Jesus I pray, Amen!

Week 8, Monday

Heavenly Father, help me to fully appreciate Your love as You quicken Your written Word by the work of the Holy Spirit. May Your Spirit touch my heart today and fill me with a fresh comprehension of Your grace, care, and love for me!

"Behold what manner of love the Father has bestowed on us,
that we should be called children of God!"
1 JOHN 3:1A

It would perhaps not surprise us to read in the Bible, as it indeed states, that we are the servants, or slaves, of God. Due to the horrible nature of our fallen sin-ridden relationship, the Scriptures also make it plain that in our natural, unredeemed state, we are the enemies of God—alienated from Him and without hope in the world.

But here the apostle John brings home the great truth that because of Christ's saving death on the Cross and His glorious resurrection—all due to God's redeeming love—we who are in Christ are now "called children of God."

What a remarkable transformation this change of relationship is! From enemies to children. And all of it is due to God's love, which drove Christ to give Himself for us as the sacrifice for sin. There is no more protective, nurturing, or caring relationship in the world than that of a parent for a child. This analogy is drawn from the apostle John's heart and the Holy Spirit, who moved upon John to reassure us of the greatness of God's love by naming us "children of God." This is God's special word for you today. Because of Jesus and your faith in Him, you are a child of God. Christian, whatever difficulty you are facing, or may certainly face before long, remember that because of God's love, you are His child. And when you face temptation, ridicule, disappointment, neglect, hatefulness, or any other of Satan's darts meant to wound or harm your confidence and faith in God's love, remember the hope—no, better yet, the *reality*—that in Christ you are a child of the eternal, omnipotent, sovereign God of the universe.

EVENING

Father, thank You for Your love! Your love has provided a full and free salvation through Jesus Christ. As I finish this day I rejoice to be called a child of God. Help me tonight to rest in this greatest of all comforts. Tomorrow empower me to live for You. Amen.

MORNING

Today, Lord, as I go about my business, whether my responsibilities are great or small, remind me of the greatness of Your works. You have made and framed the universe! You sustain and provide for it in all of its vastness and greatness. But thank You for Your thoughts toward me. Your love and care are beyond comprehension. I trust in them today. Amen.

"Many, O LORD my God, are Your wonderful works which You have done;
and your thoughts toward us cannot be recounted to You in order;
if I would declare and speak of them, they are more than can be numbered."
PSALM 40:5

Scientists tell us that from the human perspective, the universe is infinite. What a mighty God it is then who oversees and maintains it by the word of His power. Other religions give conflicting concepts of God's majestic control as Creator and Sustainer of the universe. Some say He is a heartless watchmaker who doesn't care or that everything that exists is an accident of impersonal forces!

The psalmist, however, does not necessarily consider God's work as Creator the most awe-inspiring aspect of His nature. Rather, this scripture reminds us that more inspirational is His care, love, and grace toward us. The Bible reminds us that every good and perfect gift comes from the Lord (James 1:17)! So consider each blessing that has ever touched your life—family, friends, food, health, happiness, the beauty of creation, clothing, comfort, encouragement, and the list could go on and on. This earthly life is not perfect, but the joys, happiness, and delights are all God's message to us of His love and care. The Lord's blessings are many.

EVENING

Lord, thank You for Your countless blessings. Thank You most of all for Jesus, for His love and presence. Tomorrow when I wake, give me a fresh awareness of Your love and care. Amen.

Week 8, Wednesday

Heavenly Father, I honor You as the God of history. You are in control of life and human events. Thank You that in Your providence You chose Abraham as Your special servant. Through his descendants, through Israel, You brought our Savior, Your Son Jesus, to die for our sins. Strengthen me today confidently to walk in faith and obedience in Your guiding hand, as well as in faith and obedience to Jesus. Amen.

"For what great nation is there that has God so near to it, as the LORD our God is to us, for whatever reason we may call upon Him?"
DEUTERONOMY 4:7

These words from Moses were spoken as Israel was preparing to enter the Promised Land. Through their rebellion and sinfulness they had experienced God's corrective hand. In their hour of need, traversing a desert without food or water, their Lord God miraculously provided for them.

God had promised Israel that He would be their faithful provider. It was God's personal support and care of Israel that safely saw them through the wilderness to the Promised Land. If this fact was true of Israel, how much truer is it of the one who has trusted in the Messiah of Israel as his or her Lord and Savior? The words of the New Covenant remind us that "all the promises of God in Him are Yes, and in Him Amen, to the glory of God through us" (2 Cor. 1:20).

What is your concern today? Is it small or large? Important or seemingly incidental? It does not matter to our Lord, who does all things well and waits to hear your pleas. We serve a great God who is able to show Himself strong on your behalf.

EVENING

Father, in Jesus' name, give me the faith to trust You with all of my needs. I place afresh my trust in You. Amen.

MORNING

Lord, I don't know what to expect in the day ahead. But I do know what I can expect from You. Be my Shield and Defender! Strengthen me to be faithful to You and to trust You in all I do and am. Help me to live every minute of this day in the fullness of Your Spirit and grace. In Jesus' name, Amen!

"He shall cover you with His feathers, and under His wings you shall take refuge; His truth shall be your shield and buckler."
PSALM 91:4

The psalmist draws a picture of God's care that would be familiar to anyone raised on a farm or familiar with the barnyard: a hen covering her chicks with her wings. And while a hen is certainly not the most threatening of creatures, she will guard her chicks with an unparalleled fierceness. Ah, consider this, believer in Jesus: God cares for you with as much loving grace. But He who covers you with His care and love is no barnyard chicken—He is the Lord God omnipotent! His love infinitely surpasses the natural bonds of care. They are infinite and supernatural in their intensity. He is a loving and gracious God, but one who carries a shield and wears a buckler. He is prepared to do battle with your foes and in His time to put them to flight. He will provide for and protect you. This is what this verse tells us of the ever-enduring love of God in Christ. When trouble touches our lives, we can be certain it has been filtered through God's providence. In such cases, His grace will always be sufficient.

EVENING

Father, in Jesus' name, I thank You for Your perfect love for me. I know that I am never promised release from the problems of life, but I am released from questioning or doubting Your love! Because of the Cross I am joined to You in Jesus, and in that promise I rest my cares and troubles. Thank You for loving me. In the strong and saving name of Jesus, Amen!

Father, we honor You and thank You for Your great love for us. Where would we be without Your love and forgiveness through Jesus Christ? What a joy it is to our hearts to realize that our salvation is complete and full through the greatness of Your mercy. I love You and thank You for loving me so fully and freely even while I was unbelieving and rebellious against You. May the Holy Spirit today control my life and help me to live for Your glory. Amen.

"But God, who is rich in mercy, because of His great love with which He loved us, even when we were dead in trespasses, made us alive together with Christ (by grace you have been saved)."
EPHESIANS 2:4, 5

Is there anything more amazing than the love of God? It would be quite understandable that the eternal, omnipotent, sovereign Creator of the universe would be largely indifferent to any and all human beings. Amazingly, however, the truth is that God *loves* us. And His love was and is not a superficial, emotional type of caring. Rather, this was and is the self-giving, sacrificial love that compelled Christ to go to the Cross.

Notably He did this while we "were dead in trespasses." Our rebellion against God, another way of expressing "trespass," didn't just injure or impede us; rather, it destroyed our relationship with God. Apart from the restoring, regenerating work of the Holy Spirit, we would have remained dead. By the grace of God, however, He saved us! Grace in the original Greek language is *charis*. We transliterate that word into English as *charity*. The meaning, however, translates as well. Charity means doing or giving something to someone totally incapable of repaying the gift. That is true charity.

EVENING

Thank You, Lord God, for the wonderful, free, eternal gift of salvation through Jesus Christ. I know that I can be and am saved because of what Jesus did for me on the Cross. Help me to awaken tomorrow morning freshly aware of Your grace and goodness to me!

Heavenly Father, I am so very grateful for Your love, salvation, and care for me. Without You, my life would be a disaster. With You, I am so very blessed and encouraged. Please help me this day to walk in step with Your Spirit's leadership. As I do, help me to be sensitive to the needs of others whom I might encounter. Help me to be a blessing to others! In the strong and loving name of Jesus, Amen!

"But whoever has this world's goods, and sees his brother in need, and shuts up his heart from him, how does the love of God abide in him?"

1 JOHN 3:17

The Bible, the Word of God, is so infinitely practical and personally challenging. There seems to be no place untouched or unturned when it comes to every aspect of life. It challenges our thoughts—whether they are pure; our motives— whether they are sincere; our beliefs—whether they are right; and our living—whether or not it is holy.

In this verse the Bible asks a simple question: how is it possible for those with enough to ignore Christians in desperate need? Can God's love dwell in the hearts of those who ignore a Christian brother's essentials for life? Immediately our thoughts are directed to the example of Christ: "For you know the grace of our Lord Jesus Christ, that though He was rich, yet for your sakes He became poor, that you through His poverty might become rich" (2 Cor. 8:9).

God's love fully incarnated in Jesus compelled Him to give and surrender all for us. The answer to John's question is obvious. It is impossible for God's love to fully control a person who is unconcerned about the needs of other Christians! Grace, wisdom, and discernment all go hand in hand to sensitize us about helping and supplying the needs of those who cannot help themselves.

EVENING

My Lord in heaven, thank You for Your love and provision. Lord Jesus, thank You for becoming poor so that I may become "rich" spiritually and eternally. Help me to discern the true needs of my brothers and sisters in Christ. Give me grace to help and encourage them. In Jesus' name I pray, Amen.

PHIL ROBERTS, KANSAS CITY, MO

Father, today I praise You that the substance of my faith is measurable in tangible ways. While I know that works will never save me, I thank You that my salvation will by necessity change the way I live. Help me, on this day, to demonstrate the reality of true repentance, both in my attitudes and actions. Protect me from bitterness over the consequences of my sins and give me the strength to honor You as a new creation in Christ. Thank You for giving me grace that is always sufficient. In Jesus' name, Amen.

"Therefore bear fruits worthy of repentance."
MATTHEW 3:8

Repentance is never easy. Flimsy excuses, self-righteous blame, and blind justification often minimize our behavior as anything but sin, leaving us negotiating with God rather than pleading for His forgiveness. Apparently, the Pharisees and Sadducees caught the eye of John the Baptist as he preached in the wilderness, evoking a sharp rebuke for the hypocrisy of their self-righteousness. His words cut us as well, for they serve as a reminder that the evidence of repentance is not mere confession, grief, or adherence to religious standards that are often void of heart transformation. To the contrary, life change, both inside and out, is the ultimate mark of a genuine abandonment of sin and turning toward God. The broken person knows he does not deserve forgiveness and will forsake his pride and sin in order to receive it. Good deeds born out of humility are the fruit of repentance. Religious activity, extensive sacrifice, and even diligent prayer may or may not meet this criterion. Ultimately, the key is not what people think about you, but what God knows about you. Is repentance something you do, or is it a reflection of who you are?

EVENING

Lord, as I end this day help me to abandon my prideful tendency to defend my sin and diminish Your holiness. Remind me of my need to walk in good deeds that reflect a grateful heart that is overcome with the height, depth, and width of Your love and forgiveness. Thank You for loving me for who Christ is rather than who I am. Empower me to demonstrate a changed life that bears the marks of fruitful repentance. I praise You for being a merciful God. In Jesus' name, Amen.

MORNING

Father, give me the strength throughout this day to think sanctified thoughts. Thank You for revealing much of Your will for my life within the pages of Holy Scripture. Give me eyes to see and a heart to yield to those things consistent with Your Holy Word. Protect me from the temptation of rationalizing sin, leaving me clearly outside the boundaries of sanctification. Mature me by Your grace and uphold me by Your mercy. I honor You for never leaving me or forsaking me, even when I stumble. In Jesus' name, Amen.

"For this is the will of God, your sanctification: that you should abstain from sexual immorality; that each of you should know how to possess his own vessel in sanctification and honor."
1 THESSALONIANS 4:3, 4

Like a goal that is just beyond our reach, we often portray the will of God as mysterious and even frustrating. After all, who can really know what God wants for their lives? Yet God's Word teaches that renewing our minds transforms us, making it possible to prove the "good and acceptable and perfect will of God" (Rom. 12:2). The key to finding God's will is a sanctified mind that thinks the way God wants you to think. When your thoughts operate within the parameters of sanctification, you will seek God's will less because it will be readily apparent. Such is the case regarding our sexuality. Fornication, adultery, homosexuality, and other forms of immorality should leave us seeking God, not for direction, but for the strength to yield to the clear principles of His Word. Perhaps Scripture records this example because no other sin affects us like those that are sexual in nature. Because God always wants His children to walk in holiness, praying for the power to do His will is just as important as praying for the wisdom to discern it.

EVENING

Lord, thank You for walking beside me throughout this day. Please forgive me for any attitudes and/or behaviors that did not reflect a crucified life. Renew my passion to follow You without question or hesitation, and continue transforming my thoughts as I seek to bear the mind of Christ. I praise You, oh God, for Your constant love and unwavering patience as I seek to be more like You. Amen.

ADAM DOOLEY, CHATTANOOGA, TN

Lord, today my greatest desire is to live with eternity in mind. Remind me throughout the day that I need Your grace as much as those around me. Give me a sensitivity for people who are open to the saving gospel of Jesus Christ. Protect me from apathy, fear, and laziness as I seek to be a witness for You. Empower me to walk with integrity as I seek to reflect the transforming power of Your grace. Increase my joy each time I hear what You are doing in the lives of others. Thank you for saving me. Amen.

"I say to you that likewise there will be more joy in heaven over one sinner who repents than over ninety-nine just persons who need no repentance."
LUKE 15:7

What causes you to rejoice? Which priorities rise to the top of your daily list of responsibilities? Are you preoccupied with earthly things or heavenly things? Answering these questions requires an honest evaluation of who we really are. In order to measure the health of what brings us satisfaction, we do well to consider what elicits the smile of heaven. Demonstrating that human righteousness does not impress God, Luke reminds us of the pleasure God finds in His own grace. No wonder Jesus said, "I did not come to call the righteous, but sinners, to repentance" (Matt. 9:13). Though all people are sinners, not all are willing to admit it. The gospel is for those who, in a spirit of brokenness, will call out to God for mercy as they repent of their sins. Consequently, life's greatest admission is realizing that we cannot qualify for His grace. Likewise, life's greatest ambition, outside of knowing Christ personally, is making Him known to others. Do you celebrate what heaven applauds? Are your milestones victories from an eternal perspective?

EVENING

God, thank You for the privilege of serving as Your ambassador throughout this day. Forgive me for any opportunities where I missed or neglected sharing Your gospel. As I seek to live with eternity in mind, erode any hint of selfishness reflected in my personal goals, ambitions, and joys. Give me a new passion to share my faith, along with the protection I will need to be a faithful representative of Your grace. I praise You for the privilege of being on mission with You. In Jesus' name, Amen.

MORNING

Father, I long to see Your power unleashed in my life. Help me to walk in holiness for the sake of Your name. As I do, give me the privilege of seeing Your hand, appreciating Your glory, and marveling at Your strength in all things. Protect me on this day from temptation and sin so that I will in no way hinder Your work through my life. Keep me in the center of Your will that I might experience the maximum display of Your power. I pray that today will only be the beginning of Your wonderful works. In Jesus' name, Amen.

"And Joshua said to the people, 'Sanctify yourselves, for tomorrow the LORD will do wonders among you.'"

JOSHUA 3:5

Why does the Lord require holiness from His children? The apostle Peter offers the primary answer: "Be holy, for I am holy" (1 Pet. 1:16). Sanctification is God's ultimate means of making Himself known through us. But there is another reason. Has it ever occurred to you that apart from a consecrated life we cannot see the power of God? Joshua assured the people of Israel that God would do wonders among them after they sanctified themselves. Realizing the context of this promise makes it even more amazing. The Israelites already witnessed God part the Red Sea, and He was about to divide the Jordan River in order to lead them into the Promised Land. And yet, these miracles were just the beginning. You will never experience the abundance of God's strength until you yield completely to Him. God's commandants are not designed to rob us of blessings—they are meant to unleash them. He not only intends to demonstrate His power through you, He also longs to display it to you.

EVENING

Lord, I praise Your name as the holy God of heaven and earth. Thank you for making me holy because You are holy. I worship You for allowing me to be a channel and a witness to the great things You do. Continue to sanctify my life so that I never disregard Your work in me and around me. I confess to You that my spirit is often willing, but my flesh remains weak. God, finish the work you began in me so that I might continue to see Your glory. Amen.

ADAM DOOLEY, CHATTANOOGA, TN

Week 9, Friday

Lord, I worship You as the Creator of heaven and earth. I praise You as my Maker and the Captain of my soul. Today, I recommit myself to follow You more closely, seeking greater evidence of my inheritance in Christ. Restore the joy of my sanctification, as I anticipate my future reward in heaven. Because you honor me as a sibling in Your kingdom, I will honor You by abandoning pursuits contrary to Your holiness. Thank you for walking beside me with patience and love as I try to live the Christian life. In Jesus' name, Amen.

"For it was fitting for Him, for whom are all things and by whom are all things, in bringing many sons to glory, to make the captain of their salvation perfect through sufferings. For both He who sanctifies and those who are being sanctified are all of one, for which reason He is not ashamed to call them brethren."

HEBREWS 2:10, 11

In a universe created by and for Jesus Christ, it only makes sense that salvation must come through Him as well. Like a pioneer blazing a trail where no one has gone before, Jesus is the Captain of salvation for all who will follow Him. By identifying with us through the suffering of the Cross, Christ allows us to identify with Him in the glory of His resurrection. The supreme evidence of our relationship with the Lord is that we are sanctified just as He was sanctified. The grace to be righteous is much like a present deposit on a future reward. While good works do not merit salvation, walking in holiness assures us that we are the brothers and sisters of Christ who will enjoy the bounty of His sacrificial work forever. The hope of our present sanctification is the anticipation of our future glorification. No wonder the Bible says Christ brings many "to glory."

EVENING

Father, Your goodness in my life is overwhelming. Thank you for treating me as a joint heir with Christ even though I still stumble in sin. Forgive me when my walk is inconsistent with my talk and I transgress against Your holiness. Continue to guard my heart and my mind, that my thoughts, words, and steps will be pleasing in Your sight. How precious is Your loving-kindness; I will take refuge in the shadow of Your wings. In Jesus' name, Amen.

Father, the reality of Your love is both encouraging and humbling. To think that You love us while we are yet sinners and that You delay Your judgment in mercy is more than I can fathom. I praise You that Your nature is to love and that I have experienced it personally. I pray that You will continue to be patient with others just as You are with me. Create within me a clean heart that sees the nations as You do, not rushing to judgment about others. Help me, today, as I seek to be diligent about inviting sinners to Christ. Amen.

"The Lord is not slack concerning His promise, as some count slackness,
but is longsuffering toward us, not willing that any should perish
but that all should come to repentance."

2 PETER 3:9

Though many assume a great dichotomy between the judgment of God and the grace of God, no such division exists. To the contrary, when God executes His wrath there is still evidence of His love. This does not mean that He will overlook sin and ignore His holiness, but the timing of God's reckoning reveals the abundance of His patience. While some wonder why God does not bring sinners to justice immediately, the apostle Peter reminds us that apparent slackness is really intentional mercy. God's delay is a reflection of His desire that none "should perish but that all should come to repentance." Just as God waited to destroy the earth in the days of Noah, He patiently waits today to give the world opportunity to repent. Thus, God actively demonstrates His love for all even though not all will be saved. His love by necessity demands holiness, but His holiness is always tempered by His love.

EVENING

Lord, tonight I rest knowing that there is never a moment when You cease to love me. I ask for Your continued patience as I seek to be more like Christ. Forgive me when I desire Your judgment toward others, though I continually need Your grace. I will not fret because the wicked seem to prosper. Instead, I will patiently wait on You and trust that Your ways are better than mine. In Jesus' name, Amen.

Week 10, Monday

Father, because I have been purchased with a great price and now am set apart for Your service and glory, I commit myself this day to seek first Your kingdom and righteousness. Help me this day to die to self that I might live for You. May I live this day with a heart overflowing with gratitude, free from the guilt of sin. In Jesus' name, Amen.

"Then He said, 'Behold, I have come to do Your will, O God.'
He takes away the first that He may establish the second. By that will we
have been sanctified through the offering of the body of Jesus Christ once for all."
HEBREWS 10:9, 10

Gon is holy; therefore, we are to be holy. God is separate from nature, He is separate from other gods, and He is separate from sinners—unapproachable except by mediation and sacrifice. God is set apart and set above all others. Jesus was set apart to be like no other. He came into this world, set apart to accomplish His Father's will. He was born like no other, taught like no other, prayed like no other, died like no other, was buried like no other, and was resurrected like no other. Jesus, knowing He was set apart, said, "Behold, I have come to do Your will, O God." Jesus was willing to do God's will even if it meant taking upon Himself our sin. That was His struggle in the Garden of Gethsemane and the reason He prayed, "If it is possible, let this cup pass from Me" (Matt. 26:39).

As followers of Christ we are to be set apart; we are to be unlike the people of the world. By the sacrifice of Jesus, we have been separated from the world and dedicated to God. However, like Jesus, doing the will of God often comes with challenges and soul searching. Jesus ushered in a new covenant not because animal sacrifices were wrong, just insufficient. The sacrifice of the Lamb of God is sufficient for our sanctification. The sacrifices of Old Testament lambs only covered sin, but the sacrifice of the New Testament Lamb cleanses sin. We are set apart to make a difference in the world as His ambassadors. We must be different to make a difference!

EVENING

Lord, as darkness closes out this day, I pray my life today pleased You. Amen.

Help me this day, O Lord, to be sensitive to any and all opportunities I have to meet, in the name of Jesus, the needs of others, and to share Jesus through these opportunities. May my words this day encourage others in the Lord. In Jesus' name, Amen.

"Repent therefore and be converted, that your sins may be blotted out, so that times of refreshing may come from the presence of the Lord."

ACTS 3:19

The thought behind sanctification is to get back that which was lost. Peter and John, in the name of Jesus, had just healed a lame man by the gate of the temple, which was called Beautiful. There this lame man received back that which he had lost, the strength of his legs. The people were amazed by this miracle, and the occasion gave way for Peter to preach an impromptu sermon. There are three elements in Peter's sermon:

1. Repentance. Peter told these Jews to repent, which is to change one's mind about himself and his sin. Repentance is more than contrition or feeling bad. Repentance is to turn from sin—to quit the sin.

2. Redemption. To repent means to turn from; to be converted means to turn to. Redemption is the result of turning from sin and turning to the Savior. Unless we turn from our sins, we cannot place saving faith in Jesus Christ.

3. Restoration. It is when our sins are forgiven that we experience times of refreshing. To refresh is to restore strength. Just as strength was restored to the lame man's legs, it is when our sins are forgiven that a right relationship with the Lord is restored. Restoration brings to us refreshment in the form of the outpouring of the Holy Spirit.

In this impromptu sermon, Peter calls for both individual and national repentance. Peter's point is that where there is no repentance, there will be no refreshing. One day many Jews will repent and turn to the Lord, and the Spirit of grace will be poured out upon them (Zech. 12:10). Then they will get back that which they lost: their relationship with the Lord.

EVENING

Lord, I grant You the right to point out any sin in my life. In Jesus' name, Amen.

Lord, I pray that the Holy Spirit would give me insight into Your Word so that I might correctly understand and apply Your Word to my life. I thank You, Lord, for my salvation as I commit myself to the working out of that salvation through my life today. In Jesus' name, Amen.

*"But we are bound to give thanks to God always for you,
brethren beloved by the Lord, because God from the beginning chose
you for salvation through sanctification by the Spirit and belief in the truth."*
2 THESSALONIANS 2:13

The theme of Paul's second epistle to the Thessalonians concerned their confusion about the coming day of the Lord. They had either been misinformed or they misunderstood the sequence of events around the Lord's return and were consequently idle in the Lord's work. Because wrong beliefs lead to wrong behavior, Paul writes to them about their:

1. **Conversion.** Their salvation was the result of God's love. John 3:16 tells us that salvation is grounded in God's love. God's love is *personal*—"for God so loved the world." God's love is *proven*—"that He gave His only begotten Son." God's love is *perpetual*—"that whoever believes in Him should not perish but have everlasting life."

2. **Choosing.** Love alone does not save us; God loves the whole world, yet the whole world will not be saved. God's grace gives to us what we do not deserve—salvation. God's mercy does not give to us what we do deserve—death and separation. These, God gave to Jesus on the Cross.

3. **Cleansing.** Sanctification means "purification" and refers to the work of the Holy Spirit leading the unbeliever to faith in Christ where he can be cleansed from his sin.

4. **Commission.** God has ordained the end—salvation; and God has ordained the means to the end—belief in the truth. Just as God sent Paul to the Thessalonians, He commissions us to take the truth of the gospel to the world.

EVENING

Lord, my body may often need rest, but I pray that I would never rest from sharing the truth of Your salvation. In Jesus' name, Amen.

MORNING

Lord, you have set me apart; I am no longer a part of this world, but rather a part of Your kingdom. Help me this day to represent You and Your kingdom's interest. In Jesus' name, Amen.

"As You sent Me into the world, I also have sent them into the world. And for their sakes I sanctify Myself, that they also may be sanctified by the truth."
JOHN 17:18, 19

In John 17, we have the high priestly prayer of Jesus, which is the longest prayer recorded in the Bible. In this prayer Jesus interceded for His disciples. It is the greatest prayer ever uttered and prayed by the greatest Intercessor who ever prayed.

We are sanctified to serve the Lord. Note two aspects of our service:

1. The example of our service. Jesus prayed to the Father saying, "You sent Me into the world." God the Father sent Jesus the Son into the world. And Jesus came not to be served, but to serve. Just as Jesus was set apart to serve, He sets us apart to serve. We do not send ourselves; our sending is always by divine orders. Jesus also prayed, "I have given to them the words which You have given Me" (John 17:8). Jesus was sent with a message, and we are sent with a message. Where there is no message, there is no mission.

2. The environment of our service. The place of service for both Jesus and His followers is the world. The Father sent Jesus into the world, and it was not an easy place of service. Jesus was rejected, even by His own people, and executed on a Cross. Our Lord does not send us to a place of ease and comfort. If you are looking for a comfortable and convenient environment for service, you do not understand service. Jesus had to sacrifice His life. How can we serve Him and expect to be exempt from sacrifice? We may not be received well by the world, but we must go where our Lord directs; we must share what He has given to us.

EVENING

Lord, regardless of the difficulty, may my life be useful to You. In Jesus' name, Amen.

Lord, help me this day not to criticize what You are blessing, even if I lack understanding or it is different from that which I'm accustomed. May I never contend with what You are blessing. In Jesus' name, Amen.

"When they heard these things they became silent; and they glorified God, saying, 'Then God has also granted to the Gentiles repentance to life.'"
ACTS 11:18

Something new was happening in the church, and some of the older members didn't like it. Peter had been led by God's Spirit to go to the Gentile home of Cornelius and lead him to Christ, which Peter did. When Peter returned to Jerusalem they "contended with him" (Acts 11:2, 3), meaning they opposed him and debated him. Peter's experience teaches us two things:

1. The disciples' acceptance. Our preconceived ideas and prejudices often keep us from accepting what God is doing. When someone else does church differently than we do, then they must be wrong. I wonder, if the Twelve were alive today, where they would attend church? We should always be cautious before criticizing what God may be blessing. If we are to love the lost, unregenerate man who is outside the family of God, surely we should have great love and affection for those who are a part of the family of God.

2. The Deity's anointing. We see the Holy Spirit's involvement in the commission to the saints and the conversion of the sinner.

Peter said "the Holy Spirit fell upon" the Gentiles when they believed (Acts 11:15). The Lord never commands us to be baptized by the Holy Spirit; that happens automatically at the time of our conversion. We are, however, after this baptism commanded to be filled with the Holy Spirit.

EVENING

Lord, fill me with Your Spirit and take control of my thoughts, my behavior, and my attitude. In Jesus' name, Amen.

MORNING

Lord, help me to make Your love for the church the pattern for me to love my family. Thank You for my biological family and my church family; may I be a blessing to both. In Jesus' name, Amen.

"Husbands, love your wives, just as Christ also loved the church and gave Himself for her, that He might sanctify and cleanse her with the washing of water by the word."
EPHESIANS 5:25, 26

There is no greater intimacy in our human relationships than that of husband and wife. In Ephesians 25, the apostle Paul gives to us instruction not only to enhance that relationship but also to relate to us the intimacy and love between Jesus, the Bridegroom, and the church, His bride. We learn three things here about love:

1. The command to love. We often think of love as an emotion, but we are to relate love to our will as well. Just as a husband is commanded to love his wife, we are also commanded to love the Lord. Jesus said the first and greatest commandment is, "You shall love the LORD your God with all your heart . . . soul, and . . . mind" (Matt. 22:37).

2. The commitment of love. Jesus' love was so great that He "gave Himself" for His bride. Considering Christ's great love, we find it much easier to submit to Him. Jacob so loved Rachel that he sacrificed fourteen years of labor to have and hold her.

3. The cleansing of love. In the marriage ceremony the husband is set apart to belong to his wife, and the wife is set apart to belong to her husband. This arrangement provides them with purity. In salvation, we are set apart to belong to Jesus Christ; we are cleansed in His blood to wash away our sin. Jesus demonstrated this so beautifully when He washed the disciples' feet.

EVENING

Lord, help me to be clean in this dirty world. In Jesus' name, Amen.

 *Week 11, Monday*

Gracious heavenly Father, thank You for the joy of knowing that You are My heavenly Father. As I begin this day, I ask that Your Spirit would speak to my heart and provide me with all the things necessary to please You today. I confess my sin to You because Jesus Christ is my Savior and Lord, and I place myself at Your disposal in every way. Please help me to make wise decisions and to live my life today in a manner that will be well pleasing to You. In Jesus' name, Amen.

"Therefore I judge that we should not trouble those from among the Gentiles who are turning to God."
ACTS 15:19

Millions of people throughout history have tried to find some way to justify their salvation. Classic stories abound about very sincere men and women who denied themselves in every conceivable way in an effort to find peace with God. Some starved themselves to death, some lived in caves for years, and some followed religious rituals of every kind—all in an effort to merit their salvation. The Jewish Christians certainly had many rules and regulations they had grown up with. When they converted and trusted in the Lord Jesus Christ, they really struggled to understand the difference between faith and works. Their faith was so new to them that they even thought Gentiles needed to follow their rules of religion, too. While the practice of your faith in very important, the justification of your faith is in Christ alone! Nothing we do can ever merit our salvation. Praise the Lord!

EVENING

I want to thank You, Lord, for the wonderful privilege of knowing that You have been with me today. I know I have failed You many times and, for that, I am very sorry. Please forgive me for my sins today. I am so grateful You saved me by grace alone. The good things I do for You are all because of my love for You—it grows stronger every day. Grant to me a good night's sleep, and let me wake up refreshed and ready to serve You again tomorrow. In Jesus' name, Amen.

MORNING

Dear heavenly Father, what joy to begin my day with You. Thank you for loving me the way You do, and thank You for sending Your Son to die on the Cross for my sins. As I begin this day, please forgive me for my sin. I repent before You and claim 1 John 1:9 for myself today. I need You in everything I do today, and I want You to know just how much I depend on You. Thank You for loving me despite myself. In Jesus' name, I pray. Amen.

"Our Lord Jesus Christ, who gave Himself for our sins, that He might deliver us from this present evil age, according to the will of our God and Father."
GALATIANS 1:3B, 4

To suggest that life is not busy would be the understatement of the century! Everything seems to be going on, and there never seems to be enough time in the day. The problem is the way in which we live this life and conduct ourselves as Christians. The "pull" of the world's standards and the temptation to relax our standards present a real challenge. How can we live separated lives and be the kind of people who live out the reality of our walk in Christ? This passage reminds us of three wonderful truths. First, Jesus Christ is our anchor because He is the only One who has set us free through the forgiveness of our sins. Second, we can be delivered from the temptations associated with a world without Christ. Third, our deliverance from sin and our ability to lead godly lives, in spite of the world in which we live, is the will of God for us. He designed it this way so we could live lives pleasing to Him.

EVENING

Precious heavenly Father, thank You for the day I have lived today. When I began the day, You were there for me. And now that it is ending, You are still there for me. Thank You for helping me to make it through the day. I know I sinned against You, and I confess my sin to You. But I also know You enabled me to stand up straight even when I thought I would not be able to do so. You are my strength and my tower. In Jesus' name, I pray. Amen.

Most gracious heavenly Father, I bow my head in Your presence at the beginning of a new day. You alone are the King of kings and the Lord of lords. No one can compare with You! You are mighty and powerful, and I turn to You on this day because I cannot do this on my own. There are too many challenges facing me, and I am weak and helpless without You. I will trust You completely in every way today. And I pray all of this in Jesus' wonderful name, Amen.

"Again, when a wicked man turns away from the wickedness which he committed, and does what is lawful and right, he preserves himself alive."
EZEKIEL 18:27

Every Christian should go on at least one international mission trip. It will open your eyes to many things. Perhaps the greatest impact is to see the literal transformation that takes place in the lives of those who have come to know the Lord Jesus. While speaking to many wonderful people in Central Asia, I was reminded of this. The oppressiveness of many of these governments leaves people without hope. People look miserable and never smile. The old Soviet Union taught, "Only fools smile." When talking to local people, you can immediately see those who are Christians and those who are not. Their faces tell it all without a word being spoken! God's eternal life is the abundant life of Christ. It begins at the instant moment of salvation. This is why the prophet spoke of the wonderful change that takes place when a sinner repents and turns to God. Such a person becomes alive. And this "living life" is preserved by the Holy Spirit's indwelling presence and power!

EVENING

Thank You, my heavenly Father, for allowing me to live another day "alive" in You. Thank You for the wonderful forgiveness I have enjoyed because of the Lord Jesus Christ. Thank You for opening my eyes and giving me a fresh understanding of the transforming power of the gospel. Thank You for enabling me to have the strength to stand firm and live a separated life of excellence for You. I have so many battles, but You always give me all I need to make it through. I am looking forward to another day with You at my side. Amen.

MORNING

Dear heavenly Father, as I begin this new day, I thank You for Your abiding presence in my life. I realize I have quite a lot to do today. I have decisions to make and places to go. My day will be filled with issues, and I also have burdens on my heart. I ask You to please fill me with Your Holy Spirit in such a way that I will know You are there all the time. I do confess my sin to You, and in Jesus' wonderful name I pray, Amen.

"Now may the God of peace Himself sanctify you completely; and may your whole spirit, soul, and body be preserved blameless at the coming of our Lord Jesus Christ."

1 THESSALONIANS 5:23

There is no doubt that the Lord Jesus is going to come again. When He does all people who belong to Him will be taken up into His presence to join all who are already with Him in heaven. No one knows when this will be. It could be very soon. There are many things going on in the world that match what the Bible teaches us about the signs of His coming. The problem is, you and I are still alive! We have not yet died, and Jesus has not yet come in the clouds.

How do we live as Christians in a wicked world? In this passage Paul really encourages us while we wait for Jesus. It is impossible for any of us to live perfect lives because God is the only perfect One. But we can live out our lives in a manner well pleasing to the Lord. God will do this for us through His Spirit if we are yielded to Him. Yes, in Christ, you can!

EVENING

Gracious and loving heavenly Father, how can I ever thank You enough for the gift of life You have given me through Your Son, the Lord Jesus Christ? Without Him I would be nothing! I would be helpless and hopeless, like a ship without a rudder! I find so many challenges every day, and today was no exception. I prayed to You this morning, and You made all the difference. Even though I still struggle, I go to bed knowing You are helping me live my life in a way that is pleasing to You. In Jesus' name I pray, Amen.

Week 11, Friday

Dear heavenly Father, thank You for the beginning of a brand new day. I will confess to You that there are many things I am looking forward to and many I am not looking forward to. Please forgive me today for my sin. Help me to live today as a person who knows You and has a personal relationship with You. I find this hard to do at the best of times, so I commit my day to You today with no strings attached. These things I pray in Jesus' name, Amen.

"And the hand of the Lord was with them,
and a great number believed and turned to the Lord."
ACTS 11:21

Little children are a most precious gift from the Lord. I know you feel the same as I do. My wife and I will always be grateful for our children, and now our grandson, Bolt. Guardianship remains high on any parent's list of responsibilities with little ones. I well remember a little chap coming by me in a mall in a state of unbridled panic and hysteria. He had lost his mommy! After putting my arms around him, it did not take long to find the hand of the only one who could appease his stress and anxiety. This is exactly what we are reading about today from God's Word. These people were stressed to the max! They were being persecuted and hammered from every direction because of their faith in the Lord. Today's world may not present similar persecution to some of us, but life is still tough. Marriages are under fire, teens are on the prowl for meaning, and markets are collapsing. But the hand of the Lord has not been removed! Place your hand in His!

EVENING

Most gracious heavenly Father, how can I ever thank You for all You do for me? I am so grateful for all of the blessings I have and enjoy. I realize there are so many people around the world who are less fortunate and face so many more troubles than I ever could imagine. But this is my world, and I need to thank You for guiding me and holding my hand. You have held my hand in my storms, and You have held my hand in my blessings. As this day closes, I thank You in the name of Jesus, Amen.

MORNING

Most gracious and loving heavenly Father, I begin this day in prayer. I want to consult with You, and I want You to know that I cannot go through any day without You. I have tried many times before and realize You are the only One who can help Me do the things I need to do in a manner that will be pleasing to You and a testimony to others. I commit all I do today to Your counsel, and I trust You. In Jesus' wonderful name I pray, Amen.

"Then God saw their works, that they turned from their evil way; and God relented from the disaster that He had said He would bring upon them, and He did not do it."
JONAH 3:10

I have preached alongside our people in hundreds of prisons across the United States of America. Talking about sin seems logical! Thousands of inmates have repented of their sins and have come to accept Jesus Christ as their Lord and Savior. I always remind them, "The only difference between the best of us in here and the worst of them out there is the grace of God." Amens abound! Needless to say, you and I do not need to be incarcerated to be in need of God's forgiveness. All of us are guilty as charged. Just like the Ninevites in Jonah's day, we are expected to turn away from our sin. Like them we are under the threat of God's judgment because He is righteous. He hates all sin! Repentance changes God's mind. When we repent and confess, He forgives and reconciles us to Himself because of the sacrifice of Jesus. What a wonderful God and Father of our Lord Jesus Christ!

EVENING

Gracious and loving heavenly Father, how can I ever thank You enough for the wonderful gift of salvation You have given to me in and through Your Son, the Lord Jesus Christ? I have repented of my sin, and I know my name is written in God's Book of Life in heaven. Tonight, as I go to bed, I repent of my sin as a Christian. I realize the sin in my life robs me of my joy. I want to have a full and meaningful life. I want to have real purpose and experience real joy. I love You in Jesus' name, Amen.

Precious Lord, I praise You for having a plan and a purpose for my life. Your ways are so different than my ways and Your thoughts so above my thoughts. You are my guide, my compass, my GPS, and my traveling companion. Lord, thank You for that today. You will lead me beside still waters and in the right paths I should follow. Use Your Word to give me direction for today's journey and for decisions about tomorrow. I am so blessed to know that You blaze a trail for me today. Thank You, Lord. Amen.

"I thought about my ways, and turned my feet to Your testimonies."
PSALM 119:59

Have you ever been traveling on a journey and realized you may not be going in the right direction? At that moment you have two choices: turn around or continue traveling and hope that you will eventually arrive at the right destination. The psalmist tells us four steps to follow when traveling on life's journey. We begin with *concentration.* He says, "I thought." One thing our Enemy does not want us to do is to stop and think about the direction we are traveling. He surrounds us with thousands of amusements in order to keep us from thinking.

His thoughts led to a *culmination.* He says, "I thought about my ways." Have you taken the time to be quiet and ask, "Where is this path taking me?"

Once he discovered he was heading in the wrong direction, he made a *correction* in his journey. He said he turned his feet. Here is the point of decision, the crossroads. Ask yourself, "Am I determined to keep going in the same direction knowing the destination is not good, or am I going to turn around?"

Finally, the psalmist did not make his decision based on man's philosophy, but according "to Your testimonies." His only *consideration* was the Word of God.

EVENING

Thank You, Father, for Your unfailing love and for never giving up on a prodigal child. Even when I make wrong turns, You are there to correct me and get me back on the right path. I am forever grateful to You because You are my light and my salvation, and I never have to travel in the dark. You will show me the way of life, granting me the joy of Your presence and the pleasures of living with You forever. Amen.

MORNING

Good morning, Father. You alone are God, and besides You, there is no other. I praise You for Your patience with my human failures, for Your gentleness with my compulsiveness, and for Your grace with my weaknesses. I choose to live for You alone, to live to please You alone, and to serve You above everything else today. My heart is Your throne today, and nothing else is there but You. Be magnified in my absolute abandonment to You. In the name of Jesus, Amen.

"Do not turn to idols, nor make for yourselves molded gods: I am the Lord your God."
LEVITICUS 19:4

India has more idols than the United States has citizens. A traveler throughout Asia and parts of Africa will encounter many objects of worship. These images cannot see, cannot hear, and cannot help. Sadly, in desperate situations people turn to all sorts of things looking for contentment and satisfaction.

However, the most dangerous idols are not carved into the form of a deity or made of silver, wood, or metal. The most insidious idol is the one that lingers in our heart. Ezekiel was brokenhearted that the men of his day had "set up their idols in their hearts" (Ezek. 14:3). An idol is anything we trust in when we do not trust in God.

Can a Christian have idols? John ended his first letter by saying, "Little children, keep yourselves from idols" (1 John 5:21). Could it be that God is using present day circumstances in our world to encourage us to turn from our idols of materialism and place all our trust in Him? William Cowper wrote in 1772, "The dearest idol I have known, whate'er that idol be, help me to tear it from Thy throne, and worship only Thee."

EVENING

Precious Father, You have always been and You will always be, and You have blessed me by manifesting Your presence in my life today. I praise You for seeing everything in my life, for hearing everything I say, and for caring about even the details in my life. Help me to keep my heart uncluttered. Give me grace to trust in You and You alone for all the decisions and details of my life. You are able to handle anything that I may face tomorrow because You are the almighty God. I love You, Lord. Amen.

MICHAEL CLOER, ROCKY MOUNT, NC

What a great morning You have given me, Father. Thank You for giving me this privilege of life, of knowing You, of serving You, of having You with me constantly. I praise You for being always present at all places at all times. A building or a body cannot contain all of You. O God, I present my body to You as a living sacrifice today, totally and unreservedly. I pray You will be comfortable dwelling in me and that I would be a holy habitation that honors You. Amen.

"For now I have chosen and sanctified this house, that My name may be there forever; and My eyes and My heart will be there perpetually."

2 CHRONICLES 7:16

What self-respecting woman would not want to keep her house as clean and uncluttered as possible? She constantly picks up, puts away, dusts, vacuums, and mops. She loves her family and wants them to live in the most sanitary and comfortable surroundings. She also knows that company could drop in at any moment, and she wants her house to glorify her Lord at all times. She does all this for her family's name, and for His name, and often she sees this as a privilege and not just a responsibility.

While maintaining a clean house for the Lord's glory is a worthy aspiration, we understand that the house where we live isn't God's primary concern. He cares much more about the state of the house where He lives—our heart.

If I am called a "Christian", then I bear Christ's name at all times. My body is His house, and I should care more that this house stay clean and uncluttered than I do for my own house. It is not my weekly chore, but my daily privilege.

EVENING

Precious Father, what an honor to be chosen by You as someone You wanted to live inside. I can never thank You enough for this privilege. Continue to point out what needs repairing, cleaning, polishing, and replacing in my life. I want my life to be a place You can rejoice in and use for Your glory. I know even when I am sleeping that Your eyes are always upon me. I praise You that my life is not a hotel, but it is a home where You will abide forever. You are my owner and caretaker. I love You. Amen.

MORNING

Precious Lord and Savior, thank You for calling me to Your service. Thank You for giving me a purpose that is beyond this earth and for allowing me to invest my time, money, and talents into something that is eternal. I am willing to be thought of as "different" for You, in order that You may do all You desire through my life. Lord, I am available for You to use today as a messenger of the gospel in someone's life. For Jesus' sake, Amen.

"That I might be a minister of Jesus Christ to the Gentiles,
ministering the gospel of God, that the offering of the
Gentiles might be acceptable, sanctified by the Holy Spirit."
ROMANS 15:16

What an awesome privilege we have to be priests unto God. The Old Testament priests wore different clothing, lived in different places, and performed different tasks than anyone else. They were set apart for this unique function of ministering to God on behalf of the people. Their main task was to offer sacrifices and offerings that were acceptable to God.

As God's servants today, we need not offer blood sacrifices, because the perfect sacrifice has already been offered through Jesus Christ. Instead, we are to offer up to Him those who have been won to faith in Christ through the gospel. Being set apart for this special task, every Christian is to present the Good News to those who are lost, so that we can bring to Him lives that have been made holy and acceptable by the Holy Spirit.

Both the priest and the offering were sanctified, which means both the soul winner and the new believer are to be totally consecrated to Jesus Christ. When you see Him, how many offerings will you present to Him?

EVENING

Father, I bless Your name for being my rock and my fortress; You are my exceedingly great reward. I thank You for entrusting me with such a great treasure when You gave me the Good News of salvation. Father, thank You for using someone to tell me about You and Your kingdom. Thank You for Your providence in allowing me to have all the many blessings and opportunities in this day. I offer all that I am and all that I have to You. You are worthy of my life. In Jesus' name, Amen.

MICHAEL CLOER, ROCKY MOUNT, NC

Heavenly Father, thank You for allowing me to enjoy the freedom I have in You. Thank You for the liberty of worship, singing, praying, and enjoying fellowship with You. I praise You for Your providence in planting this nation, for protecting this nation, and for providing for this nation. Father, I am burdened for this nation, and I plead with You that Your people will be the ones You use to cause this country to turn back to You. For Jesus' sake, Amen.

"Turn from your evil ways, and keep My commandments and My statutes, according to all the law which I commanded your fathers, and which I sent to you by My servants the prophets."

2 KINGS 17:13C

The righteousness of God demands that His people be holy. With loving-kindness He warns that judgment follows sin as night follows day and that this is just as true in a country as it is in an individual. Those who bring sin into a nation or family bring a curse into it and will have to answer for all the calamity that follows.

In spite of all the blessings of God upon Israel, His people had followed the evil ways of other nations; they had forsaken His absolute statutes and had forgotten their heritage. As a result, they would have to forfeit their land to their enemy.

How can we avert the judgment of God on our nation or upon us? We must begin with *convincing repentance* and turn from our evil ways. This change must take place in our thoughts, our attitudes, and our beliefs as well as in our behavior. God also requires *complete obedience.* The word "all" means that in God's assessment, partial obedience is whole disobedience. Then we must have *continual faithfulness* in following the heritage of our godly forefathers.

EVENING

O God, our help in ages past, our hope for years to come, thank You for Your patience, Your forbearance, and Your longsuffering with us. Thank You that You have not dealt with us according to our iniquities, but according to Your loving-kindness. I pray that my children will dwell safely in the land and that their descendants will be established before You. I pray that my descendants will be found faithful. In Jesus' name, Amen.

MORNING

Good morning, Lord. I thank You for being all that I need in this world and the next. You make it possible for me to be right with the Father and with anyone on earth. I praise You for being my wonderful Counselor. There is nothing I will face today that You do not already know. Thank You for guiding me, for leading me, and for showing me. I pray that today I will focus more on what I have in You than on what I have from You. Amen.

"But of Him you are in Christ Jesus, who became for us wisdom from God—and righteousness and sanctification and redemption."
1 CORINTHIANS 1:30

Those of us who are born again have all we need in Jesus Christ. He not only gives us what we need, but all we will ever need is in Him. Jesus is wisdom incarnate. We are told in Colossians 2:3 that in Christ are "all the treasures of wisdom and knowledge." Everything I need to know in this world, He is able to explain to me.

In contrast to the false wisdom of this world, the very mind of God is ours by virtue of Jesus Christ living within us. As a result, everything we need for fellowship with God is available to us—righteousness, sanctification, and redemption.

Righteousness speaks of what we had immediately at the moment of salvation. Sanctification is what we have progressively as we become more and more conformed into the likeness of Jesus Christ. However, redemption covers the entire scope of salvation. We have been delivered from the bondage that sin caused in our spirit; we are being delivered in our souls by sanctification; and we will be delivered from the bondage in our bodies when we see Him. Hallelujah, in Jesus we have everything!

EVENING

Lord, You are more valuable than gold and silver. Lord, You are more precious than any earthly possession or relationship. Lord, You are incomparable, indescribable, and incomprehensible. Tonight, I am secure in the fact that I am in You and that no one is able to take me out of Your hand. You are my Sabbath, and I am not resting in who I am or what I have done; my rest is in who You are and what You have done on my behalf. Thank You, precious Lord. Amen.

MICHAEL CLOER, ROCKY MOUNT, NC

Week 13, Monday

Father, I praise You for Your love, which is perfect and unconditional. I thank You for forgiving my sin. I thank You for the gift of salvation. You have given me a gift I could never merit nor earn. Help me today to live in response to Your love. Help me to love people the way You love them. Help me to be open to share the story of Your love with people I meet who do not know You. I pray for the wisdom to live according to Your Word. Amen.

"For God so loved the world that He gave His only begotten Son, that whoever believes in Him should not perish but have everlasting life."
JOHN 3:16

In this world, love is often conditional. A person's love is based on performance or merit. God, on the other hand, loves unconditionally. God's love is more than mere words. His love is backed by incredible proof. He proved His love by sacrificing His Son on a Cross for all mankind. There is no greater love than the love of the One who is willing to give His life that others may live. He has demonstrated His love by accepting all who will believe in Jesus. No one is exempt. Mankind is often exclusive; God is inclusive. There is no one who cannot be saved who comes to Jesus in faith. Because of the unconditional love of God, sin is forgiven and eternal life is granted. There is no sin so great that God will not forgive it. There is no one who is beyond the love of God. In a culture where bad news is very commonplace, this is incredibly Good News. God's love is the most powerful form of love a person will ever experience.

EVENING

Lord, thank You for this day, for leading me through it. Thank You for the people I met today, the challenges I faced, and the wonderful assurance of Your constant presence. Your love is powerful and brings peace to my life. I pray for rest tonight that will prepare me for tomorrow. I pray that my mind and my heart will be renewed and my body refreshed. I pray for my friends who still do not know You. I pray for the Holy Spirit to continue to work in their lives. Thank You, Father. Amen.

Lord, I come to You today thanking You for Jesus. I thank You that my salvation resides in Him and Him alone. My sin separated me from You, but You did not leave me in my sin. You gave Jesus in order that I may be forgiven and have eternal life. I can only boast in Jesus because He is my life. I am grateful for my salvation. I don't deserve what Jesus has done for me. I desire to live this day as a reflection of the life You have given me. Amen.

"He who believes in the Son has everlasting life; and he who does not believe the Son shall not see life, but the wrath of God abides on him."
JOHN 3:36

Eternal life is in the Son. Jesus is not merely a way to God, or even the best way to God. He is the only way. God's plan for mankind's salvation resides in His Son and His Son alone. All who believe in Him have eternal life. Believing is more than the intellectual belief that Jesus existed. Belief that leads to salvation is based on trust. It is the act of trusting Jesus with one's life. When you believe Jesus is the only way, a relationship with God is possible. When you place your faith in Jesus for forgiveness of sin, you then begin to experience eternal life. This is critical because apart from the Son, the relationship with God that has been broken through sin can never be repaired. John records Jesus' words on this subject: "I am the way, the truth, and the life. No one comes to the Father except through me" (John 14:6). Are you depending on Jesus alone for eternal life?

EVENING

Lord, I want to thank You for Your presence throughout the day. There was never a moment when You were not there. I sensed Your presence many times. When I got so busy that I wasn't sensitive to You, You were there. Father, I am grateful that eternal life doesn't begin at my death, but it began the moment I placed my trust in Jesus. I failed You at times today. I ask You to forgive me and to give me the strength to overcome my sin and to live a life that is pleasing to You. Amen.

Week 13, Wednesday

MORNING

Dear God, I fall terribly short of Your standard of righteousness. I am guilty of sin. My only hope is in Christ's death on the Cross. You have redeemed me. You have, by Your grace, given me new life. Lord, this life is too wonderful to keep to myself. Please show me today how to influence others for You. Teach me how to share the Good News of redemption with people around me who have not personally experienced Your grace. Lord, help me to live today as one who has been redeemed. Help me to not, in any way, disgrace Your name. Amen.

"For all have sinned and fall short of the glory of God, being justified
freely by His grace through the redemption that is in Christ Jesus."
ROMANS 3:23, 24

Think of the best person you know, the person who does the most good deeds, helps others, and is morally clean. He or she, as the case may be, is still guilty of sin. How can that be? When you read the verse carefully, you begin to understand. The measuring rod is the perfection of God. The world is quick to make judgments based on comparisons with other people. This scripture teaches that the only accurate comparison is God, and all fail to live up to His standard. If everyone is guilty of sin, where is hope to be found? Hope is possible through Jesus' death on the Cross. There He redeemed us. He paid the penalty for our sin. The Scripture says, "You were bought at a price" (1 Cor. 7:23). Although all people fall short of God's standard, He freely forgives all who trust His Son.

EVENING

Dear Lord, another day has come to an end. Today has been a mixture of success and failure, wins and losses, accomplishments and struggles. Through it all, You have been God. You are still on the throne, and nothing has escaped Your attention. You have been true to me even when I have failed. You are a great God. It is an honor to serve You. It is my desire to know You more intimately and to bring glory to Your name. You deserve all the honor, glory, and praise. May I always live to praise You. Amen.

MORNING

Father, You are the God of grace. As I begin the day, I worship and praise You as the greatest gift giver in this universe. I am a recipient of Your grace. When I look at my life, I cannot understand how You could love me the way You do. You have given me the most wonderful gift—the gift of salvation. Lord, as a recipient of grace, I desire today to extend grace to others. Help me to be patient with people, to love people the way You love them, and to act graciously toward the people You bring into my life. Amen.

"For by grace you have been saved through faith, and that not of yourselves; it is the gift of God, not of works, lest anyone should boast."
EPHESIANS 2:8, 9

Grace is a powerful word. In a culture where acceptance and love are often based on merit, it is even more powerful and appealing. When applied to one's salvation, it is very personal as well as powerful in meaning. As a young Christian, I was taught this definition for grace: **G**od's **R**iches **A**t **C**hrist's **E**xpense. Grace is a gift from God. No one can boast that he or she is more favored by God than someone else. Grace treats everyone equally. God's grace gift is centered totally in His Son. He gives to anyone who will receive His Son the gift of salvation. There is nothing one can do to earn God's grace. A gift cannot be earned; it can only be received. If you are a Christian, it is because of grace. If you are not a Christian, you can become one by freely receiving the greatest gift available to mankind. The gift is God's Son. Simply receive Him into your life by faith.

EVENING

Lord, thank You for the blessing of another day. As this day draws to a close, I want to thank You for the people in my life. Family, friends, church family, and peers are blessings You allow me to enjoy. I thank You for these relationships. You created us to live in relationship with other people. Community is so important to You. Help me never to take for granted these relationships. Remind me constantly of what Paul said to the Christians at Philippi: "I thank my God upon every remembrance of you" (Phil. 1:3). Amen.

LARRY WYNN, DACULA, GA

Week 13, Friday

Heavenly Father, I thank You so much for sending Jesus into the world, not to condemn it but to save it. This is the motivation I need to face this day. Help me to remember that in whatever situations I find myself, You are for me, not against me. With You on my side, I can face life with a positive outlook. I can be confident in making decisions, handling tasks, and dealing with issues that arise. Help me to keep a short account of sins, so I can be usable to You today. I thank You that my sin is under the blood of Jesus, so there is no condemnation. Amen.

"For God did not send His Son into the world to condemn the world,
but that the world through Him might be saved."
JOHN 3:17

People wanted Jesus to fit many different roles while He was on earth. Most folks wanted Him to be a political leader. What they failed to understand was that Jesus had one mission to carry out. He came to earth for one reason. He came to be the Savior of the world. "For the Son of Man has come to seek and to save that which was lost" (Luke 19:10). The religious leaders of Jesus' day were quick to condemn people, but offered very little hope, if any. Jesus did the opposite. He offered hope to the hopeless, not condemnation. He continues to do the same today. In Jesus you will find salvation, not condemnation. "There is therefore now no condemnation to those who are in Christ Jesus, who do not walk according to the flesh, but according to the Spirit" (Rom. 8:1). Jesus is Good News for the world. He is the answer to life's deepest and greatest needs. You can trust Him. He is for you, not against you.

EVENING

Dear Lord, another day has come and gone. Throughout this day You have manifested Yourself in many ways. Some of them I recognized and others I failed to recognize. But no matter what, You have shown Yourself strong. Lord, in order to be truly successful I must keep You at the center of my life. It is so easy to get distracted by the demands of life. Help me to stay focused on You and to live to please You at all times. Amen.

MORNING

"This is the day the LORD has made; we will rejoice and be glad in it" (Ps. 118:24). Father, You have created this weekend for Your purpose. You bless me by allowing me to participate in it. In a world filled with bad news, it is Your desire that I as a Christian be Your ambassador of Good News. Give me the courage to share with people that they do not have to live separated from You for all eternity. Through Jesus they can go to heaven, where there is no more sin or suffering. Amen.

"For the wages of sin is death, but the gift of
God is eternal life in Christ Jesus our Lord."
ROMANS 6:23

How often have you heard it said, "Do you want the bad news first, or the good news?" Most of us want the bad news first. This scripture in Romans 6 handles it that way. First the bad news: "the wages of sin is death." Left to ourselves, we have to pay for our sin. The payment is death. Death in this verse refers to separation from God. Apart from the gift of life found only in Jesus, there is no hope but eternal separation from God. That is extremely bad news.

But hold on, that is not the end of the story. There is very good news, and it is this: "the gift of God is eternal life in Christ Jesus." He reverses the death process. The moment You trust Christ, Your spirit becomes alive in Him. Ultimately, so will your body. For the Christian, physical death is not an end—it is only a doorway to life without end, life with God in His heaven. Now, that is the best news of all!

EVENING

Dear Lord, help me to prepare myself for worship. I pray that as I attend church, I will be open to all You want to teach me. Lord, please let me never forget that I am to be constantly on the lookout for people I can influence with the gospel. I know this is the highest calling for a Christian. I thank You that I am going to heaven one day. I want to be part of seeing as many people as possible go there as well. I pray for the gospel to reach the unsaved as the pastor speaks. Amen.

LARRY WYNN, DACULA, GA

Father, thank You for being the giver of life. Thank You for the gift of abundant life that comes through knowing Your Son. As I begin this new day, may I experience all that You desire for me and have a heart full of gratitude for the joy of living an overflowing life in You. Amen.

"The thief does not come except to steal, and to kill, and to destroy. I have come that they may have life, and that they may have it more abundantly."

JOHN 10:10

Do you have a "bucket list"? This term has been popularized by Justin Zackham's book and a recent blockbuster movie in which people leap from planes, drive race cars, eat caviar, motorcycle on the Great Wall of China, and trot by other wonders of the world before they "kick the bucket." This premise resonates. Millions of people have a dream "to-do" list. Namely, all the things they think it takes to "really live life" to the fullest. These lists tend to feature acts of fancy, courage, and delight and are full of punch and flavor, adrenalin and imagination—but is that what it means to really live?

Jesus Christ made a powerful statement that answers the question, "What does it mean to really live?" He began by identifying Satan as a thief. Satan seeks to steal from us the truth of what it really means to live—to live life to the fullest. Jesus said that He came to give life, and the life He gives is full, complete, and satisfying. The life lived outside of Jesus Christ will always result in emptiness and a futile search that sadly leads to an empty well and bucket. The apostle Paul in his letter to the Colossian Christians said that Jesus "is our life" (Col. 3:4). If you are looking for life, you will find it only in Christ. Jesus not only gives "real life"—He will overflow your bucket!

EVENING

Father, today You have filled my day with Your fullness. My heart is overflowing as I consider the "full bucket" of blessings from Your good hand. Thank You for the gift of Your precious Son who enables me to live a life that is worth living. Thank You for being my life. In Your name I pray, Amen.

Week 14, Tuesday

Jesus, I begin this day with the acknowledgement that I am a sinner. I rejoice in the fact that You are not flawed. You are the perfect Son of God who came to take away my sin. You are the answer to my sin problem. Thank You for being the strong Son of God. Amen.

"Therefore, just as through one man sin entered the world, and death through sin, and thus death spread to all men, because all sinned."
ROMANS 5:12

Welcome to the club of the flawed. All members of Adam's race are members of this group. No one escapes—even the strongest among us are dripping with sin.

Achilles was a hero in Greek mythology. He was described as extremely handsome but driven by his passions. He was almost immortal, since his mother had dipped him into the river Styx as a baby. Holding the child by his heel when putting him into the water, she made Achilles' whole body, except the heel, impervious to injury or death.

When the kidnapping of Helen ignited the war against Troy, Achilles went to fight for King Agamemnon. He could not be defeated in battle, killing the Trojan hero Hector out of revenge for the death of his closest friend. Achilles' victory, however, was short-lived as an arrow guided by the Greek goddess Aphrodite pierced his only weak spot—his Achilles' heel.

Achilles' heel may be a myth, but each one of us having Adam's sin nature is a fact. We all inherited it from him—we are all flawed. We sin because we are sinners. Sin has entered the heart of all of us. This is the reason we need Jesus to enter our hearts, to heal us of our sin sickness. The arrow of judgment doesn't pierce the heart that is occupied by Jesus. He took that arrow when He was pierced for our sin (Is. 53:5). At the Cross, Satan may have bruised His heel; however, He crushed Satan's head (Gen. 3:15). We now have victory in Jesus.

EVENING

Jesus, I thank You for being my personal Savior. Thank You for entering my heart and transforming my life. Please forgive me for not expressing that enough and for not sharing this wonderful news with others. In Your strong name I pray, Amen.

JEFF CROOK, FLOWERY BRANCH, GA

Week 14, Wednesday

Lord, I begin this day in amazement that You love me and gave Your life for me. Thank You for demonstrating Your love at the Cross. Thank You for showing me love each and every day. Help me to show and speak Your love to others this very day. In Your loving name I pray, Amen.

"But God demonstrated His own love toward us,
in that while we were still sinners, Christ died for us."
ROMANS 5:8

Have you been captured by the love of God? You will be when you consider "the width and length and depth and height" of the love of Christ (Eph. 3:18,19). It seems today that many are superficial when communicating what they love. They're just words that we say—a shallow expression. Do you want to see authentic love? Go to Calvary, the place where God exhibited and proved His love by giving His own perfect Son to die for imperfect sinners. How much does God love us? His Son answered from the Cross with arms stretched wide: "This much!"

What extravagant love was displayed on the Cross. May extravagant love be demonstrated from each of us as grateful recipients.

EVENING

Father, thank You for showing Your love with the gift of Your Son. Jesus, thank You for expressing Your love on the Cross. Holy Spirit, thank You for pouring God's love into my heart. I am filled with amazement. May I continue to be amazed. Amen.

MORNING

Jesus, thank You for allowing me to begin this new day with Good News—the Good News of the gospel. Your death on the Cross and Your triumph over the grave have profoundly changed my life. Amen.

"Christ died for our sins according to the Scriptures, and that He was buried, and that He rose again the third day according to the Scriptures."
1 CORINTHIANS 15:3B, 4

It was July 17, 1945, and World War II raged on in the Pacific. President Harry S. Truman would write in his diary about a meeting of future superpowers that would shape the course of history:

"I looked up from the desk and there stood Stalin in the doorway.
I got to my feet and advanced to meet him. He put out his hand and smiled.
I did the same, we shook, I greeted (Soviet Foreign Minister Vyacheslav)
Molotov and the interpreter, and we sat down."

The meeting between the American president and the intimidating Soviet leader was set to discuss a post–World War II Europe. Truman wanted to know what Stalin wanted to do with the parts of Europe now under his control.

The gospel's simplicity is amazing. It can be described in just twenty-six English words in 1 Corinthians 15:3, 4, and yet it is so profound that all the libraries cannot describe its depths. It's so simple that a child can hear the gospel message and be eternally saved, yet so profound that theological scholars cannot touch the bottom of this ocean of truth. The apostle Paul expressed this when he wrote, "Oh, the depth of the riches both of the wisdom and knowledge of God!" (Rom. 11:33). Jesus died, Jesus was buried, and Jesus is risen. To embrace this simple truth will result in a profound transformation in your life!

EVENING

Jesus, thank You for the power of the gospel. Help me to be passionate about the gospel. May I continue to be in awe of what You did for me. May I also be compelled to tell others what the gospel can do for them. Amen.

Jesus, You are the greatest gift I have ever received. Thank You for making me Your child. As I begin this new day, may I live with deep gratitude for the privilege of being in Your family. Amen.

"But as many as received Him, to them He gave the right to become children of God, to those who believe in His name."
JOHN 1:12

Roy Collette and his brother-in-law have been exchanging the same pair of pants as a Christmas present for eleven years, and each time the package gets harder to open. It all started when Collette received a pair of moleskin trousers from his brother-in-law, Larry Kunkel. Kunkel's mother had given her son the britches when he was a college student. He wore them a few times, but they froze stiff in cold weather. So, he gave them to Collette. Collette, who called the moleskins "miserable," wore them three times, wrapped them, and gave them back to Kunkel for Christmas the next year.

The friendly exchange continued routinely until one year when Collette twisted the pants tightly, stuffed them into a three-foot-long, one-inch-wide tube and gave them back to Kunkel. Not to be outdone, the next Christmas, Kunkel compressed the pants into a seven-inch square, wrapped them with wire, and gave the "bale" to Collette. Back and forth the pants have been exchanged.

This past Christmas, the pants were delivered to Collette in a drab green, three-foot cube that once was a 1974 Gremlin with ninety-five thousand miles on it. A note attached to the two-thousand-pound scrunched car advised Collette that the pants were inside the glove compartment.

Unlike these unwanted pants, salvation is a gift that never stops giving and never gets old. Have you received the gift? No gift can compare to being a forgiven child of God's forever family. "Thanks be to God for His indescribable gift!" (2 Cor. 9:15).

EVENING

Jesus, thank You for the gift of this moment to express to You again my love and gratitude for the joy of being Your child. The gift of Your love is truly amazing. I praise Your name. Amen.

MORNING

Jesus, as I open the door to this brand new day, I thank You for being in my life. You are the strength of my life. I love you, Lord Jesus. Amen.

"Behold, I stand at the door and knock. If anyone hears My voice and opens the door, I will come in to him and dine with him, and he with Me."
REVELATION 3:20

Who's knocking at your door? It could be the Publishers Clearing House Prize Patrol. Born in the advertising department, the Prize Patrol has been a staple of American family life for two decades. The Prize Patrol knocks on the door of a recent entrant of the company's sweepstakes and surprises the family with the news that they are the winners of millions!

The Prize Patrol began appearing in 1989, but really became popular when they began surprising unsuspecting families during the Super Bowl halftime. Prior to the creation of the Prize Patrol, Publishers Clearing House notified winners of major prizes by phone, and then later brought them to New York to film scripted television commercials. In 1988, the northern New Jersey location of the company's first Ten Million Dollar winner provided a unique opportunity for Dave Sayer to notify the winner, Barbara Armellino, with the exciting news that she had won the sweepstakes. No cameras were present for this notification, but after hearing about all the excitement that transpired when Mrs. Armellino was informed of her good fortune, the Prize Patrol was born.

The chances of the Prize Patrol knocking on your door with a check for the company's top prize are 1 in 1.75 billion. But there is Someone who is always knocking. Revelation 3:20 says that our Lord Jesus stands and knocks. For the non-Christian, the knock is that of hope and healing from the death sentence of sin. For the Christian, the knock is that of abiding fellowship with the Lover of your soul. Take a moment and listen. Do you hear a knock at the door of your heart? Jesus wants your heart to be His home.

EVENING

Jesus, I praise You for Your constant presence. I rejoice in the fact that once You come in, You are there to stay. I rest in You. In Your secure name I pray, Amen.

JEFF CROOK, FLOWERY BRANCH, GA

Week 15, Monday

Lord, thank You that You have saved me and given me the precious joy of sharing my story with others. May I always remember that confessing You before others is not only a privilege but also a solemn responsibility. May I never forget that if I am to one day hear You confess me in heaven, I must be faithful to confess You on earth. As I begin this day, please open some door of opportunity that I may tell the amazing story of Your love for all mankind. In Jesus' wonderful name I pray, Amen.

"Therefore whoever confesses Me before men, him I will also confess before My Father who is in heaven."
MATTHEW 10:32

One of the most obvious evidences of authentic conversion is a verbal confession of it. While some would suggest that a person's faith is personal and private and should be quietly kept within, the Bible knows nothing of that kind of salvation. A saving faith is a talking faith.

While it is possible to talk a lot about Jesus and not be saved, it is unlikely one can be saved and not talk a lot about Jesus. Telling a new convert not to speak about what has happened in his or her life would be as silly as lecturing an erupting volcano on the virtues of being calm!

When Annas the high priest commanded Peter and John "not to speak at all nor teach in the name of Jesus," those courageous disciples majestically replied, "We cannot but speak the things which we have seen and heard" (Acts 4:18, 20). Those transformed followers of Christ had been given a dose of "can't help it!" There raged in their souls a burning passion, and like Jeremiah they could only say, "But His word was in my heart like a burning fire shut up in my bones; I was weary of holding it back, and I could not" (Jer. 20:9). May that same fire burn within us!

EVENING

Dear Jesus, at the close of this day, I want to thank You that Your sweet Spirit has caused me to be mindful of Your love and mercy and that You have granted me the joy of confessing You before others. If I have unknowingly failed in any way to do that, before I sleep tonight, please forgive me. I pray in Your name. Amen.

MORNING

Loving Father, as I rise from my bed of rest and prepare for today's activities, may I be conscious of Your precious will in every detail of my being. As the servant looks to the hand of his master for instruction, may my eyes be turned to Your ways and may my ears be open and obedient to Your soft and gentle guidance. Give to Your servant a listening spirit and an obedient heart. I sincerely ask this in Jesus' name—the name above all names. Amen.

"He who has the Son has life; he who does not have
the Son of God does not have life."
1 JOHN 5:12

As contradictory as it may sound, a man can be alive and yet not have life. For life does not consist of *what one has—but Whom one has.* How much a man has in his pocket is a poor judge of how much he may have in his heart. If a man's wealth consists solely in how much he can count, he probably doesn't count for much. Those who are always quick to tell just how much they are worth generally aren't worth very much!

The psalmist summarized that truth so concisely when he said, "A little that a righteous man has is better than the riches of many wicked" (Ps. 37:16). Apart from Jesus, life at its very best is an endless quest—an agonizing journey through a confusing maze of unsatisfied desires and unquenchable thirsts. It is a lonesome street to nowhere.

But for those who have the Son, life is better than the riches of many wicked, for the Master said, "I have come that they may have life, and that they may have it more abundantly" (John 10:10). Some have much abundance but no life—but for those in Christ, we have life and much abundance!

EVENING

Dear Jesus, thank You that when I have nothing, in You I have everything. When I am hungry, You are the Bread of Life. When I am thirsty, You are the Water of Life. When I am weary, You give me rest. When I am lonely, You stick closer than a brother. Thank You that You never leave me nor forsake me. I lie down tonight in the confidence of that precious truth. Good night, Jesus. I love You. Amen.

JUNIOR HILL, HARTSELLE, AL

Week 15, Wednesday

Dear Lord, as I begin this new day, please help me remember to number my days so that I may "gain a heart of wisdom" (Ps. 90:12). Help me live today as if it were my last. Grant that my words will be kind and loving, that my eyes may look in the right direction, and that my thoughts may be stayed on You. If I displease You in any way, remind me quickly so that I may repent and ask Your forgiveness. I pray this in Your dear name. Amen.

"Jesus said to him, 'I am the way, the truth, and the life.
No one comes to the Father except through Me.'"
JOHN 14:6

Few things are as offensive in today's religious culture as is the exclusiveness of Jesus Christ. It is one thing to say that Jesus is the Savior of the world—but it is something else to say He is *the only* Savior of the world. And yet, that is precisely what Jesus taught.

The words "except through Me" in today's scripture leave no room for anyone else. Those who are serious about following Jesus must believe that, accept that, and unashamedly proclaim that. And once we do, hatred, ridicule, and hostility will inevitably follow. That is why Jesus so solemnly warned His followers, "If the world hates you, you know that it hated Me before it hated you" (John 15:18). Those who are unwilling to bear that kind of harsh animosity by the world are not worthy to be identified with the Savior. And sadly, there are many who are hesitant to pay that price.

Criticism and derision are powerful tools that often silence the clear and forthright proclamation of the gospel, and many professed believers have succumbed to them. The Bible says, "Even among the rulers many believed in Him, but because of the Pharisees they did not confess Him, lest they should be put out of the synagogue; for they loved the praise of men more than the praise of God" (John 12:42, 43). When it comes to serving Jesus, whose praise do we really seek?

EVENING

Loving Father, thank You that Your hand has guided me through another day. You have given breath to my body, direction to my paths, and peace to my heart. I lift my hands in gratitude to You. In Jesus' name, Amen.

MORNING

Heavenly Father, thank You for the rising of the sun and the promise of a new day in which I may serve You. Grant that Your dear hand may order my steps and that I will honor and please You in all that I do. Give me Your wisdom and discernment that every decision I make today will be centered in Your will. Keep me from presumption. Make me kind and sensitive to all those whom I shall meet. I ask all of this in Your holy name. Amen.

"If you confess with your mouth the Lord Jesus and believe in your heart that God has raised Him from the dead, you will be saved."
ROMANS 10:9

One of the major problems faced in sharing the gospel is the natural inclination to complicate it. Thankfully, God never does that. While we take simple things and make them hard to understand, the Bible takes hard things and makes them easy to understand.

And in no other area is that more clearly demonstrated than in the matter of salvation. Jesus said being saved is as simple as a hungry man eating bread: "I am the bread of life. He who comes to Me shall never hunger" (John 6:35).

Jesus also said being saved is as simple as drinking water: "Whoever drinks of the water that I shall give him will never thirst. But the water that I shall give him will become in him a fountain of water springing up into everlasting life" (John 4:14).

Trusting Christ is as simple as receiving a gift. Paul said if anyone believes that God raised Jesus from the dead and is willing to confess that with his mouth, he will be saved. That is the gospel clear and simple. Don't complicate it—just believe it and share it.

EVENING

Faithful Father, once again Your gracious hand has guided and sustained me through another day. You have given me strength to do the work You have provided. Your grace has encouraged me, and Your sweet presence has ministered to my oft-weary soul. Thank You for reminding me that my help comes from the Lord. I love You, Jesus. Amen.

JUNIOR HILL, HARTSELLE, AL

Precious Jesus, as I open my eyes today, I praise You that I see. I rejoice that I had a bed in which I could rest my weary body last night. I am thankful that I can begin this new day with the wonderful assurance that if I should die, I know where I will go—and with whom I shall be. And best of all, dear Savior, I rejoice that I know who made it all possible. Thank You for Your wonderful death on the Cross. May Your mighty name be praised! Amen.

*"But if the Spirit of Him who raised Jesus from the dead dwells in you,
He who raised Christ from the dead will also give life to
your mortal bodies through His Spirit who dwells in you."*
ROMANS 8:11

Few promises are as precious to the child of God as that of eternal life. It is the crown jewel of salvation. While all those who are truly saved are blessed to love, serve, and fellowship with the Lord through this brief earthly journey, that pilgrimage is made so much more precious by the comforting assurance that it will never end. Though our bodies will ultimately die, our spirits are alive forevermore.

When Christ triumphantly came out of that grave alive and well, it was our guarantee that we shall do the same. Thank God, if the grave could not hold Him, then neither will it be able to hold us! The same Spirit that raised Jesus from the dead will one day do the same in our own mortal bodies. No wonder Paul could so majestically write, " 'O Death, where is your sting? O Hades, where is your victory?' The sting of death is sin, and the strength of sin is the law. But thanks be to God, who gives us the victory through our Lord Jesus Christ" (1 Cor. 15:55–57). Hallelujah, He arose! And one day, so shall we!

EVENING

Dear Lord, as I lay down to sleep I am grateful that Your Word says, "He will not allow your foot to be moved; He who keeps you will not slumber" (Ps. 121:3). Even as I sleep, Your loving eye will watch over me. Thank You, dear Jesus, that when I slumber You are always awake. Praise Your holy name! Amen.

MORNING

Faithful Master, Your Word says, "The steps of a good man are ordered by the LORD" (Ps. 37:23). I thank You as I begin this new day that I can rest in that comforting assurance. You see and watch over me. Therefore help me today that I will not fear whatever may befall me. I ask this in Your precious name, Amen.

"For if we live, we live to the Lord; and if we die, we die to the Lord.
Therefore, whether we live or die, we are the Lord's."
ROMANS 14:8

When the late Dr. Adrian Rogers learned that he had terminal cancer, he said to one of his friends, "I find myself in a win/win situation! If I live, I win—and if I die, I win!" Those who have learned to live in that sublime submission to God's sovereignty have come to fully understand what this brief stay on planet Earth is all about.

At the very best, this short voyage we are all taking through this terrestrial globe is but a preparation period for the eternity to come. We are not designed to live indefinitely in this fallen world. We are pilgrims who are merely "passing through." And since we will not be here but a few short and fleeting years, we would be wise to treat all that we see and hold as fleeting and temporal. We entered this world with empty hands—and we shall leave it the same way.

EVENING

Lord Jesus, I realize this world is not my home—and yet sometimes I tend to forget that. My burdens and cares are often heavy and difficult to bear. But in those hardest of times, You have a remarkable way of coming to my rescue. Thank You that You have done that today—and better yet, that You will do it again tomorrow. I praise You for loving me. In Jesus' name, Amen.

Week 16, Monday

Lord Jesus, I ask You to fill me with Your Spirit and help me to handle anything that comes my way today with Your strength. May I walk in such a way that people are pointed toward the Cross and drawn to You. May I praise You through not only the good times in my life, but also through the bad times. Use the valleys in my life to bring me closer to You and to draw those that don't know You to their own "mountaintop meeting" with You. Amen.

"So they said, 'Believe on the Lord Jesus Christ,
and you will be saved, you and your household.'"
ACTS 16:31

In Jesus' day, the Roman soldiers were brutal men who had no mercy. They were feared because of their cruelty and their disregard for human life. Paul and Silas experienced this cruelty firsthand as they were severely beaten on their backs with rods and thrown into prison for boldly preaching and seeing lives transformed.

At midnight in the jail cell, a praise and worship service erupted, and God began to move. After seeing the power of God demonstrated and listening to the apostle Paul preach the gospel, the Philippian jailer was saved. Shortly after his conversion, through his testimony and Paul's preaching, the jailer's entire family received Christ! One man's genuine conversion led to his family being converted. When you experience the life-changing gift of salvation, you will not be able to rest until those closest to you also meet Christ.

Have you believed on the Lord Jesus? I am not speaking of an intellectual sense with knowledge of the facts, but a sincere belief and trust in the death, burial, and resurrection of Jesus Christ. If the answer is yes, then rejoice over the miracle of salvation that you have experienced, no matter what trying times you may be facing in your life. What friends or family members still need to hear the message from someone who is genuinely concerned about their soul?

EVENING

Thank You, Jesus, for saving me. Thank You that through the darkest times of our lives, You have remained faithful and carried us through. I commit myself to You as an empty vessel to be used for Your glory, even if that means You must break me to use me. Amen.

Week 16, Tuesday

MORNING

Thank You, Jesus, for Your grace. Thank You that even though I deserve death, hell, and judgment, You paid the price for me that I might go free. Help me today to be sensitive to everyone around me who is in need of Your grace. Forgive me for not caring like I should for those who do not know You. Amen.

"And Jesus said to him, 'Assuredly, I say to you, today you will be with Me in Paradise.'"

LUKE 23:43

Jesus is hanging on the Cross. He has been laughed at and ridiculed. He has been mocked and spat upon. Nails have been driven through His hands and through His feet. A crown of thorns has been thrust upon His brow. He winces in agony as blood and sweat trickle down His face. He experiences darkness and alienation from His Father as God is forced to turn away from the ugly sin that is cast upon His Son. He hangs on the Cross, His life slowly ebbing away. Even in this moment with death approaching, He looks down at the crowd with eyes of love and forgiveness.

Jesus is hanging between two thieves. One is belligerent, and one is humble. One chooses to reject Jesus, and one accepts His love and forgiveness. This was certainly an "eleventh hour salvation experience." What a day this thief experienced—that morning, he was a lost and condemned creature; at midday, he was covered by a blanket of grace, and the blood of Jesus was applied to his life, erasing his past; and by the time evening arrived, he was in Paradise with Jesus. What a journey!

The mission of Jesus was to seek and to save the lost (Luke 19:10). Even in the last hour of His life on earth, Jesus sought to reach those who were lost and separated from Holy God by sin and flesh. Even as He hung on the Cross dying, He pleaded with His Father to forgive the very ones who sought to kill Him.

EVENING

Father, thank You for sending Your Son to die for me. Thank You for supplying salvation through Jesus, knowing that it would cost You the ultimate sacrifice. Please do not allow me to be content because I am saved, but give me a burden to tell others about You. I love You, Lord Jesus. Amen.

STEVE FLOCKHART, HIRAM, GA

Heavenly Father, thank You for the message and gift of eternal life. Thank You for loving me when I was unlovable and still in my sin. I praise You for forgiving me and for the privilege of starting a new life. Lord, help me today to see others pass from death unto life. Use me to share boldly with others Your love and gift of eternal life. Help me to live in the power of the resurrection. Amen.

"Most assuredly, I say to you, he who hears My word and believes in Him who sent Me has everlasting life, and shall not come into judgment, but has passed from death into life."

JOHN 5:24

The Bible teaches us in Ephesians 2:1–3 that we were dead in our trespasses and sin before accepting Christ. That is graphic language to describe a tragic condition. We were dead. We had no capacity for God or spiritual things. Our sin had separated us from a loving heavenly Father. Our eternal destiny was judgment and hell.

When we hear or read the word "judgment," it conjures up many emotions. All of them seem to be negative. The word "grace" brings pleasant thoughts, the word "love" brings pleasant thoughts, but the word "judgment" brings thoughts of condemnation.

The One who judges has the perfect character to do so. He has been given the right to judge (John 5:22). God judged Jesus as He hung on the Cross, bearing our sin. "He made Him who knew no sin to be sin for us" (2 Cor. 5:21). Jesus took our judgment upon Himself. Christ experienced death, hell, and judgment for you and for me.

Thanks be to God that we heard the Word of God and believed the message that Jesus Christ loves us, died for us, and rose again. From that death comes the gift of life. We who once had no capacity for God are now the vessel in which God lives! Have you passed from death unto life? If not, let today be the day!

EVENING

I praise You, Father, that I am Your child. Thank You for Your precious Word, Your love letter to us that directs us to Christ and helps keep us close to Him. Thank You for salvation, for the opportunity to allow the old man to die and the new man to be born again in the Lord Jesus. Amen.

MORNING

Father, I know what I should do, but it is such a struggle. I know Your plan is best for me. Forgive me for resisting You and ignoring Your calling. God, please help me to surrender. Help me to let go of my life and experience all that You have for me. I am tired of living on my own and trying to be in control. I release my agenda and yield to Yours. Amen.

"He who finds his life will lose it, and he who loses his life for My sake will find it."
MATTHEW 10:39

The phrases, "commitment", "sacrifice", "taking up your cross", "putting to death the old man," and "surrendering to God with reckless abandonment" are ones we often read and talk about but have a hard time living. We love and live for this life we have. We are confident in our jobs, our family relationships, our church attendance, and our service. God has so much more in store for us when we are willing to relinquish control, let go of what we have, and totally surrender to all that He is. Then we will truly experience His life. His life is a life of humility, surrender, and dependence. It is a life of power—not power for you, but power to affect others with the message of the gospel. It is a great paradox, but nonetheless true. You lose your life and discover His. What an amazing exchange!

The question on the table today is, are you willing to make the exchange? Do you really believe that God is the rewarder of those who seek Him (Heb. 11:6)? Do you really believe that God has your best interests at heart? Let go, step out, and give Him your entire life, not just a portion or a percentage, but your total being. Give your whole life to Jesus—He gave you His! The exchange is worth it!

EVENING

Lord Jesus, thank You for allowing me to live another day. I desire for my life to count. I understand that I need to change, so please help me to change and to truly lay down my life and allow You to live through me. Help me to be dead to sin and dead to self. Help me to live each moment dependent on You and trusting in You. I surrender to You this day. Amen.

STEVE FLOCKHART, HIRAM, GA

Father, do a deep work in my life today. May I move past the surface and experience Your life deep within my soul. I thank You for the great work of salvation that You have worked in me. I am forever saved! May I take what You have put in me and release it in an appealing manner that draws others into an overwhelming desire to possess the same relationship with You. Amen.

"Therefore, my beloved, as you have always obeyed,
not as in my presence only, but now much more in my absence,
work out your own salvation with fear and trembling."
PHILIPPIANS 2:12

The average Christian's life is a series of ups and downs, but should instead be considered a process of ins and outs. God works it in, and we work it out. Paul doesn't say we need to work for our salvation. Our salvation was purchased on the Cross of Calvary. After we receive the gift of eternal life, we work out what God has placed in us. The word "work" speaks of constant energy and effort to finish a task. It speaks of working in a mine gathering the valuable minerals, jewels, or other items.

Those of us living in the 21st century are not familiar with the commitment and sacrifice of panning for gold. In the 1800s, people would rise at the crack of dawn and pan for gold until it became dark in the evening. Each day in the scorching heat, they dipped those pans in the water and swirled them around and around for hours working diligently and tirelessly in hopes to "get out that which was in"—gold! We cannot work for our salvation, but we must work *at* our salvation.

The idea is simple: as a believer, you need to make a continuous effort to work out what God has put in you. When that happens, your life will be an example on the outside because of the power on the inside.

EVENING

Lord Jesus, may every word that I speak and every action bring You glory. I pray that everyone around me will observe my salvation and that it will attract others to You. Help me to enjoy my salvation as Your gift to me but to work at it as I seek to be more like You. Amen.

MORNING

Lord Jesus, please help me be sensitive to all of those around me. Give me a greater desire to tell others about You. Help me get in on Your plan and Your agenda of saving people. Forgive me for not possessing a burden like I should. Help me today to be salt and light to the world around me. Amen.

"For this is good and acceptable in the sight of God our Savior,
who desires all men to be saved and to come to the knowledge of the truth."
I TIMOTHY 2:3, 4

The Father, the Son, and the Holy Spirit have come together in a rescue mission to redeem a lost world. The Trinity is actively involved in getting people saved. The Father planned it, the Son accomplished it, and the Spirit draws, convicts, shines the light on the dark heart, and magnifies the individual's ultimate need for Christ. The Spirit also seals you when you say yes at the moment of salvation.

To each of us who has been born again, God has given the responsibility of sharing Christ with a lost and dying world. We are His messengers. He has provided everything we need to present the gospel with others. He has even promised to give us boldness through His Holy Spirit (Acts 1:8)! God does not want anyone to perish but desires that all would come to repentance.

It is the will of God that all people be saved. Will that happen? Of course not, but we must be in the business of praying and actively sharing our faith with others. God sends hurting people into our lives every day. Some are family members or close friends. Many are people we meet briefly in our daily comings and goings. May God help us to share the truth with each of these people.

EVENING

Father, I pray that You will give me Your heart to see others saved. May I not get so busy that I am distracted from the thing that brings You the greatest joy—bringing others to the saving knowledge of Jesus Christ. Help me never to be satisfied in sharing my faith, and help me to stay sensitive to the fact that there are men, women, boys, and girls on their way to hell. Thank you for the privilege to serve as Your messenger and deliver the Good News to them. Amen.

STEVE FLOCKHART, HIRAM, GA

God, this day is all about You! You are worthy of my focus and attention. Please help me to depend on You in everything I do today. In Jesus' name, Amen.

"Not by works of righteousness which we have done, but according to His mercy He saved us, through the washing of regeneration and renewing of the Holy Spirit."

TITUS 3:5

Ever heard, "Pull yourself up by the bootstraps"? All of our lives we are taught to take care of ourselves. From childhood, we are ingrained with the importance of a "can do" attitude. Unfortunately, the things we must do, we can't do. The most important thing in our lives cannot be accomplished by our works.

"Not by works . . . which we have done." Nothing we "can do" will determine our relationship with God. This is especially encouraging in light of what we have done. The apostle Paul wrote this verse with a fresh awareness of His past sinfulness. The sins he mentions we have all battled: "We ourselves were also once foolish, disobedient, deceived, serving various lusts and pleasures, living in malice and envy, hateful and hating one another" (Titus 3:3). Aren't you grateful your relationship with God is not based on what you have done?

"But according to His mercy." A decisive change takes place when we recognize that His mercy supersedes our works, both righteous and unrighteous.

Have you opened the door to the new way of living His mercy offers? Stop trying to "do" whatever it takes to be right with God. There is nothing you can do but bathe in His mercy and let Him cleanse you, inside and out.

EVENING

Jesus, thank You for loving me in spite of my sin. Thank You for Your mercy and grace. Please cleanse me once again and renew me by Your power. Amen.

MORNING

Lord, I want You to be in control of this day. Please help me to live this day without regret. Thank You for another opportunity to rest in You. Amen.

"For godly sorrow produces repentance leading to salvation,
not to be regretted; but the sorrow of the world produces death."
2 CORINTHIANS 7:10

How many times have I heard, "I'm sorry," from one of my children, realizing that they did not mean one word of that two-word confession? How many times have I uttered that empty apology just because it is expected?

It is possible to express frustration over the consequences of our attitudes and actions while not experiencing sincere remorse of the pain we have caused. God's Word teaches that we should beware of such ungodly and meaningless sorrow.

We should long for sorrow that *produces repentance*. Why? Because true repentance leads to times of refreshing in our lives (Acts 3:19). James MacDonald defines repentance as "recognition of sin followed by heartfelt sorrow culminating in a change of behavior." Have you experienced the overwhelming blessing of being made right with God through repentance?

Most of us have sinful choices in our lives we wish we could undo. "If I could go back in time I would certainly do things differently . . ." But we would not give anything for the change God has brought about in us because of a repentant spirit.

Perhaps you are in need of a good dose of R&R—repentance and refreshing. May God give you awareness of any area of your life that needs godly sorrow today.

EVENING

Heavenly Father, thank You for Your grace. It is Your grace that has been sufficient for me this day. Please help me live with a constant knowledge of my need for Your grace. Even now, refresh me anew and make me aware of any area of my life that necessitates repentance. In Jesus' name, Amen.

PAUL PURVIS, FORSYTH, MO

Father, thank You for the gift of this new day. My prayer is simple: "Create in me a clean heart, O God, and renew a steadfast spirit within me" (Ps. 51:10). I look forward to the new things You are going to do in me today! Amen.

*"Therefore, if anyone is in Christ, he is a new creation;
old things have passed away; behold, all things have become new."*
2 CORINTHIANS 5:17

There is something special about newness, whether it's a new car, a new house, or a new baby. Things can look new, they can feel new, and some things even smell new. Did you know that God's Word teaches you can become brand new?

The first use of the English phrase "brand new" is found in a sermon by John Foxe in 1570: "New bodies, new minds and all things new, brand-new."

"All things"—that includes every area of your life. When Jesus Christ infiltrates who you are, He makes *all things* new. He gives you new attitudes and new actions; He gives you new habits and a new heart.

What is the result of the new you? The old you passes away. God cleans your closets; He takes out your trash; He sweeps the very floor of your former existence with the powerful vacuum of His grace; and in the greatest of all extreme makeovers, He makes you brand spanking new.

Are you in Christ? If so, smell and touch and see the newness that only He can offer you today! If not, ask God to create a brand new you today!

EVENING

Precious Lord, thank You for giving me this day to live "in You." Please forgive me for those choices I made that were not of You. As You forgive me of my sins, please cleanse me of all unrighteousness. Thank You for the opportunity to begin again. Amen.

MORNING

Father, You are the Holy One! Please speak Your truth into my life today. Allow me to live in salvation and strength. Give me the quiet courage to trust Your plans. In Jesus' name, Amen.

"For thus says the Lord GOD, the Holy One of Israel: 'In returning and rest you shall be saved; in quietness and confidence shall be your strength.'"
ISAIAH 30:15

Rebellious people are not looking to hear from God, but He refuses to sit silently by in the midst of their rebellion. The people told the prophet Isaiah that they did not want to hear God (Is. 30:10), but it was the Word of God they needed the most. And so He spoke. The Sovereign God earnestly desires to speak into your life and bring you closer to Him, but the pathway to His presence may not be what you think it is.

Throughout history people have attempted to experience salvation in a variety of ways. In this passage of Scripture the people had trusted in "swift horses" (Is. 30:16). Today trust is often placed in possessions, pleasure, or even other people. God's Word teaches that some of these ways may seem right, yet they still lead to death (Prov. 16:25).

We must be careful about devising our plans without God's input. Isaiah states that the end result of this rebellious attitude is shame and sorrow. But that's not the way it has to be. You can experience salvation and strength—you simply have to trust Him.

God again reminds His people that salvation is not experienced as a result of hard work but as a consequence of rest in Him. Our strength today does not come from awareness of our abilities, but in our quiet confidence that He is able. Ask God to give you salvation and strength in Him today.

EVENING

Jesus, thank You for Your word today. Forgive me for the moments of stubbornness when I did not listen. Forgive me for trusting in my plans rather than Yours. Even as I prepare for physical rest please draw me close to You and restore my strength. Amen.

Jesus, I praise You as the victorious King. Thank You, God, for giving me another day to worship You. Help me this day to demonstrate Your presence and power wherever I go. Amen.

"For we are to God the fragrance of Christ among those who are being saved and among those who are perishing."
2 CORINTHIANS 2:15

D o you know what it's like to stand in the winner's circle and enjoy the smell of victory? For the champion, victory is "oh so sweet," but for the defeated person, the same celebration breeds bitterness.

God's Word teaches that Christ followers put off a sweet scent to those who have experienced the victory of knowing Him. Your life should be a pleasing fragrant reminder of Jesus to your brothers and sisters in Christ. However, the scent is different to those who don't know our Lord.

At certain times of the year I expect to pass a dead skunk during my daily drive. It seems these creatures overwhelm our community. The first time this occurred I instantly recognized the odious and yet familiar scent. Even in death the little skunk was making a statement.

The fragrance exuded by Christ followers is not sweet to those who do not know Him. It is the bitter smell of defeat and death. And yet we cannot help but live our lives as His fragrant reminder. May you impact your "corner of the world" with His scent today!

EVENING

Father, You have gone with me today as I have walked through both victory and defeat. I pray that my attitudes and actions have represented You well. Please continue to help me be a fragrant reminder of You to all I meet. May my scent draw others to You, and may You draw me closer still even now. In Jesus' name, Amen.

MORNING

Father, thank You for loving me and waking me this morning. You have given me yet another day to bask in the wonder of Your love. Jesus, please dwell in me today, so that I may accomplish the plans You have prepared for me. Give me faith to trust You no matter what this day brings. Amen

"That Christ may dwell in your hearts through faith."
EPHESIANS 3:17A

What is your life's work? For the apostle Paul, it was helping people understand and respond to God's message of Good News (Eph. 3:7). Ultimately our work as Christ followers is simple in scope, but it sometimes feels quite weighty. The burdens of this world make our tasks seem undoable and our burdens unbearable. At times we even feel as if we are "in over our heads." It is at these times that we must remember God always takes care of the details.

God in His sovereignty knows the plan(s) He has for you. Your job is simple: trust in Him so that He dwells in you through faith. How do you do this? Focus on the wonder of His love. This weekend, think about the love of God. Experience the depth, the breadth, the length, and the height of who He is and what that means. Invite Him to dwell within your heart, and live these days in the fullness of Him. When you do, He will do far more in and through you than you could ever imagine.

EVENING

Lord Jesus, thank You for giving me the treasure of this day. My life is different because of Your love. Thank You for the promise that nothing can separate me from Your love. Help me this night to rest in the peace of that promise. Amen.

Father, I praise You this morning for the gift of Your Son. I am grateful I have a Savior and I have salvation. I confess with John the Baptist that Jesus is the "Lamb of God who takes away the sin of the world," including mine (John 1:29). Amen.

*"And she will bring forth a Son, and you shall call His name JESUS,
for He will save His people from their sins."*
MATTHEW 1:21

Unlike every other human born, Jesus was not given existence at His conception—He was given incarnation, for He already existed. Had He been given existence at His conception He could not have been God. Jesus, the Alpha and Omega, the beginning and the end, the first and the last, existed from eternity past and was "the Lamb slain from the foundation of the world" (Rev. 13:8).

Unlike every other human born, an earthly mother and an earthly father could not have conceived Jesus or else He would have been the creation of humans and not God. Humans are incapable of reproducing God; we only reproduce ourselves. Matthew 1 makes it abundantly clear that Jesus was not conceived by an earthly father, but by the Holy Spirit (vv. 16, 18, 20, 23). Jesus could not have been the Seed of Adam, for in Adam all die (1 Cor. 15:22). Jesus had to be the Seed of the woman (Gen. 3:15), which necessitated a virgin birth.

Unlike every other human born, Jesus came to earth to save all of mankind from sin. We could not pull ourselves up by our own bootstraps. Since we are all sinners, we could not meet the righteous demands of Holy God and present ourselves as an unblemished sacrifice to take away our sins. Jesus came for the specific, intentional purpose to save us "from" our sins. His very name means "Jehovah is salvation."

Jesus is the eternal Son of God and was conceived in the womb of the virgin Mary by the Holy Spirit for the purpose of saving us from our sins.

EVENING

Almighty God, I have relished in my salvation all day long. The thought of Your redeeming love and grace has been my constant joy throughout the day. I thank You that because my sins are forgiven, the peace of God rules in my heart. Amen.

MORNING

Good morning, Lord. I lift up my voice to You, for You have made me glad. You have placed a song in my heart and a spring in my step. Passion for You and life flows in my veins because of the abundant life You have wrought in me. Be glorified today, Lord, in my life, and may others see Jesus in me. Amen.

"Then the angel said to them, 'Do not be afraid, for behold,
I bring you good tidings of great joy which will be to all people.'"
LUKE 2:10

People live in fear. Fear of financial loss, deterioration of health, broken relationships, death of a loved one, etc. Life is often tragic. However, the worst news of all is that we are sinners separated from a Holy God. Therefore, we need to hear Good News that can trump our bad news.

Our text gives us three key insights into Good News. First, we see the *angel*. Until the earthly ministry of Jesus, God often used angels to bring His message. Up to this point and time in history perhaps no message was as significant as the one proclaimed by the angel. The value of the message of Good News necessitated a valuable messenger.

Second, we see the *audience*. God did not choose to declare this important message to any political or financial power; He chose a group of lowly shepherds. Isn't that just like God? The Chief Shepherd makes known His Good News of salvation to common shepherds. The shepherds represent each of us who are spiritually lowly and in need of the angel's message of good tidings, because this news was for "all people."

Third, we hear the *announcement*. This was not an announcement of fear, but one of great joy. God's expressed plan of salvation is one of great jubilation! It is not a plan to strike trepidation in the hearts of His people, but elation. The two adjectives spoken by the angel—"good" and "great"—describe God. He is both a good God and a great God.

EVENING

Lord, the evening news is filled with bad news that brings immense sadness for many. I praise You, my good God for the blessedness of Your good tidings. I bless Your great name, for You have been my great joy. Your good tidings have overcome the world's bad news. Amen.

ALLAN TAYLOR, WOODSTOCK, GA

Week 18, Wednesday

Lord, speak, for Your servant is listening. I will drown out all imposters and will hear only You, for You alone are God. Therefore, as Your sheep, I will only heed the voice of my Great Shepherd. Amen.

*"And a cloud came and overshadowed them; and a voice came
out of the cloud, saying, 'This is My beloved Son. Hear Him!'"*
MARK 9:7

The world is full of many voices. They all beckon for your attention and allegiance. Viewpoints abound and philosophers are a dime a dozen. Yet there is one voice that stands above the rest—the voice of God and His Son! God the Father tells Peter, James, and John on the Mount of Transfiguration that Jesus is His Son and we are to hear Him!

If Jesus is not the Son of God, then the Father is a liar. If Jesus is not the Son of God, then He is irrelevant. But if He is the Son of God, we can do no less than to give Him our undivided attention.

We must hear His voice above all the other voices that are religious imposters. "He who does not enter the sheepfold by the door, but climbs up some other way, the same is a thief and a robber" (John 10:1). God's true sheep hear the voice of Jesus. "But he who enters by the door is the shepherd of the sheep. To him the doorkeeper opens, and the sheep hear his voice; and he calls his own sheep by name and leads them out. And when he brings out his own sheep, he goes before them; and the sheep follow him, for they know his voice" (vv. 2–4).

EVENING

Holy God, Your voice speaks truth, Your voice speaks compassionately, and Your voice penetrates my heart. No one has ever spoken to me like You. Amen.

MORNING

Sovereign God, I have no idea what this day may bring, so I cling to Your ever-sure hand. I am grateful You have promised to never leave me nor forsake me. I know You will see me through any storm that may rage against me. May I look unto You, the author and finisher of my faith. Amen.

"Then those who were in the boat came and
worshiped Him, saying, 'Truly You are the Son of God.'"
MATTHEW 14:33

In Matthew 8:23–27 Jesus was asleep in the boat when His disciples awoke Him in the midst of a storm saying, "Lord, save us!" After He calmed the wind and waves, the disciples asked, "What manner of man is this?" Later, in our text, Jesus came walking to His disciples on the water in the middle of a storm and in the middle of the night. Jesus grants Peter permission to come to Him on the water, but Peter begins to sink when he takes his eyes off Jesus. He cries, "Lord, save me!" After Jesus enters the boat with Peter and calms the tempest, the disciples answer their question from the first storm with these words: "Truly You are the Son of God."

You are either in a storm, coming out of a storm, or headed for a storm—life is stormy. In the midst of our personal storm we, too, need the One who used the sea as a sidewalk to save us; we too, need to proclaim, "Truly You are the Son of God." Only Christ can bring calm in the midst of calamity. It is not natural to have peace in the midst of a storm—it is supernatural! Human nature shuns storms; divine nature stills storms. When faith cries out, "Lord, save me!" the hand of God reaches down and picks us up. Let Jesus bring you victory in the midst of your storm today!

The evidence is in—Jesus will see you through! Like the disciples, the more we truly know the Son of God, the more we will want to worship Him and bow our knee to Him, just as the wind and waves do!

EVENING

Father, You are my Rock and my Refuge. In You I trust. Even if I walk in the valley of the shadow of death, I will fear no evil, for You are with me. Your very presence is my comfort. Amen.

ALLAN TAYLOR, WOODSTOCK, GA

Week 18, Friday

Omniscient God, before You I lay naked. As honestly as I know how, I bear my soul to You. You know the thoughts and intent of my heart. I confess my sin and iniquity and ask Your forgiveness through the blood of Your Son. May I start my day clean and fresh before You. Amen.

*"Nathanael answered and said to Him,
'Rabbi, You are the Son of God! You are the King of Israel!'"*
JOHN 1:49

Most skeptics are biased and ingenuous. Their approach to Christ is "my mind is already made up, so don't confuse it with the facts." Nathanael, however, was a sincere skeptic. He doubted anything good could come out of Nazareth but was willing to take Phillip's simple invitation to "come and see" (John 1:46). Nathanael was an open book before Christ, being transparent, vulnerable, and candid. When Nathanael came to Jesus, he discovered that Jesus already knew about him! How could this Man whom he had never met already know everything about him? He must be the Messiah! Only omniscience could know this, and only God is omniscient. Therefore, Jesus had to be the Son of God. This led Nathanael to a personal conviction and a personal confession: "You are the Son of God! You are the King of Israel!" (v. 49).

Like Adam and Eve, we often take fig leaves in an attempt to cover something from the all-seeing eyes of God. Of course, we only deceive ourselves, because nothing can be hidden from an omniscient God.

Are there any doubts in your heart today about Jesus? Any skepticism? Any reservations? Will you "come and see" with an honest, open heart? God is a reasonable God. Life is too short and eternity too long for you not to give Jesus an honest look. What is your personal conviction and confession about Jesus?

EVENING

Merciful God, I thank You for the sweet fellowship of abiding in Christ. My soul stands cleansed of sin through Your mercy and grace. I have tried Jesus and found Him to be everything I need. Amen.

Father, I recognize my propensity to sin. I sense the constant battle between good and evil that wars within me. So I lean on Your Word and place my life under the lordship of the Son of God. In Jesus' name I commit this day to You. Protect me today from myself, and place Your hedge of protection around me. Amen.

"He who sins is of the devil, for the devil has sinned from the beginning. For this purpose the Son of God was manifested, that He might destroy the works of the devil."
1 JOHN 3:8

The devil is a great hunter. He sets his trap and baits it with that which is alluring to us—the lust of the flesh, the lust of the eyes, and the pride of life (1 John 2:16). Our natural man is drawn to his bait like an animal is drawn to the food in a hunter's trap. Why are we naturally attracted to sinful desires? Because the seed of sin is in us. The man who continually, habitually practices sin is of the devil. "You will know them by their fruits . . . Every good tree bears good fruit, but a bad tree bears bad fruit . . . By their fruits you will know them" (Matt. 7:16, 17, 20).

Enter the Son of God. Jesus invaded this world to do for us what we could not do for ourselves—destroy the works of the devil. Jesus counters and overcomes the purpose of Satan. After the original sin in the Garden of Eden, God declared war on Satan and promised ultimate victory (Gen. 3:15), which was fulfilled in the death, burial, and resurrection of Christ. The incarnate Christ was revealed for the very intention of destroying the destroyer! A true believer cannot habitually live in sin, because the One who abides in us destroys the works of the devil. We are no longer powerless and helpless, but strengthened by the power of His might. Because Jesus came and fulfilled His purpose, we can now fulfill our God-given purpose, too!

EVENING

Lord, today You have kept me from evil, and the seed of Your Word and Your Spirit has given me the victory over the works of the devil. I praise You for the impartation of Your divine nature. Amen.

Lord, help me to not suffer from spiritual amnesia, forgetting who You are and why You came to this perishing planet. Open Your Word and reveal Yourself in this day as well. In Jesus' name, Amen.

*"For there is born to you this day in the
city of David a Savior, who is Christ the Lord."*
LUKE 2:11

The Son of God was the God-Man, which sounds like an oxymoron, like "jumbo shrimp" or "civil war." But Jesus was born with no midwife, anesthesia, epidural, fetal heart monitor, and even among the animals. God took an ordinary night and revealed His Son's birth to common shepherds. God often uses common everyday events and people to carry out His great plan for humanity. "You shall call His name Jesus, for He will save His people from their sins" (Matt. 1:21).

The Lord of the heavenly hosts has become the Friend of the outcasts. He is big on personal pronouns. Counting your five fingers on one hand reminds you: "The Lord is my shepherd." On the other hand, "He has chosen sinful me." Today's verse says He came "to you." "You shall call His name JESUS, for He will save His people from their sins" (Matt. 1:21).

Christ as Messiah came to reign not only over Israel but also over "all people" (Luke 2:10). He did not come to stay in a stable, but to be exalted on the throne of heaven. There is a difference between "Jesus <u>is</u> Lord" and "Jesus <u>as</u> Lord." He reigns supreme whether you recognize it or not, but He desires to be Lord over every aspect of your life today.

EVENING

Lord, thank You for living in and through me. Thank You for sending angels to common shepherds in order to announce the birth of Your most precious Gift, Jesus. I pray you continue to use the common, ordinary events in even my life to reach the lost. In Jesus' name, Amen.

MORNING

Father, I pray like Jehoshaphat facing the evil coalition: "We have no power . . . nor do we know what to do, but our eyes are upon You" (2 Chr. 20:12). Father, may Your Holy Spirit teach me what to pray for and how to ask. I place a "Help Wanted" sign over my heart. In Christ's name, Amen.

"Likewise the Spirit also helps in our weaknesses. For we do not know what we should pray for as we ought, but the Spirit Himself makes intercession for us with groanings which cannot be uttered."
ROMANS 8:26

We often feel like ants before the mountain of prayer or like babies with little language to communicate. God's promise of help in weakness means that we can pray even if we are sick and dying. Unfortunately, many do not pray until they are sick or dying. We are not to rely on eastern mantras, glib religious clichés, or even written devotionals. We are indwelt by the Spirit, our divine Prayer Partner, who enables us to pray "in the Holy Spirit" (Jude 20). Therefore, we petition: "Lord, teach us to pray" (Luke 11:1).

"Helps" is the word picture of two men carrying a log or two horses in a harness, working together to carry the load. The Holy Spirit comes to our side and takes hold of our prayer load. He prays with and through us, interceding to the Father for us. The Spirit interprets God's will to us, helps us express it, and puts it in perfect form. But we must be "born of the Spirit" (John 3:6) and "filled with the Spirit" (Eph. 5:18) to live and "walk in the Spirit" (Gal. 5:25).

EVENING

Father, I pray in the mercy, authority, name, and blood of Christ. Cleanse today's sins, interpret my prayers, and direct them into Your will. Help me to awaken in the morning with a fresh assurance that my weakness is an opportunity for You to reveal Your power not only in my prayers but also in every problem. In Christ's name, Amen.

Lord, help me to deal with sin's inevitable defilement by having a clear conscience before You. Help me today to have quick restoration of fellowship. In Jesus' name, Amen.

"How much more shall the blood of Christ, who through the eternal Spirit offered Himself without spot to God, cleanse your conscience from dead works to serve the living God?"
HEBREWS 9:14

Our consciences leave a legacy of guilt. Long after the sins entered the mind or the hands and seem to have faded in memory, the stains still remain upon the conscience, leaving guilt and dead defilement. But through the ages, saints have overcome Satan "by the blood of the Lamb" (Rev. 12:11). Overcomers do not look within as much as they look back to the Cross.

Jesus became the unblemished Lamb of God as our sacrifice. God does not welcome you to His throne because of your discipline, depth of knowledge, or degree of victory but because of His blood. Hebrews 9:14 says that any attempt to satisfy God other than through the blood is simply "dead works." There are wicked works (Col. 1:21) and good works (Eph. 2:10). Standards are commendable, but we cannot stand on dead works and ground that has not been covered by the blood. Condemned consciences can be liberated through repentance, which is available to all who love the Lord.

The ashes of an animal sacrifice were used for cleansing in the Old Testament, but far superior to that is the cleansing power of the sacrifice of Christ on the Cross. At Calvary the wrath of God against sin burned itself out. We cannot look at the blood without seeing the ashes of His finished work. Cleansing took place once and for all.

Therefore, we "serve the living God" not out of dead duty, but in delight.

EVENING

Lord, I ask that You cleanse my conscience and empower me to serve You tomorrow without the baggage of guilt. In Jesus' name, Amen.

Lord Jesus, I come to You in awe that as Son of God and Son of Man, You died for me. Help me to live this day in Your humility and under the shadow of the Cross. In Jesus' name, Amen.

"And being found in appearance as a man, He humbled Himself and became obedient to the point of death, even the death of the cross."
PHILIPPIANS 2:8

In the workplace, people desire the upward mobility of climbing the ladder. Lucifer boasted, "I will ascend into heaven, I will exalt my throne above the stars of God" (Is. 14:13). But God's plan of salvation involved the downward mobility of Christ's Incarnation and Crucifixion.

Today's verse says Jesus came "in appearance as a man." His inner nature was God, but not His external appearance. All that God is, Christ was, is, and always will be. Jesus "became obedient to . . . the death of the cross." He did not obey death but His Father. Some idealistically say He died as a revolutionary or a martyr or a hero ahead of His time. He was not murdered but willingly laid down His life for us (John 15:13) in the torturous death of a Roman cross.

As a kidnapper holds his victim for ransom, Satan held us bound in his piracy of this planet, Jesus paid the ransom to redeem and liberate us (Matt. 20:28). As the slave spiritual song declares, "Free at last, free at last; thank God almighty, I'm free at last."

EVENING

Lord, I have sought to humble myself today just as You did, giving up my rights to be more like You in Your world. Just as You surrendered the independent exercise of Your divine attributes, I declare dependence on You tonight and again tomorrow. Before I lay down in bed, I again thank You for laying down Your life for me. In Jesus' name, Amen.

Week 19, Friday

Father, remind me today that You are for me and that it doesn't matter who is against me. I choose in prayer today to draw near to You through the blood, the name, and the high priestly work of the Lord Jesus. In Christ's name, Amen.

"Therefore He is also able to save to the uttermost those who come to God through Him, since He always lives to make intercession for them."
HEBREWS 7:25

Few things have thrilled me more than when in 1976 Dr. T.W. Hunt, the great teacher of *The Mind of Christ* and *Prayer Life,* promised to pray for my family and me each day. He has never broken that promise and is the godliest prayer warrior that I have ever known. Far more wonderful is that Jesus died for us to save us forever and continually intercedes for us as High Priest.

When Satan, "the accuser of our brethren" (Rev. 12:10), condemns us before God, the Judge declares that Satan's evidence against us is inadmissible in court. I can hear Jesus, my divine Defense Attorney, say, "Your Honor, I object…point of order…Hayes' sentence has been served on My Cross." The prosecutor has no claims against the defendant, because the Counsel for the defense pleads for me in His "intercession," a legal term for pleading for acquittal on the basis of the evidence. This present ministry has limitless power (Heb. 7:25) and is based on Christ's sinless character (v. 26) and His perfect offering (vv. 27, 28). He is in my corner!

EVENING

Lord, thank You for being my heavenly Prayer Partner today and for continuing Your work of salvation, not only from the penalty but also the power of sin. Thank You for being my Defender in court today and for rebuking the accuser on my behalf. I have sung again, "Oh happy day, when Jesus washed my sins away; He taught me how to watch and pray." In Christ's name, Amen.

MORNING

Jesus, You came as a baby, lived as a man, died, and raised as Lord. I worship You, because You gave up Your heavenly position to be an example for me. Help me today to surrender my rights to Your lordship. In Jesus' name, Amen.

"Let this mind be in you which was also in Christ Jesus, who, being in the form of God, did not consider it robbery to be equal with God."
PHILIPPIANS 2:5, 6

Today's verse says Jesus was "in the form of God." Whatever could be said about God the Father and God the Spirit could be said of God the Son. Apart from Christ's human nature, He possessed all the characteristics and qualities belonging to God because He is, in fact, God. He was and is equal to the Father in holiness, love, and the other attributes.

The Greek word is translated as "robbery" here, because it originally meant "a thing seized by robbery." Through history, the word came to mean anything clutched, embraced, or prized, and sometimes translated "grasped" or "held onto." Even though Christ had the rights, privileges, and honors of diety, He didn't cling to those things or His position, but was willing to give them up for a season.

Jesus lived His life as the ultimate example of selfless humility. If we truly let Christ's mind be in our mind and we think His thoughts, we will understand and see this, and then we will now see that it is God working in us to do His good pleasure.

EVENING

Lord, it is sometimes tough to live in selfless servanthood today. I thank You that You have helped me to live a life pleasing to You. Lord, when You knelt before Your disciples and washed their feet, You demonstrated Your humility. I thank You that I am growing a little more into Your likeness every day. In Jesus' name, Amen.

Week 20, Monday

Father, You sent Your only Son to earth to take on humanity at its fullest. Even in the very circumstances of His birth, You chose to show the world that He came thinking not about Himself, but His mission. May that be my attitude today. Help me to have that type of humility and reflect the character of the Lord Jesus. Amen.

"And she brought forth her firstborn Son, and wrapped Him in swaddling cloths, and laid Him in a manger, because there was no room for them in the inn."
LUKE 2:7

If you go to the Holy Land today, you will see a place that scholars believe is somewhat similar to the place where Jesus was born. In our culture babies are born in the most sterile, controlled environments available. It is hard for us to imagine a baby being born in a stable. But this was the plan of God. Seven hundred years earlier the prophet Micah had foretold His birth location. The Son of God was wrapped in whatever they could find and laid in a manger that had just been used to feed the animals. Today's verse says this happened "because there was no room for them in the inn."

This story has been told countless times, and His birth is celebrated all over the world, but the truth is that in so many cases we don't have any room for Jesus in our lives. As followers of Christ we are amazed when we are reminded how He humbled Himself in order that we might gain heaven and have the abundant life He promised. The Bible tells us that Jesus humbled Himself, and that began right there in the stable. We must make sure there is room for Jesus in every part of our lives. He was born in a stable and laid in a manger, but He is to have a place of prominence in everything we do, for He is Lord!

EVENING

Lord, my life is filled with all types of activity, but I pray that I will always make room for You in every area. In every situation help me to think first of what You would have me to do, and in so doing honor You as my Savior. Amen.

MORNING

Father, this is a day that will be filled with opportunity and challenge. Help me to share with someone today my story of how You have forgiven me. Amen.

"Therefore I will divide Him a portion with the great, and He shall divide the spoil with the strong, because He poured out His soul unto death, and He was numbered with the transgressors, and He bore the sin of many, and made intercession for the transgressors."

ISAIAH 53:12

Just like His birth, Jesus' death was a part of the plan of God. Today's verse comes at the end of the servant poem, which was a prophecy of Jesus' death on the Cross. Jesus came to die as a sacrifice for the sins of the world. The death of the sacrificial Servant points out His glory and the eternal blessings of those who accept Him. The image here is of the victorious conqueror sharing the victory with his allies. But it came at a great price.

Jesus was numbered with the transgressors in that while innocent, He was charged with the sins of mankind and so bore their penalty. But Jesus didn't stop there. Not only did He suffer and die for sinners, but He also took on the role of Intercessor for them. Imagine having to pray for those who not only despised you, but also crucified you! Yet Jesus prayed for the Father to forgive them as He was doing the very thing upon which their forgiveness, and the forgiveness of others, was to be founded—His death on the Cross. He paid the ultimate price, and it is because of His sacrifice and His sacrifice alone that we can have eternal life when we put our trust in Him. We have a fresh start and a second chance because He loved us.

Jesus died for the sins of the world, but He also died for our sins individually. It was our sin that put Him on the Cross. He has won the victory, and we have the chance to share in that victory as we put our trust in Him.

EVENING

Lord, thank You for what You have done for me through the sacrifice of Your Son. I pray that I will be able to do as He commanded and take up my cross daily and follow Him. Amen.

MIKE HAMLET, SPARTANBURG, SC

Week 20, Wednesday

Father, Your love never wavers. That is hard for me to understand. You are so consistent. You have never loved me more than You do right now, and at the same time, You have never loved me less than You do right now. I know that when You love, You go all the way! You have made it clear to me that I can trust You with everything in my life because of Jesus Christ. Amen.

"He who believes in Him is not condemned; but he who does not believe is condemned already, because he has not believed in the name of the only begotten Son of God."
JOHN 3:18

Despite what some people tend to think, God is not looking for a reason to condemn us. We have already condemned ourselves through our sin. He is not looking to condemn us but to save us. We have a tendency to think that we have all the time in the world to make a choice about whether we will serve the Lord. This verse says that if we have not made that choice, then we have already made the choice! In other words, to not decide is to decide. We stand condemned already for our sins because we have not put our trust in "the only begotten Son of God."

This verse does away with the idea that religion is sufficient. We live in a religious culture. Religious people will surround you today. But being religious is not the same as having a relationship with the living Christ. It does make a difference what you believe, and it makes a difference where you put your trust. If a person has not trusted Christ, he or she has already made the wrong choice. It is our responsibility to share the truth with them. When someone views our life, do they see someone who is religious, or do they see someone who has a relationship? May our desire be that they see Christ in us!

EVENING

Lord, I've accepted the pardon. You've offered me eternal life through Your Son, Jesus Christ, and I've taken it! Thank You! Give me a passion to share this message with others. So many stand condemned before You and don't even know it. Help me to show them Your Son, the only source of life! Amen.

MORNING

Father, thank You for being willing to come to earth and dwell among us. Thank You for experiencing life in a way that gives me confidence that You can identify with me in every way. May I rejoice today in the fact that I serve a God who can relate to everything I am going through. You are all I need, Lord. Amen.

"And the Word became flesh and dwelt among us, and we beheld His glory, the glory as of the only begotten of the Father, full of grace and truth."

JOHN 1:14

This is the most incredible and amazing event in all of history. The omnipresent, omniscient, eternal Son of God took on human nature and lived among men as one that was both God and man at the same time as one person. The verse today shows us that Christ came to dwell among us, and while doing so, He revealed to us the Father's glory. The term "dwelt among us" means that He pitched His tent among us. God could have sent an angel or created a special being to come, but He chose to send the very best, the only begotten Son of the Father.

In our world we are accustomed to people paying or providing the minimum in terms of what is required. No one wants to pay full price. We like to pay or contribute as little as possible, but God did exactly the opposite. He sent the very best—"full of grace and truth." He is the ultimate revelation of God's grace and truth. He is the ultimate. He is greater than any other person in history. This is a picture of how much God loves us and what He was willing to do in order to have a saving relationship with us.

EVENING

Lord, how awesome it is that You were able to be fully human and fully God at the same time. And how comforting to know that You can understand me completely through Your humanness, yet You have the power to change my circumstances and my life through Your deity. Thank You for the way You've already used both to reveal the Father to me. I know I've only seen a mere glimpse of His glory—how exciting that there's so much more to come! In Jesus' name, Amen.

MIKE HAMLET, SPARTANBURG, SC

Father, as I go about my day today, keep me mindful of the fact that I serve a God who has experienced and who truly understands the temptations I will be facing. And as I face them, may I call upon Your power to resist the urge to give in, no matter how alluring the opportunity or situation might be. You fought temptation on earth, and You were victorious in every way. Help me to claim that same victory today.

"For we do not have a High Priest who cannot sympathize with our weaknesses, but was in all points tempted as we are, yet without sin."
HEBREWS 4:15

Jesus came to identify with us. And because He took on flesh and dwelt among us, He experienced life as we do in every way. As we've seen this week, He experienced our emotions and frustrations. He even experienced our temptations. This One who serves as High Priest on our behalf has been where we have been and has been tempted in every way, just as we are. Therefore, He can understand our situation and is able to sympathize with our weaknesses. Yet unlike us, He was without sin, never responding wrongly to any of His temptations. It seems that only One who has fully resisted temptation can know the full scope of its force.

Jesus has also given us help in handling temptation. First Corinthians 10:13 says, "No temptation has overtaken you except such as is common to man; but God is faithful, who will not allow you to be tempted beyond what you are able, but with the temptation will also make the way of escape, that you may be able to bear it." All of us face temptation, but we are able to respond correctly because He has provided us with the power.

EVENING

Lord, thank You for walking through my day with me today. Thank You for the strength to fight temptation that You make available to me at all times. I can't do it alone, but I know I serve a risen Savior who has already won the victory and walks with me every step of the way. Amen.

MORNING

Father, You are Lord over life and death. Because You experienced death and then rose again, I can now experience a life that death cannot conquer in any way. When I think about how wonderful this promise of eternal life for me really is, I am overwhelmed. Thank You for the wonderful assurance that comes from serving a risen Savior! Because You live, I can also live! Amen.

"Jesus said to her, 'I am the resurrection and the life. He who believes in Me, though he may die, he shall live. And whoever lives and believes in Me shall never die. Do you believe this?' She said to Him, 'Yes, Lord, I believe that You are the Christ, the Son of God, who is to come into the world.'"
JOHN 11:25–27

Because Jesus is the Creator of life, He has power over life and death. Who else could restore life except the very One who is life? In today's verse, Jesus tells Martha that because her brother Lazarus had been a believer in Him, even though he died, he would live. Jesus has the same message for us today—anyone who believes in Him will live eternally even if his or her body experiences physical death here on earth.

This is a real encouragement to us for our daily living. Perhaps you are facing a serious problem or challenge in your life right now. The good news is that if our Lord Jesus can conquer death, then there is no problem that He cannot handle. When Martha faced the death of her brother, Jesus asked Martha if she believed what He told her about eternal life. Her response was emphatic: "Yes, Lord, I believe." Her statement of faith is exactly the response that Jesus wants from us. This should be a real affirmation for us. Whatever you are facing today, the power of the living Lord Jesus is more than adequate to handle it.

EVENING

Lord, help me to live in the midst of resurrection power. May my belief in You not only affect the way I view death, but also my daily life. Help me to live the abundant life that You provide for me. I know it can only be found in You. Amen.

MIKE HAMLET, SPARTANBURG, SC

Father, I am so grateful this morning that as I face another day that is filled with uncertainty, a world that is filled with upheaval, and a culture that is filled with ungodliness, Your Word still stands. You have indeed spoken through the written Word, so that uncertainty is met with biblical assurance, upheaval is met with personal confidence, and ungodliness is met with divine providence. I pray today that Your Word would be a lamp unto my feet and a light unto my path to know and to do the right before You and all that I come in contact with in a world that needs to hear Your voice both through my lips and my life. Amen.

"But these are written that you may believe that Jesus is the Christ, the Son of God, and that believing you may have life in His name."
JOHN 20:31

I was recently preaching in a crusade in south Georgia and two young men came forward at the invitation who were instantly recognizable by their dress as, shall we say, "missionaries from another faith." I was asked if I would talk with them. When I sat down with the gentlemen, I asked if they had indeed repented of their sins and trusted Christ alone to save them, and the men insisted that they had. When I asked them if they *knew* they were going heaven, the pair reverted to their former "faith" which taught them no one could have that assurance. They used phrases such as "I feel," "I believe," and "I think." I then asked a question that stopped them in their tracks. I said, "What matters more—what you or I think or what God says?" I then had them read John 20:31 and 1 John 5:13. The men agreed that they did indeed possess eternal life at that very moment. I then said, "If you are being truthful, I have some good news and some better news. You are no longer a _____; you are now a Christian!"

EVENING

Father, I thank You as I close this day that Your Word says that I can sleep with the peace of knowing absolutely that if I don't wake up again on this earth it will only be because I am spending my first day with You in Your holy presence. Amen.

MORNING

Good morning to the One who is both crucified Savior and risen Lord! Today I begin this day as one who is so very grateful for on old wooden Cross that stood somewhere just outside an ancient Jerusalem gate some two-thousand-plus years ago. I thank You, precious risen Lord, that I have responded to the message of that Cross and now live in its shadow daily. Today I pray that You will crucify me with You on that Cross that I may die to all that would keep me from Your will. May I live in such a way that I always reflect Your glory. Amen.

*"For the message of the cross is foolishness to those who are perishing,
but to us who are being saved it is the power of God."*
I CORINTHIANS 1:18

Have you ever stopped to consider the fact that every major religion and ideology has had or does have its own particular visual symbol? For example, Buddhism uses the lotus flower with its shape of a wheel. Judaism, of course, is known by the Star of David and Islam by the crescent. Even secular ideology has its own visual signs. Marxist communism had the hammer and sickle. Nazism had the infamous swastika, and on it goes. Christianity, too, has its symbol, a cross, but not just a cross—the Cross of Jesus Christ. The message of that Cross is at one and the same time the most *controversial* message to some and the most *comforting* message to others. Why? Because this message is God's first and last word of salvation. It is only when we come *before* the Cross and place our sins *beneath* the Cross that we can go *beyond* the Cross and have a relationship with the God who sent His son to the Cross that we might know Him. The Cross tells us there is no "Plan B" to salvation. That is why the Cross is more than an ornament on a chain around our neck—it is to those of us "who are being saved the very power of God" (1 Cor. 1:18).

EVENING

Good night to the Son of God, who by His blood turned an instrument of death into a fountain that gives off the fresh water of eternal life to those who drink from it. Keep me near the Cross forever! Amen.

JAMES MERRITT, DULUTH, GA

Father, as I think of the ways You have revealed Yourself to me, I am so very thankful. Thankful that I can look around to a world that is clearly Your handiwork that declares unmistakably Your power, grandeur, and glory. I am grateful that You have spoken so clearly through a Book that bears all the marks of coming from a divine hand; a Book that pulsates with supernatural truth and unmistakably carries the sound of Your voice. I am humbled that You spoke last but not least through Your Son, who is my Lord. In every way You choose today, speak to me and through me. Amen.

"God . . . has in these last days spoken to us by His Son, whom He has appointed heir of all things, through whom also He made the worlds."
HEBREWS 1:1, 2

One of my favorite sayings, "There is nobody like Jesus!" One I often use when I am getting off the phone with my friends or as I am starting a message. Indeed, my entire life is built around my belief in those five simple words. There never has been, there isn't now, and there never will be anybody like Jesus. God has spoken through Jesus unlike any One else because Jesus was not just a prophet or just another messenger—He was God's unique Son—God in human flesh. He is the heir of all things because He created all things and He owns all things. The Christ of the New Testament is none other than the Creator of the Old Testament. That is why Jesus is not just God's best Word to the human race; He is God's last Word to the human race. After Jesus, even God has nothing else to say because when you have said "Jesus," you have said it all. So to a world that offers other holy books and other holy prophets we say, "No thanks"—in the Word of God and the Son of God we have all we need.

EVENING

Lord, You speak to me so clearly through Your Son, Jesus. I end this day thankful that I am an heir with the One who is the heir of all things. Forgive me when I am tempted by the sound of other voices. Remind me that the only One worthy of my worship is Jesus. Amen.

MORNING

My Sovereign Lord in heaven, I come to You saddened at the thought of the times in my life when I rejected You, Your Word, Your will, and Your witness. My heart breaks when I remember the times that I hid my face from You and the times I did not esteem You or show by word and deed that You are my first love. Lord, today as I go out into a world that still despises You and rejects You, give me the power and strength to stand for You and speak for You at every opportunity. Thank You for giving me another day to show my allegiance to You. Amen.

"He is despised and rejected by men, a Man of sorrows and acquainted with grief. And we hid, as it were, our faces from Him; He was despised, and we did not esteem Him."

ISAIAH 53:3

Without question, it is one of the most devastating things that can happen to anyone at any age regardless of the reason. I know because I have experienced it during my elementary, high school, and post-college years. It can destroy your self-confidence, devastate your self-esteem, and deface your self-image in a nanosecond. So quick to strike but so lingering in its effects, it can take years to recover from its force—and some never do.

I am talking about rejection. Until I finally developed athletically, my peers didn't want me on their team. The first girl I ever asked out on a date flatly refused, and the first job I interviewed for after college went to someone else. I can't even begin to imagine what a spouse feels after being rejected for another man or woman, or what a person with a physical handicap feels after being rejected by the circus stare or the cold laughter.

But Jesus knows exactly how you feel—He above all others experienced the ultimate rejection by the entire human race, and yet at the height of that rejection offered His life never ending and His love never failing. The good news is He will never reject you!

EVENING

Dear God, I thank You that You are not a God that holds grudges. Precious Jesus, thank You for not rejecting me even as I rejected You. I now completely forgive all who have rejected me as You have forgiven me. Amen.

Week 21, Friday

Heavenly Father, the longer I live the more I see just how precious this thing called life really is. The passing years remind me of its brevity; good health reminds me of its quality; children remind me of its sanctity; youth reminds me of its vitality. This prized and precious possession causes me to praise You all over again that Your Son gave His life for mine. It truly is a debt of love that I could never repay—even if I had an eternity to do so. Lord, thank You for giving Your perfect life for imperfect me, and thank You for giving Your love to undeserving me. The love You have shown me, show through me to others today. Amen.

"By this we know love, because He laid down His life for us.
And we also ought to lay down our lives for the brethren."
1 JOHN 3:16

Talk is cheap. And when it comes to love, perhaps never more so. I heard about a guy who was really pouring it on with a beautiful girl he wanted to impress. He was always telling her, "Baby, I love you so much I would die for you!" He said that to her every day, several times a day, until one day she finally said, "You know, you are always saying that, but you never do it!"

When Jesus Christ, the Son of God, literally laid down His life for us, He was saying, "This is how much I love you—more than My own life." Think about it. God didn't just say He loves us (though His Word should be sufficient)—He *showed* He loves us. To do so, He didn't send an angel or appoint an ambassador—He gave His Son. On the other hand, Jesus didn't send a substitute—He *became* our substitute and thereby settled His love for us once and for all. If God's Son loved us like that, how much more should we also love our spiritual family? When the world sees that kind of love, they will truly believe we are His disciples.

EVENING

Lord I end each day as I begin it—knowing that You love me unconditionally. I cannot doubt Your love because of the Cross, and I will not doubt Your love because of Your compassion. With that same love lead me to love others. Amen.

MORNING

Father, as I walk through this world and face the burdens of making a living as well as making a life, it seems as if at times the mountain gets higher, the burden gets heavier, and the road gets longer. I confess that He is the Christ, the Son of the living God. I face life today knowing that Your Son will guide me and guard me, and because of His presence I will overcome anything life brings to me every day. Amen.

"Who is he who overcomes the world,
but he who believes that Jesus is the Son of God?"
1 JOHN 5:5

I have learned during my years as a pastor that life is full of battles and storms. My mentor, Adrian Rogers, said that we only have three problems: sin, sorrow, and death. He was right. Talk to anyone long enough, and everyone has been affected by all three of those problems—and if not, give them long enough and they will!

One of my all-time favorite movie stars is Clint Eastwood. In the movie "The Outlaw Josie Wales" there is a scene where he and his friends are in a cabin awaiting an attack by a band of cutthroat renegades. He tells them they have to believe they will win because "if you quit you neither win nor live." The minute he said that, I was reminded of the importance of faith—and particularly faith in Christ—for facing and fighting successfully every foe life brings.

There is a reason why your faith is so important to you on a daily basis. Do you realize that Jesus never failed to overcome anything, including death itself? When you place your faith in the undisputed, undefeated champion of love who is the ultimate overcomer, you, too, will find through His power and presence that you will be an overcomer. So replace your fear with faith and see God's Son make you the overcomer you were meant to be.

EVENING

Sovereign God, I get so very weary of the fight, so tired in the battle that life brings. Yet I am thankful that my faith in You brings with it the power to overcome this world and all that is in it. Amen.

Week 22, Monday

Lord, fill Your temple today and glorify Yourself through everything I do. Amen.

"Or do you not know that your body is the temple of the Holy Spirit who is in you, whom you have from God, and you are not your own?"

1 CORINTHIANS 6:19

I will never forget witnessing a well-intentioned man asking a teenager to remove his cap inside the church building. He used solemn words: "Son, take off your cap in God's house." The man was very sincere in his desire to honor the house of God. But we must realize the true house of God and honor it by living obediently to our Lord.

The true house of God is you and me, the saved. God has come to dwell with us in the person of the Holy Spirit. Jesus our Lord promised His disciples in the Upper Room shortly before His Crucifixion that He wouldn't leave them as orphans. He revealed to them it would be to their benefit that He depart. He desired to complete His redemptive work and come to dwell within every follower, not just the Twelve, in the person of the Holy Spirit.

When you accepted Jesus as your Savior, the Holy Spirit came to live within you. He won't leave. We may hinder His influence over us at times with our lack of surrender, but He doesn't leave. Because He lives in us, we must care for the temple. Remember you are special. God has chosen to dwell with you. Care for His temple, your body. We must remember the commission of the temple. According to the verse that follows our text today, that commission is to glorify God. Every day in everything we do and say, we must glorify God. This commission becomes natural when we give way to the Holy Spirit's control of His temple—us!

The Holy Spirit lives in us; therefore, there is comfort in being His temple. You and I will never go anywhere and never do anything without God being with us. When we are submitted to Him, we do not live, work, play, or minister on our own power, but His. He empowers His temple to serve Him. It is an incredible blessing to be His temple. He dwells in us and with us.

EVENING

Lord, may Your temple rest tonight for another day of glorifying You. Amen.

MORNING

Father, I need the anointing presence of the Holy Spirit to fill my life. I want to be effective for You today. Therefore, I surrender completely to Your control. Fill me, Lord! In Jesus' name, Amen.

"And the Holy Spirit descended in bodily form like a dove upon Him, and a voice came from heaven which said, 'You are My beloved Son; in You I am well pleased.'"

LUKE 3:22

Have you ever thought, *I want to make a difference. I want my life to count for something?* Certainly we live in a time when Christians need to be effective. How can our lives be effective for the Lord? How can we impact people around us? The answer is revealed in the text for today.

Jesus' baptism inaugurated His ministry. The event has symbolism for us. If we are to be effective in life and ministry, it will be the result of utter surrender to the Holy Spirit who lives in us. The fact that the Spirit descended in bodily form like a dove emphasizes the reality of His presence. He is not some figment of the overactive imagination of religious people. He is real! Receiving the anointing power for effective life comes when we submit to that anointing. We give up all rights to self, and all we desire is the will of God. The Spirit pervades all areas of our existence. We become mightily anointed for ministry.

We also act like true sons and daughters of God. The evidence of the Holy Spirit in us manifests that we are heirs of God. I can't help but think the world isn't impressed with the Lord because they aren't impressed with us. They will be when we are living under the anointing of the Spirit.

God announced His great pleasure with His Son at Jesus' baptism. Living life in the Spirit, under His control, is how we please God. The key to life is not living for personal pleasure but to please God; that is the deepest form of human fulfillment and effectiveness.

EVENING

May all You have used me to do today continue to have lasting fruit. May people be drawn to You by the activity of today. I pray people were impressed with You because they saw You in me. Amen.

MIKE ORR, CHIPLEY, FL

Father, my time of prayer is often filled with personal desires. I pray that one of my greatest desires will be to fully enjoy the gift of the Holy Spirit. May I desire His influence over my life more than any possession, practice, or probability. In Jesus' name, Amen.

"If you then, being evil, know how to give good gifts to your children, how much more will your heavenly Father give the Holy Spirit to those who ask Him!"
LUKE 11:13

One of my favorite times of the year is Christmas. I remember as a child the excitement of Christmas morning. My parents always gave us the coolest gifts. I never remember being disappointed. We appreciated what we were given, and my parents worked hard to discover and purchase the things we would enjoy the most.

If my parents wanted to do that, how much more will my heavenly Father? He is perfect and has all resources and knows exactly what I need and desire. He didn't spare His own Son for me or for you.

The Lord has promised to provide for our needs, and He will even, at times, grant our desires. Matthew's record of this verse states it this way: "How much more will your Father . . . give good things to those who ask Him!" There may be something on your heart today you desire greatly. If it is in your best interest and will glorify Him, He will grant that desire. Luke has in mind the most important of "things," and that is the gift of the Holy Spirit. If we were to regard the Holy Spirit in terms of the great gift He is, we would desire His influence over us. When this occurs other desires lose their attractiveness, as we have discovered the real source of fulfillment in life. It is not possessions; it is being possessed by the Lord. Our desires overwhelm us at times because they are for possessions and practices related to the world. Real fulfillment is learning to enjoy the great gift of the Holy Spirit. He has multiple ministries for us to benefit from. Learn to desire the influence of the Holy Spirit daily.

EVENING

Father, I desire to recognize the benefits of Your presence in my life. Thank You for the great gift of the Holy Spirit. Amen.

Father, I surrender completely to You. May Your Spirit fill me, and may I be further transformed today into the image of Your Son. In His name I pray, Amen.

"Then Peter said to them, 'Repent, and let every one of you be baptized in the name of Jesus Christ for the remission of sins; and you shall receive the gift of the Holy Spirit.'"
ACTS 2:38

Today's text is from Peter's sermon to those in Jerusalem on the Day of Pentecost. The listeners had been "cut to the heart" by the message Peter proclaimed and cried out to know what to do in terms of dealing with their sin. Peter's response was for them to repent and exercise faith, for being baptized in Jesus' name was a symbol of faith in Him.

Repentance is necessary for salvation; that's why it is critical for people to realize their sin. The Spirit of God uses the Word of God to reveal it. Repentance is a turning away from sin, but the turning away from sin is not possible without turning to Jesus in faith. Therefore, to be baptized in Jesus' name means that one has responded to Jesus in faith, confessed Him as personal Savior, and submitted to Him as personal Lord. The result of repentance and faith is forgiveness of sin. Every sin is dealt with completely. Other passages in the New Testament teach us that we are declared righteous as well as forgiven.

Another gift is received at the moment of salvation, and it is the gift of the Holy Spirit. This gift isn't just for an elite group, but for all believers. The Holy Spirit regenerates us, unites us as the church, empowers us, and transforms us. When one experiences genuine saving faith, transformation takes place in our personal lives. This process of transformation continues for a lifetime.

This is one reason why we must continually surrender to God's will, not our will, or this continual process will be interrupted. Daily submission to the will of God enhances the Spirit's work of transformation or growth in us. Daily we submit, daily we serve, and daily the Spirit sanctifies us.

EVENING

Father, thank You for Your transforming work in my life. May that work continue tomorrow. Amen.

Week 22, Friday

Father, I do not want to fear the wonderful practice of witnessing for You. It is an honor to testify of Your grace and greatness. Help me depend daily on the power You provide to be an effective witness. Amen.

"But you shall receive power when the Holy Spirit has come upon you;
and you shall be witnesses to Me in Jerusalem, and in all
Judea and Samaria, and to the end of the earth."

ACTS 1:8

I remember the first time I went out on outreach visitation when it was my turn to share the gospel. On the way to that visit I remember praying, "Lord, don't let them be at home." Why did I pray this? I was terrified!

All of us have experienced witnessing anxiety at some point in our Christian walk. We are commanded to make disciples, which means we must share the gospel first. We are charged to be witnesses for Christ. It can be scary, and yet so fulfilling.

Much of our anxiety can be eliminated when we embrace this truth: we are empowered to witness for Christ by God Himself. Today's text reveals we have power to witness from the Holy Spirit. He is in every believer. We must learn to trust Him and rely on His power. The moment we realize our weakness and depend on Him is the moment we will become a powerful witness for our Lord. We are to be a witness for Him everywhere!

No matter where we go, we have the authority and power to be witnesses for our Lord Jesus. Whether to family or friends, God enables us to be effective as witnesses for Christ. There is nothing more fulfilling than sharing the gospel of Christ. So no more excuses—let's witness in the power of the Spirit.

EVENING

Father, may the seeds of the gospel You planted through me today come to harvest. May I be a witness for You tomorrow in the power of Your Holy Spirit. Amen.

Father, help me walk in truth by sharing the truth that Jesus is the only way to God. In His name I pray, Amen.

"Jesus said to him, 'I am the way, the truth, and the life.
No one comes to the Father except through Me.'"

JOHN 14:6

Despite this truth's lack of popularity today, it makes perfect sense that Jesus is the only way to God. Why would there be another valid way to God if Christ was the only worthy sacrifice for our sins? Does it make sense that Jesus would have to suffer if there were some other way? Does it make sense that you could gain access to God without ever acknowledging and accepting Christ's sacrificial work on our behalf?

The Gospels are reliable, as is all the Bible; it is the Word of God, and the record of Christ's claims are clear. He claims to be the way. He cannot lie—He's God!

Jesus Christ is the exclusive way to God and inclusive in offering the way to all. He is the *way*. We cannot have fellowship with God apart from Him. Jesus is the *truth*. We cannot know levels of truth without Him. He is *life*. It is impossible to have eternal and meaningful life without Him.

There is one way to the one God who lives in a real and exciting place called heaven. We were created for eternal fellowship with God. The only way to experience it is to acknowledge our dilemma. We are separated from God because of our sin. We must recognize God's provision, which is the death and resurrection of Jesus, to provide forgiveness and righteousness. We must receive Jesus as our Savior.

I must ask two questions. First, have you come by way of Christ alone? If not, you are not there. You must come to God through Him. Second, are you revealing to others that Jesus Christ is the only way? If not, you have succumbed to the influence of the world over the influence of Christ. He is the way. In case you haven't done so and you desire to accept Jesus, pray this: "Lord, I know I'm a sinner. Please forgive me. I believe in Jesus and His work, and I surrender to Him now. Lord Jesus, be my Savior."

EVENING

Thank You Jesus for being the way, the truth, and the life. Amen.

MIKE ORR, CHIPLEY, FL

Lord Jesus, thank You for the ability to get out of bed this morning and sit down before You and Your Word. Please give me the ability to comprehend Your ways and will for my life. May Your Spirit speak into my life and give me direction as I start my day. In Jesus' name, Amen.

"I indeed baptize you with water unto repentance, but He who is coming after me is mightier than I, whose sandals I am not worthy to carry. He will baptize you with the Holy Spirit and fire."
MATTHEW 3:11

Among the ways in which the Messiah would be mightier than John would be in His baptism with the Holy Spirit. John's word about the Holy Spirit must have been comforting and thrilling to the faithful Jews among his hearers, those who hoped for the day when God would pour out His Spirit on all mankind (Joel 2:28). The people longed for God to "sprinkle clean water" on them, give them "a new heart," and put "a new spirit" within them (Ezek. 36:25, 26). In that day they would at last be baptized with the very power and Person of God Himself.

John's baptism was a baptism of repentance, looking forward to Jesus' coming. John knew who he was, and he also knew his role. The real question to ask is this: "Do we really know who we are and who Jesus is?" Just as John came to discover that he could do nothing on his own without the power of the Holy Spirit, we must come to the same conclusion. Jesus does in and through us what we could never do ourselves, and the only way for that to continue is to live a life yielded and surrendered to the Holy Spirit.

What an incredible message of hope this is! John got it right: "He must increase, but I must decrease" (John 3:30). When my children were small, I always said to them, "Remember who you are and whose you are!" It would do us all good to remember that today.

EVENING

Lord Jesus, thank You for being my provision and provider this day. Thank You for the opportunities You gave me to share Your Name with a lost and dying world. Thank You for loving me in spite of all my imperfections. I love You! In Jesus' name, Amen.

Lord Jesus, thank You for the night's rest and for watching over me while I slept. It is so comforting to know that You never sleep or slumber. Thank You for the ability to trust You and Your grace during the night as well as during the day. May I dress myself in the armor of God this morning as I appropriate Your Word into my life. In Jesus' name, Amen.

"Jesus answered, 'Most assuredly, I say to you, unless one is born of water and the Spirit, he cannot enter the kingdom of God. That which is born of the flesh is flesh, and that which is born of the Spirit is spirit.'"
JOHN 3:5, 6

Nicodemus was puzzled by the words "born again" (John 3:7). He did not know what Jesus meant. He understood Jesus to be saying that a man must be born a "second time." How could a man possibly start all over, or go back to the beginning?

Jesus was telling him that accepting God's salvation was not a matter of adding something to all his efforts or topping off his religious devotion; rather, salvation means canceling everything and starting all over again. Jesus was asking for something that was not humanly possible (to be born again); He was making entrance into the kingdom contingent on something that could not be obtained through human effort. Jesus challenged this most religious Jew to admit his spiritual bankruptcy and abandon everything he was trusting in for salvation.

Being "born of water and the Spirit" means that a person must be cleansed spiritually and that is made possible through the Holy Spirit through the Word of God at the moment of salvation.

EVENING

Lord Jesus, thank You for the times today You guarded my steps and initiated my starts. Thank You for living Your life in me and through me. Let the words of my mouth and the mediation of my heart be acceptable in Your sight today. In Jesus' name, Amen.

Week 23, Wednesday

Lord Jesus, I praise Your name for being my provider and protector as I seek to live for You this day. I ask You to deliver me from evil and to enable me to finish my race with joy. I desire to finish strong and influence the lives of the people You have placed around me during my journey here. I submit myself to Your leadership and grace this morning. In Jesus' name, Amen.

"But the anointing which you have received from Him abides in you, and you do not need that anyone teach you; but as the same anointing teaches you concerning all things, and is true, and is not a lie, and just as it has taught you, you will abide in Him."

1 JOHN 2:27

All of us want to be able to speak and say things that will make a difference in the lives of the people we cross paths with. We talk in terms of a man or woman having charisma. If he or she does not have charisma, they will never go very far in today's culture. "Anointing" is the Greek word charisma. The word literally means to "smear on"; it means to take an ointment and smear it on or to anoint yourself with medicine.

In the Old Testament, the Israelite priests were anointed with oil, and it indicated in a physical way that they were specially endued by the Holy Spirit to perform a certain function. Likewise, John is reminding us that at salvation we have received an anointing as well.

The important thing to note here is that John is not saying that we do not need teachers. We do need teachers, but the greatest teacher we will ever know is the Holy Spirit, our resident truth teacher. Ask the Spirit of God to teach you and lead you. If you don't understand something, get down on your knees and say, "Lord, I don't understand this. Make it real to me."

Lord, I thank You for all the godly people who have influenced my life through the years. But most of all, I thank You for the investment of the Holy Spirit in my life. I received Him at salvation, and He will never leave me nor forsake me. In Jesus' name, Amen.

MORNING

Lord Jesus, I thank You for loving me in spite of me and for always forgiving me when I truly repent of my sin. I ask You to give me the ability through the power of the Holy Spirit to do for others today what You do for me. In Jesus' name, Amen.

"Now may the God of hope fill you with all joy and peace in believing, that you may abound in hope by the power of the Holy Spirit."
ROMANS 15:13

Today is without doubt a day of fear, panic, and hopelessness throughout our nation. Everywhere we turn we are hearing the message of doom and gloom. Our economic system has failed us and caused us all to see that we didn't have what we really thought we had to begin with. The Bible tells us that God is the God of hope! He is also the foundation of our hope, the builder of our hope, and the finisher of our hope.

In today's verse, the great apostle Paul prays a prayer that would be good for all of us to pray. The things Paul mentions cannot be possessed apart from God, and we can possess them only as He gives them to us. None of us will ever have peace, hope, or joy apart from a relationship with Jesus Christ and the power of the Holy Spirit. We do not have to pray for hope, joy, or peace because Jesus becomes all of that for us when we trust Him at salvation. Indeed, Jesus is all we need!

The child of God need never fear because he finds in this passage the Rock of Ages who is the shelter in the time of storm for us all. Paul shares his heart with the church at Philippi in a very similar fashion: "And the peace of God, which surpasses all understanding, will guard your hearts and minds through Christ Jesus" (Phil. 4:7).

EVENING

Lord Jesus, thank You for giving me the ability through Your Spirit to trust You today through all my life's experiences and challenges. It is so comforting to know that You are my peace, joy, and hope through everything I face. I love You and thank You for being my best friend! In Jesus' name, Amen.

Week 23, Friday

Lord Jesus, thank You for being my God and my guide. Thank You for giving me the precious ability to read and comprehend Your Word as the Holy Spirit enables me to understand its depths and meaning. Please guide me into all truth today and prepare me for the things You have prepared for me. In Jesus' name, Amen.

"Jesus answered and said to him, 'If anyone loves Me, he will keep My word; and My Father will love him, and We will come to him and make Our home with him.'"
JOHN 14:23

Love is a word that is thrown around today so freely that it has lost its true meaning and identity. Until we know and experience the love of God, we will never have the ability to love others with a true biblical love. True love is always accompanied with a desire to please its object. I love my wife, therefore, I desire to please her in all that I do and say. If we treasure God's Word and obey it, then the Father and the Son will share their love with us and make their home in us. Can you imagine that? The Father and the Son will come and set up camp in our lives. Wow!

When the sinner trusts Christ, he is born again, and the Spirit immediately enters his body and bears witness that he is a child of God. But as we yield to the Father, love the Word, pray, and obey, there is a deeper relationship with the Father, Son, and Spirit. Salvation means we are going to heaven, but submission means that heaven comes to us!

The only way the world is going to find out about the love of the Lord Jesus is through us, and obedience is imperative. Your profession is not worth anything and neither is church membership. The issue is this: is our love for Him evidenced by our obedience?

EVENING

Lord Jesus, thank You for loving me and giving me the desire to please You and to obey Your Word. I realize that I could never know or experience Your love apart from a saving relationship with You. Please give me the ability to love others the way You love me. Help my life to always reflect the love of Jesus Christ. In Jesus' name, Amen.

Lord Jesus, today "I will lift up my eyes to the hills—from whence comes my help" (Ps. 121:1). May my life be a reflection of Your love and grace as I bump shoulders with all the people You will allow me to meet today. I acknowledge You as the sole purpose of my life and being. In Jesus' name, Amen.

"However, when He, the Spirit of truth, has come, He will guide you into
all truth; for He will not speak on His own authority, but whatever
He hears He will speak; and He will tell you things to come."

JOHN 16:13

One of the benefits of taking a tour is the blessing of a good guide. A guide takes all the stress out of our trip because he or she has already gone before us and has the knowledge that we do not have about the trip. As a preacher of the gospel of Jesus Christ, it is comforting to know that I do not have to preach on my own. As the Holy Spirit guides me, He also provides me the words that God Himself would speak if He were here in the flesh.

Our Lord was always careful to give His disciples the right amount of truth at the right time. The Holy Spirit is our teacher today, and He teaches us the truths we need to know exactly when we need them. It is impossible for the Spirit of truth to give us error.

The twenty-first century has afforded us a day of e-mail, text messaging, and Internet. However, the Bible remains truly unique and separate from all other forms of information. The Bible is the Word of God, inspired by the Spirit of God, and invested with the power and authority of God. It is infallible, inerrant, and sufficient for all our needs in life. Only the Holy Spirit knows what God knows, and He alone is the only One who is qualified to reveal divine truth to our lives.

EVENING

Lord, I take comfort in the fact that You have gone before me and intervened in situations that I will never even know about. I also take comfort in the fact that You will tell me what to say and when to say it as long as I fill my heart and mind with Your inspired Word. In Jesus' name, Amen.

TIM ANDERSON, ATHENS, AL

Father, make me strong in the Lord and in the power of Your might. Give me courage to face life's pressures. When I am tempted to give up and give in, help me to trust in You. In Jesus' name, Amen.

"Have I not commanded you? Be strong and of good courage; do not be afraid, nor be dismayed, for the LORD your God is with you wherever you go."

JOSHUA 1:9

Press *on in spite of your problems.* Moses, the great leader, deliverer, and interceder was dead, but *God was not!* Joshua had been a slave, a servant, a soldier, a spy, and now Moses' successor. God wants us to look to the future, learn from the past, and live in the present. Appreciate the past, but never abandon it or make an idol of it. Joshua needed encouragement and so do we. At every turn in life, in every problem, God is there.

Press on in light of His promises. It was time to enter the Promised Land. God has given it to us, but it will never be ours until we step forward. God asked the Israelites in today's verse, "Have I not commanded you?" The command was to cross over. One never stands still in the Christian life. You are either going forward or backward. God promises victory over the Enemy when we go forward in faith.

Press on in the might of His presence. Joshua did not assemble the leaders to ask for their opinion. Israel disobeyed forty years prior because of unbelief. Failure to obey God is fatal—an entire generation died. God raised up a new generation. We should never get set in our ways and become more of a hindrance than a help. Attitude is the issue, not age. Caleb and Joshua were the oldest in the camp! When we have God's presence, we have His power, peace, and provision available for every need. Man may mislead and forsake you, but God will never leave or forsake you.

What unclaimed territory do you need to claim? Are you facing a crisis? Leaders rise in times of crisis. Don't overreact. Don't panic. Don't look back. This is your opportunity. Seize the moment. Press on!

EVENING

Father, thank You for giving me Your Word of assurance. You are my strength and my shield; My heart trusts and rejoices in You. Amen.

Father, give me a clean heart and clean hands to worship You all throughout the day. Amen.

"God is Spirit, and those who worship Him must worship in spirit and truth."
JOHN 4:24

The emphasis is God's Spirit. Worship should never be business as usual. I am reminded of the old deacon who prayed, "Lord, please let something happen today that is not printed in the bulletin." You can predict what will happen in many churches before you arrive. Worship is an expression of who God is, but God isn't dull, boring, or dead! Why should worship ever be that way? Worship is "worth-ship." Our worship will never equal His worth, but we should strive for excellence.

How tragic when churches experience "worship" wars. Some churches have enthusiasm without truth. Others are straight as a gun barrel doctrinally and just as empty. What is "spirit" and "truth?" The word "spirit" is not capitalized. It refers to man's spirit. It indicates man's innermost being. We are emotional about the things that matter most. Spirit-led worship is more than outward rituals and formality. When it comes to worship, your heart must be in it.

The word "truth" points to the Bible. Make sure you are in a church that preaches and believes the Bible. God has told us in His Word what is acceptable worship. Our worship should not be based on personal preference or prejudice. The Word of God is our guide. Watered-down church where the Bible is not read may be entertaining, but it is not life changing. People are turned off to dead religion. They have seen what it did (or did not do) for their parents. They are looking for genuineness and authenticity.

There is no substitute for Spirit-anointed preaching, praying, praise, and worship. Where the Spirit is there is liberty and life. Where the Spirit is there are changed lives. Where the Spirit is there is lasting spiritual impact. Only the Holy Spirit can enable sinful man to be transformed and worship a holy God.

EVENING

Help me worship You with my whole heart. May worship always be a priority in my life, family, and church. Amen.

GRANT ETHRIDGE, HAMPTON, VA

Lord, I put on the whole armor of God. I take every thought captive to the obedience of Christ. I plead the blood, resist the devil, and claim the victory in Jesus' name. Amen.

"You are of God, little children, and have overcome them,
because He who is in you is greater than he who is in the world."
I JOHN 4:4

The Bible teaches us about God and Satan, heaven and hell, holy angels and fallen angels. Some say, "I don't believe in demons. I can't see them." You believe in the wind and a God you've never seen. The Christian life is not a playground. It is a battleground. The things that never bother you seldom happen. The things that bother you most happen all the time. That is not coincidence. We have an Enemy, but people are not our problem. Our real Enemy is Satan. He was the archangel who tried to overthrow God. One-third of the angels followed him, and they were cast out of heaven. The devil is not omnipresent. He works through fallen angels. The thief comes to steal, kill, and destroy. He wants to steal your understanding so you will not think correctly. He wants to kill your joy. Ultimately, he wants to destroy God's purpose for your life.

At least nine times in the Gospels, Jesus cast out demons. He never laid hands on a person. He rebuked the Enemy verbally. In the last days, demonic activity will increase. Satan knows his time is short. God has equipped His children to battle against the flesh, the world, and Satan. Our weapons are not carnal, but mighty through God to the pulling down of strongholds. Daily use your spiritual weapons: *the blood of Jesus,* we overcome through the blood of the Lamb; *the Cross of Jesus,* die to self daily; *the name of Jesus,* there is power in no other name; *the Word of God,* "it is written." Repent, rebuke, and rejoice everyday. It's amazing what praising can do! The devil cannot hang around where Jesus is exalted. Satan may be stronger than us, but he is no match for the One who lives inside us!

EVENING

Father, I ask for your hedge of protection. Have holy angels stationed to minister to me and drive the Enemy away. I repent of my sin and confess Jesus Christ is Lord. Amen.

Father, I praise You that I am under no condemnation since giving You my life. Help me to walk in the Spirit. Spirit of the living God, pray through me according to Your will. Amen.

"The Spirit Himself bears witness with our spirit that we are children of God."
ROMANS 8:16

Romans 8 is one of the greatest chapters in the Bible. It begins with "no condemnation" in verse 1 and ends with "no separation" in verses 38, 39. We are saved, sanctified, strengthened, sealed, and secured by the Spirit.

The only way to enter God's family is through the new birth. At salvation, we receive the gift of a Person. At a wedding, the minister says, "Who giveth this woman to be married to this man?" You cannot be a husband without the person of your wife, and one cannot be a Christian without the Person of the Holy Spirit.

Referring to the lost, Jesus said, "You are of your father the devil" (John 8:44). As Christians, we have a new Father. "Abba" is the Aramaic term equivalent to our word "daddy." This is the word Jesus used in Gethsemane. In Roman culture, witnesses were required for an adoption to be legal. The Holy Spirit confirms the validity of our adoption, and being adopted is a wonderful thing! You may hear about an unwanted pregnancy, but never an unwanted adoption.

Pray before any decision—the Holy Spirit will guide you. The Spirit forbade Paul to preach in Asia but opened the door to Macedonia (Acts 16:6). Don't get upset over closed doors! All things are working together for good because you love God and are called according to His purpose.

The Holy Spirit witnesses to us (Heb. 10:15), and the Holy Spirit also witnesses *in* us (1 John 5:10). In today's verse, we learn the Holy Spirit witnesses *with* us. Thus, the Holy Spirit gives us the fact, faith, and feeling of our salvation.

EVENING

Thank You, Father, for adopting me into Your family and giving me an inheritance in heaven that is incorruptible. Nothing I encounter shall be able to separate me from the love of God that is in Christ Jesus our Lord. I rest in the joy of Your salvation. Amen.

GRANT ETHRIDGE, HAMPTON, VA

Week 24, Friday

Father, Your Word says that "nothing good dwells" in our flesh (Rom. 7:18). So help me walk in the Spirit and not fulfill the lust of the flesh. Amen.

"If we live in the Spirit, let us also walk in the Spirit."
GALATIANS 5:25

My wife's parents once came for a visit the day after we bought a new vacuum cleaner, and they decided to help by vacuuming the house while we were at work. When we came home, they were sitting on the couch, red faced, sweating, and exhausted! "That new vacuum cleaner is so heavy that we can hardly push it! We had to rest after vacuuming each room." Tammy and I began to laugh! The problem was simple—they tried to vacuum the entire house in neutral. They never put it in drive. The vacuum is designed with "Tech Drive Power Assist," making vacuuming almost effortless! It only takes a featherlike touch to push the system! We all had a big laugh, but then the thought occurred to me, *That is exactly what it is like when we try to live the Christian life without the supernatural power of the Spirit.* The power was there all the time—they simply did not appropriate it.

Can you imagine what our home, work, church, and relationships would be like if we were filled with the Spirit? One moment we can be walking in the Spirit, and the next, walking in the flesh. How is this possible? We leak! Everyday we have to be filled with the Spirit afresh and anew.

Over the years, I have heard people say, "I can't help it preacher; I am just weak in the flesh." The fact is they are strong in the flesh and weak in the Spirit. Say no to your flesh. The only way to crucify our fleshly, carnal desires is to stop feeding them. Die to selfish ambitions, desires, and opinions.

Growing up as a child, you had to learn how to walk. As a child of God, we have to learn how to walk in the Spirit. If you are exhausted by trying to live the Christian life in your own strength, walk in the Spirit!

EVENING

Lord Jesus, help me to deny myself, take up my cross, and follow You. I must decrease, and You must increase. Amen.

MORNING

Father, order my steps today. Open doors that no man can shut. Close doors that no man can open. I wait on You, knowing it will be worth it! Amen.

"Your ears shall hear a word behind you, saying, 'This is the way, walk in it,' whenever you turn to the right hand or whenever you turn to the left."

ISAIAH 30:21

Over the years, when I did not know what to do, I have prayed, "Lord, You make the decision for me. Left to myself, I will make the wrong choice. You know what is best for me, my family, and the kingdom work." God has always honored that prayer.

The Lord blessed us with the privilege of serving Him in four churches. In each one, we watched God do "exceedingly abundantly above all" that we could ask or expect (Eph. 3:20). He grew His church and many souls were saved. At each church, we were committed to stay until God moved us or called us to heaven. After serving a wonderful church in Arkansas for almost twenty years, God began to stir our hearts that He wanted us to move to a church in Virginia. We had never stepped foot inside the church! My wife, Tammy, had been diagnosed with a brain tumor and was recovering from major surgery. There were many good excuses as to why we did not want to move. It was the only home our children had ever known. We were very happy and blessed.

Overwhelmed with emotion, we started to call the church in Virginia and tell them we had decided not to come. Before making that phone call, we asked God to speak to us through His Word. Our devotion that day was Jeremiah 1:7, "You shall go to all to whom I send you." We smiled at each other through the tears. God's Word had settled it. He does all things well. God has confirmed that decision over and over again in so many ways. We are glad we listened to His voice and obeyed.

Our heavenly Father makes no mistakes! Get alone with God. Listen to His still, small voice. He will show you what to do.

EVENING

Lord, I trust You with all of my heart. I lean not on my own understanding. In all my ways I acknowledge You. Please, direct my path. Amen.

GRANT ETHRIDGE, HAMPTON, VA

Week 25, Monday

Father, as I begin this new day, I give You praise and thanksgiving for a good night's sleep. Thank You, heavenly Father, for the opportunities You'll place in my path throughout the day. Help me to be sensitive to Your Spirit that I might use godly discernment as You direct my steps. Help me, O Lord, to be a godly influence in the lives of those I encounter this day. In the precious name of Jesus I pray. Amen.

"This is the word of the LORD to Zerubbabel:
'Not by might nor by power, but by My Spirit,' says the LORD of hosts."
ZECHARIAH 4:6

In God's vision to the prophet Zechariah, He delivered a word to Zerubbabel, the governor of Judah. God presented a lampstand in the tabernacle with extra features. This unique lampstand collected a continual supply of oil from the two trees, which kept the lamps burning. This golden lampstand symbolized God's purpose for the Jewish nation in becoming a light unto the Gentiles.

In the same way, God's Holy Spirit is in constant supply for His people today. Even in our weakness God is not hindered, nor is God aided by our strength! Too often in our lives and churches, we've become more dependent upon our affluent resources rather than the power of God through His Holy Spirit. The apostle Paul, the great evangelist, finally came to the realization that his Hebrew pedigree and intellectual knowledge was no comparison against the mighty power of God's Holy Spirit. He later penned these words in Philippians 4:13: "I can do all things through Christ who strengthens me." The next time you feel helpless and weak, be reminded that God's oil (Spirit) is available in abundant supply.

EVENING

Heavenly Father, I praise You for the blessings of this day. I thank You also for the people You've allowed me to minister to and influence. I pray You'll continue to empower me with Your Holy Spirit that I might be a vessel You can use for kingdom glory. Grant me a good night's rest that I might be refreshed and ready for the challenges of tomorrow. Bless my family and continue to protect them from the Evil One. Thank You, Father, for all You do for me. You're such an awesome God. I love You with all my heart! Amen.

MORNING

Father, thank You for getting me up early this morning to hear from You. Your Spirit has drawn me to my prayer room. Help me today to hear exactly what He has to say to me. O Lord, speak Your truths into my heart and grant me wisdom to respond to Your will and direction. Use me for Your glory and honor. Thank You, heavenly Father, for speaking to my heart. I love You and praise Your holy name. Amen.

"These things we also speak, not in words which man's wisdom teaches but which the Holy Spirit teaches, comparing spiritual things with spiritual."

1 CORINTHIANS 2:13

The canonicity of Scripture is a composite of God's Holy Word written to reveal His person and purpose to those who desire to know Him. But how are we in our finite minds able to grasp and understand a God who is infinite in wisdom and truth? The apostle Paul explains in today's verse that the Holy Spirit teaches us spiritual things according to His wisdom, not ours. Jesus promised that the Spirit would teach us (John 14:26) and also guide us into truth (16:13). Through the Bible we have been given the inspired Word of God (2 Tim. 3:16), which means "holy men of God spoke as they were moved by the Holy Spirit" (2 Pet. 1:21). Therefore, we as Christians have been taught the Word of God that in return we're able to teach others also.

My youngest grandson, Lincoln is one year old and is learning to talk. He utters words that I cannot fully understand. But his mother usually knows what he's trying to say and interprets his words to me. How does she know? Lincoln has her DNA deposited within him! His mother gave him birth and therefore knows his words. Likewise, the Holy Spirit gives discernment to God's Word, which speaks the words of life to those who desire to fully know Him. So if you truly desire to know God, then pray for the Holy Spirit to teach you His Word.

EVENING

Thank You, Father, for my Bible. Your precious Word is truly is "a lamp to my feet and a light to my path" (Ps. 119:105). My pathway and direction comes from walking with You and being taught by Your Holy Spirit. Amen.

Week 25, Wednesday

Father God, I come before You this morning to say thank You for a brand new day. I look forward to the opportunities of this day. I ask You to guide me by Your Spirit throughout the day. Help me, O Lord, to be salt and light before those I encounter that I might represent and reflect the life of the Lord Jesus Christ. I praise You and give You glory. In Jesus' name, Amen.

"That the righteous requirement of the law might be fulfilled in us who do not walk according to the flesh but according to the Spirit."
ROMANS 8:4

On September 22, 1862, President Abraham Lincoln issued the famous "Emancipation Proclamation," which abolished the law of slavery. The apostle Paul also experienced this same emancipated freedom, as he, too, had been set free from the law of religious legalism. The Mosaic Law was given by God to reveal and expose the sins of the Israelites, although the Law couldn't set the people free from their sin. The Law could not save; it could only condemn. But thanks be to God who sent His Son to save us and do what the Law could not do. Today's verse says that Jesus Christ fulfilled "the righteous requirement of the law" at Calvary's Cross! Therefore, the Law no longer has any jurisdiction over us because we are now dead to the Law (Rom. 7:4) The righteousness of the believer is not produced by "our good works" but stems from the indwelling of God's Holy Spirit. God's controlling Spirit enables the believer to "walk in the Spirit" and "not fulfill the lust of the flesh" (Gal. 5:16). When Christians truly come to the realization that we are no longer under the Law but under the new nature of God's grace, then we can rejoice with confidence as did the apostle Paul in Galatians 5:1: "Stand fast therefore in the liberty by which Christ has made us free, and do not be entangled again with a yoke of bondage."

EVENING

I thank You, O God, for the truths of Your Word. Your truth has made me free. I pray for our churches to preach and teach Your Word in truth and in spirit. I pray You would bless our nation and draw us closer to You through the power of Your Holy Spirit. Amen.

Lord, as I bow humbly in Your presence, speak to my heart this very moment. Lord, remind me of Your goodness and mercy. Fill me with Your Holy Spirit power. Open my eyes to the needs and hurts around me. Guide me by Your Spirit to those who are in desperate need of the Savior. Use me as Your vessel to make a difference. Grant this prayer, O Lord. Amen.

"The wind blows where it wishes, and you hear the sound of it, but cannot tell where it comes from and where it goes. So is everyone who is born of the Spirit."

JOHN 3:8

Jesus was the master teacher. He often used object lessons to teach spiritual truths to His disciples. The Jewish ruler Nicodemus was about to encounter His first in-class session with Jesus. Nicodemus came to seek Jesus at night. The wind was swirling with a stiff easterly breeze as the two rabbis conversed concerning the mystery of life's new birth.

Class was now in session. Jesus utilized the mystery and symbol of the wind to explain just how an individual is transformed from flesh to spirit. This would be an object lesson the Jewish ruler would never forget! Jesus clarified how the wind that blows is a typology of the Spirit of God. They are both are invisible, yet extremely powerful forces. Both are directed wherever God chooses. Although they are both invisible to the eye, the aftereffects of each are highly visible. The sound of the wind gives evidence that it's a supernatural force, as does God's Spirit the moment a new birth transpires. Just as God's power is present in the blowing wind, God breathes His Spirit upon His newborn children (John 20:21, 22).

EVENING

Thank You, Father, for breathing Your life into me and transforming my life through Your Word and Your Spirit. May that transformation be easily visible to all who witness my daily walk. In the precious name of Jesus I pray, Amen.

Week 25, Friday

As I awake this morning, O Lord, I give You praise for another day of life. Thank You, Father, that I can live for You because Your Son, Jesus, died for me! May my life be a living sacrifice for You, and may my actions glorify Your name. Amen.

"But you are not in the flesh but in the Spirit, if indeed the Spirit of God dwells in you. Now if anyone does not have the Spirit of Christ, he is not His."
ROMANS 8:9

Of all the saints, no one was more qualified to speak personally and directly concerning the dichotomy between the flesh and spirit than the apostle Paul. As a strict, religious "Hebrew of the Hebrews" (Phil. 3:5), Paul had been well trained in the ritualistic formality of the Law. It wasn't until his Damascus road experience that Paul soon realized that the presence of the indwelling "Spirit of Christ" (Rom. 8:9) was his only guarantee of life in Christ.

Paul would later write, "If anyone is in Christ, he is a new creation" because he no longer lived in the flesh but in the newness of God's Spirit (2 Cor. 5:17). Paul validated his new position in Christ in Galatians 2:20 when he wrote, "It is no longer I who live, but Christ lives in me." Paul had learned one of life's most valuable principles: before a believer can be in Christ, he must be filled with the Spirit and emptied of self!

EVENING

Father, I praise You for Your mighty hand of protection upon me and my family. Bless us as we faithfully serve You and Your glorious church. Grant us good rest through the night that we might rise to serve You another day. Thank You, Father, for Your peace and comfort and for the total assurance of knowing that if we don't rise here, we will surely arise there! Amen.

MORNING

Father, You are an awesome God! I give You praise and glory for the powerful moving of Your Holy Spirit within my heart. You have blessed my life beyond measure. You have endowed me with an abundance of joy and peace. My cup is running over! If only I could convey the depths of my soul with others so they, too, might know Your grace and mercy. I am of all men most blessed. I praise You in the morning as I look forward to the beauty of this day. Hallelujah!

"But God has revealed them to us through His Spirit.
For the Spirit searches all things, yes, the deep things of God."
1 CORINTHIANS 2:10

Many people are oftentimes frustrated with religion because they say they cannot comprehend God or understand His Word. They work frantically to perform good works and try to live the best they can. Some would even protest that the Bible isn't relevant and is very outdated. To them, God and the Bible are a mystery. The same was true in Corinth. In today's verse, Paul states that God only reveals the deepest "hidden truths" of God to those who are indwelt by His Spirit. Paul goes on to reveal the secret of this mystery in verse 11 by proclaiming, "No one knows the things of God except the Spirit of God."

Paul reveals this same truth to the Colossian church in Colossians 1:26: "The mystery which has been hidden from ages and from generations, but now has been revealed to His saints." One can only know God and God's Word though the power of being indwelt by His Holy Spirit. Even Jesus' disciples didn't fully know Him until the Holy Spirit anointed them. This is the reason why "the natural man does not receive the things of the Spirit of God, for they are foolishness to him; nor can he know them [the mysteries], because they are spiritually discerned" (1 Cor. 2:14).

EVENING

Thank You, heavenly Father, that You came to us in the Person of Jesus Christ in order to reveal Yourself to those who would believe in You by faith. I praise You for Your precious gift of salvation. Thank You for Your Holy Spirit that teaches us Your will and Your way. In the name of Jesus our Lord and King, Amen.

DUSTY MCLEMORE, ATHENS, AL

Father, this week is Your week. Speak truth and hope into my life. Give me ears to hear You speak. Grant me discipline to open Your Word in order to listen to Your voice. Whatever is before me, give me what I need at that moment. Even now, I listen to You. May You alone be praised. Amen.

"Is anyone among you suffering? Let him pray. Is anyone cheerful? Let him sing psalms. Is anyone among you sick? Let him call for the elders of the church, and let them pray over him, anointing him with oil in the name of the Lord."

JAMES 5:13, 14

Effective prayer occurs when you talk to God and listen to what God is saying to you. When a need arises today, talk to God about it. Upon the authority of God's Word, when you are sick, request your spiritual leaders to pray over you. Prayer should be your first choice, not your last. Something special happens when we pray. Even medical science recognizes that prayer can be an asset to and for the sick. People are in need all around us today. Whatever their need may be, our course of action must get beyond pity or sympathy and move to the highest level of all. What is that level? Calling upon the God of heaven, God Almighty, to step into their situation personally and miraculously.

You will have needs today. You may have needs right now. Personal pride will call you to try to work it all out yourself. Stubbornness will just try to wait it out, thinking things will improve. Consider God's way: talk to Him about it right now and then open His Word, letting Him speak promise into your day. When you do, the Holy Spirit will do what only He can do in your life. He will move upon you with peace and give you confidence that God is with you.

EVENING

In the name of Jesus tonight, I call upon You. Help me see people the way Jesus sees them and minister to them in the midst of their need by praying for them. As my own needs arise today, I commit to talk to You first about those needs. For Your glory alone, I choose calling upon You first, above all else. Amen.

Dear Lord, I bless You on this morning for being with me all the time. I thank You that whether I am on the mountaintop or in the valley, You are there. I pray this morning that I will live out my faith today. I pray my life will be known as a living testimony for You. May I be able to comprehend the privileges afforded to me by You. Amen.

"Pray without ceasing, in everything give thanks;
for this is the will of God in Christ Jesus for you."
1 THESSALONIANS 5:17, 18

You can go to God anytime, anywhere, about anything. The privilege given to you by Him is that fellowship with Him is yours all the time. Without interruption today, pray. Continually and repeatedly, choose prayer today. Be conscious of God's presence—you are in constant fellowship with Him. No, you don't have to walk around saying words out loud all day, hoping that you are fulfilling these verses. You fulfill the heartbeat of this passage when your focus and concentration is on the Lord—when you consistently, yes even persistently, talk to God. Do not give up in prayer. Pray it through!

Joining that joyful privilege of being in communion with God should be a thankful heart. A thankful heart to God turns His heart toward you even more. When you have done something for someone and they eventually look you in the eye and utter with sincerity the powerful words, "Thank you," you want to do even more for them. Praise the Lord, He is far more loving and reliable toward us, whether we thank Him or not. Yet He desires our praise and thanks.

My friend, God has given to you a winning combination. Praying about everything and being thankful for everything can send your spiritual life not just to the next level, but even beyond. Oh yes, you can go to God anytime, anywhere, about anything. And when accompanied with a thankful heart, now that is a winning combination.

EVENING

Oh Father, even in the night, may I know I can talk to You. In the midst of the darkness, may my heart be overflowing with gratitude to You. Thank You for the winning combination of prayer and thankfulness. Help me to live it out daily. In Jesus' name, Amen.

Week 26, Wednesday

Good morning, Lord. Speak to me today; Your servant is listening. My heart is open, and my ears are ready to hear You today. Give me the power to not only hear You but also obey You. In Jesus' name, Amen.

"Therefore I say to you, whatever things you ask when you pray,
believe that you receive them, and you will have them."
MARK 11:24

No bounds exist in prayer. God is able to do anything, anytime, anywhere. He is who He says He is, and He can do what He says He can do. There is no one like Him. There are no bounds on your requests to God. He will hear you about anything and will answer you with yes, no, or wait. Whatever the answer is, He does so by His will. While He is impressed with your dependence and faith to call upon Him, He always goes by His Word and always does what is best for you.

Trusting in the Lord while you pray is essential to effective praying. Your trust means that you cast your cares upon Him, leaving all in His hands and trusting that He will do what is best for you. While we live life on the ground in the midst of the challenges, He sees all from His place beside the Father. He sees tomorrow, while we live today. He sees next year, while we live this month. He sees eternity, while we live on this earth. This is why we must trust Him at all times, receiving His answers to our prayers with a confident heart.

The longer I live, the more I know I can trust Him. Thank God He has not given me everything I have requested through the years; otherwise, I would be in one bad deal after another. While years ago I struggled when I did not get my way, today I trust Him through it all. No one knows what is best for me more than Jesus. The same is true for you.

EVENING

I place all my questions, burdens, and worries in Your hands tonight, O God. You alone hold the future in Your hands. Therefore, I trust You. I will rest not only physically, but also spiritually, knowing You will do what is best for me. In Jesus' name, Amen.

MORNING

Dear Lord, on this day, I will practice what God's Word says to me. I will follow Your will and Your Word. Give me the power to do that as I pour out my heart to You. In Jesus' name, Amen.

"Then you will call upon Me and go and pray to Me, and I will listen to you."
JEREMIAH 29:12

M oments of greatness are experienced in prayer and from prayer. The great word given in our passage today follows a promise that God will give you a future and a hope. Knowing that God will do what is best for you, granting to you *His* future and hope for you, He provides for you the privilege to call upon Him. Yes, prayer becomes the channel and experience where you can cry unto God with your all, entering into His presence in Jesus' name, and talk to Him. Just think, you who are limited enter into the presence of the unlimited, and the result is that He provides you an unlimited life. Why? Well, it is simple. If God is for you, who can be against you (Rom. 8:31)?

The privilege of prayer is not only you talking to God but also God listening to you. Listening to your burdens, visions, and dreams. Listening to even your whining and complaining. You serve a God who is so incredible, He listens to you at all times. Today, practice calling upon the Lord. With great intensity and focus, call upon the Lord with your all. Share with Him your number one burden. Leave it there. Share with Him your number one need. Leave it there. Share with Him your number one vision. Leave it there. Let this day be the day when you take your burdens to the Lord and leave them there.

While your spouse, your friend, your mentor, or even your pastor may not always listen to you, God always does. Pour your heart out to God today. He will listen to you.

EVENING

O precious Lord, Your Word instructs me to call upon You and You will listen to me. As I stand on that promise tonight, I share with You my dreams, visions, hopes, mistakes, concerns, burdens, and pains. I present them to You in Jesus' name. I leave them with You. Do with them and do with me whatever pleases You the most. Amen.

RONNIE FLOYD, SPRINGDALE, AR

This is Your day, O Lord; let me live it for You. Teach me how I can be a greater warrior in prayer. Change my attitude and heart to be all You want me to be. By Jesus' power and in His name I pray, Amen.

"Confess your trespasses to one another, and pray for one another, that you may be healed. The effective, fervent prayer of a righteous man avails much."

JAMES 5:16

Passivity does not lead to a successful prayer life. Passivity never takes the time to even write down various requests we want to take to God. Passivity does not consider our sins against God and others; in fact, it just acts like they do not exist. Passivity minimizes what God can do. Passivity never leads to a passionate prayer life. What God wants from you in your prayer life is for you to be effective and passionate. So effective that you take it seriously. So passionate that you put your heart and energy into it when you talk to Him.

How can we not be energized? We can share our mistakes with one another. We can pray for one another. We can be healed. We can have an effective prayer life. We can be passionate about all we are talking to God about. All of this is possible because, through Jesus, we are in right standing with God, and He gives us the privilege of going to Him anywhere, anytime, about anything. What happens? Results! When we get into our prayer life, take it seriously, deal with our stuff, and learn to pray for one another, our God gets involved with us. He answers us. He gives results. This is the heartbeat of James 5:16.

Could it be your prayer life is stale because you are more passive than passionate? Could it be that your heart is insensitive because of an ineffective prayer life? Well friend, if either of these is true, change it today. Change it now. Get fired up and passionate today when you talk to God. You are talking to the King of kings, who is able to do whatever He wills. Perhaps if our attitude and heart was more "into our prayer life," the results might be different.

EVENING

O Jesus, resurrect my heart toward You in every way. Build me into being a mighty prayer warrior. Amen.

Thanks, Lord, for the weekend. Rest and refresh me in these hours. Speak to me. Build in me godliness and holiness. Raise me up to be a warrior in prayer. Amen.

*"Be kindly affectionate to one another with brotherly love,
in honor giving preference to one another; . . . rejoicing in hope,
patient in tribulation, continuing steadfastly in prayer."*
ROMANS 12:10, 12

What kind of prayer ministry does your church have? How do you practice prayer in your venues of worship on a weekly basis? How serious is your church about prayer? The apostle Paul and the New Testament church were very committed to prayer. In our passage today, Paul talks to the church about how to treat one another and the need to continue in prayer at all times. You will never read the New Testament without realizing the high commitment the church had to prayer. Daily, I ask God to raise up a mighty prayer movement in our church. While venues of worship can incorporate prayer, other venues committed to nothing but prayer need to be raised up. We have seen this on both of our campuses through Tuesday and Thursday night prayer gatherings. These gatherings are committed to one thing—praying for our church.

Just think what would happen in your church if gatherings would begin to occur weekly where five, ten, or one hundred people just committed two hours every week to enter into our centers for worship to pray. It does not have to be an organized gathering as we are so used to. Give the Holy Spirit the opportunity to create something. There is an army of your people that God will raise up. You know, He may want you to be a part of it. While individually we need to continue in prayer, let me remind you, so does the church. Pray for your church today.

EVENING

Dear Father, raise up my church with a revival of prayer. I pray for our church to experience a mighty touch of God this weekend. Anoint our pastor with God's power as he proclaims God's Word. Amen.

Lord, as I begin my day, I thank You that nothing will cross my path that is not Father-filtered. I praise You that You stand ready to guide, protect, and answer me when I call upon You. Thank You for the strength that is mine for the asking. As we walk together today, may I be mindful of Your grace that makes all of this possible. In the wonderful name of Jesus I pray, Amen.

"In the day when I cried out, You answered me,
and made me bold with strength in my soul."

PSALM 138:3

King David wrote this psalm while his enemies surrounded him. Hezekiah added it to the hymnbook in the midst of his troubles, surrounded by his enemies, when in all likelihood he was forced to evacuate Jerusalem.

Let me share with you a poem on problems. Ready? It's short and to the point: "Problems . . . Adam had 'em." And so do you and I. I've got some bad news and good news. The bad news is that man born of woman has trouble. The good news is that we have an *ever-present, promising,* and *powerful* God who stands ready to do for us what He did for the apostle Paul's "thorn in the flesh" (2 Cor. 12:7). God answered no but then gave him a promise that His grace would be sufficient.

In today's verse, David said, "In the day when I cried out." That tells us God's a *present God.* "You answered me" tells us He's a *promising God.* "And made me bold with strength in my soul" tells us He's a *powerful God.*

God answers our prayers the same way He answered David's prayer. He didn't remove his problem, though He did in time. Instead He strengthened David in his soul, which makes us even stronger believers. Have you noticed that often our Sovereign God answers our prayer by giving us what we need in order to live with the problem?

EVENING

Father, today we've walked together, and Your grace has been sufficient. You were very present, kept Your promise, and gave me strength in my soul. You really are powerful! Today I cried out. Today You answered me. Goodnight, present, promising, powerful God. How I worship You. Amen.

MORNING

Lord Jesus, I confess that sometimes in the midst of my pain, I cry out and it seems heaven is silent. Today I ask for Your wisdom to discern, Your patience to be still, and Your faith to believe that Your delays are not always Your denials. I submit my life and all that my day holds for Your glory and my good. I ask this in the powerful, matchless name of our coming King, Jesus Christ. Amen.

"O Lord, God of my salvation, I have cried out day and night before You.
Let my prayer come before You; incline Your ear to my cry."
PSALM 88:1, 2

The psalmist confesses he's been crying out day and night, and it seems God's ear is closed and darkness is hiding His face. Ever been there? Sure you have. There today? Maybe not, but if you've walked with God any length of time, you will be. Heaven is as brass, and you find yourself literally crying out both day and night. Listen, darkness can hide you, but it cannot divide you. It may hurt you, but it cannot harm you.

God's plan is bigger, broader, and better. Let's consider three truths about darkness as you start your day. First, *God's choicest servants* go through darkness. Moses, Elijah, David, and Jeremiah experienced it. Even Jesus on the Cross in darkness said, "My God, My God, why?" (Matt. 27:46). Those of greatest devotion may know the deepest darkness. Secondly, *God's clearest teachings* are spoken in darkness. Have you learned that faith born in the light often grows best in darkness? When do we see God's beautiful stars? When do we rest? Thirdly, remember *God's closest fellowship* happens in darkness. Jesus took your darkness, so as children of light you and I will never sit in darkness. You may not see Him or feel Him today, but trust me, He's as close as the mention of His name. He promises never to "leave you nor forsake you."

EVENING

Father God, while I didn't see You today, I knew You were there and Your ear was inclined to mine. As I rest tonight, thank You that You give Your beloved sleep. The dawn will come, and the sun will rise. The Lord God of Israel never slumbers nor sleeps. No sense both of us staying awake. Goodnight, Lord—I rest in You. Amen.

KEN WHITTEN, LUTZ, FL

Week 27, Wednesday

MORNING

O Lord, the psalmist tells me You know everything about me (Ps. 139:1–4). As I begin my day, I am so grateful You know my needs, hopes, and desires; and You know all of them even before I ask. Today I submit to Your lordship and care. Thank You for Your loving hands and heart. You are good—all the time. Amen.

"And whatever things you ask in prayer, believing, you will receive."
MATTHEW 21:22

I have a confession to make about prayer. Prayer is a mystery! In my family, I'm the emotional one. My wife Ginny is the logical one. But my guess is that even to the logical one in your family, some days prayer doesn't make sense. Let's see if I understand this mystery of prayer: First, God knows what I need before I ask. He already knows if and when He desires to meet those needs. But He still desires I come to Him and ask.

Here's the beauty of prayer: prayer isn't always logical, but it is spiritual. When our Lord told us "whatever things you ask in prayer, believing, you will receive" in today's verse, He was not telling us He is a heavenly bellhop and whatever our little hearts desire, if we could just muster up enough belief, He's obligated to grant it.

He is reminding us that prayer is three things: Prayer is *relational.* We pray in the Spirit, to the Father, and through the Lord Jesus Christ. Prayer is also *personal.* Because He knows my needs in advance, He desires I personally come to Him for the meeting of those needs. Lastly, prayer is *circular.* Here's the key that unlocks the logic of prayer: the prayer that gets to heaven starts in heaven! It is God who knows. It is God who puts the desire in my heart. And it is God who answers the requests that are in His will. Whether you're dealing with moving mountains or moving the hearts of men, you can always pray.

EVENING

God, You are my Father, who knows the very hairs upon my head. Thank You that the prayer that gets to heaven starts in heaven. I will sleep well tonight knowing You always love to make intercession for Your children. It is in Your Spirit, for Your glory, and through Your name I pray. Amen.

ONE YEAR DEVOTIONAL PRAYER BOOK

MORNING

Father, I greet You this morning with praise in my heart for the privilege of prayer. As we walk together today, may I be mindful that at any time, anywhere, and for anyone, I can come to You in prayer. Please don't let me miss the opportunity and the obedience of this blessing. Amen.

"Therefore I exhort first of all that supplications, prayers, intercessions, and giving of thanks be made for all men."

1 TIMOTHY 2:1

The apostle Paul, in his exhortation to young Timothy, gave him the *priority* and the *parameters* of prayer. Paul wants us to know that prayer is our first choice, not our last chance. It is a "first of all" kind of habit. When I depend on programs, I get what programming can do. When I depend on people, I get what people can do. But when I depend upon prayer, I get what God Almighty can do. We have all met people who, instead of being humbly grateful, were grumbly hateful. Thanksgiving is not something we do at the end of our request. It is an attitude of our life that's reflected in our conversation and conduct with the Lord at all times.

Today's verse says we need to draw near to God with a heart of thanksgiving for "all men." My prayers are not only a priority but also a strategy. "All men" is a great reminder that there is no one outside the influence of prayer. My family, my friends, my enemies—they all become not only the concentration of my heart but also the circumference of my prayer. Sometimes people will say to me, "Pastor, I prayed for you today." Wow! What a privilege to make anyone's prayer list. Besides, I need the prayer, and they need the practice. So, who's on your list today?

EVENING

Lord God in heaven, the thought that people who love me prayed me for today is so overwhelming. You even mentioned my name to the throne as well. Today I felt Your prayers and protection. Help me to make prayer not only a priority in my life but an everyday reality as well. Amen.

O Lord, thank You for equipping me with the whole armor of God. I put on the helmet of salvation, the breastplate of righteousness, the belt of truth, the gospel shoes of peace, the shield of faith, and the sword of the Spirit—and now I am dressed and ready for battle. It is in Your victorious name I pray. Amen.

"Praying always with all prayer and supplication in the Spirit, being watchful to this end with all perseverance and supplication for all the saints."
EPHESIANS 6:18

When Paul wrote, "We do not wrestle against flesh and blood" (Eph. 6:12), he was describing the battle we face against Satan. Paul was availing his readers to the supernatural warfare they were engaged in. We are at war, and we have an Enemy. It is not our boss at work, our spouse at home, or a friend at church. It is the sinister minister of fear and destruction himself, the devil. And prayer is our strategy and priority for victory.

Let's consider the six disciplines of prayer: *The Persistence of our Prayer.* Paul uses the word "all" four times in today's verse. We must constantly be in prayer because we are constantly in danger. *The Possibilities of Prayer.* Paul says "all prayer." We pray on all occasions, in all places, at all times, and for all things. I call God in the morning, and I don't hang up until evening (1 Thess. 5:17). *The Power of Prayer.* Prayer's power is "in the Spirit." *The Precision of Prayer.* Be vigilant, diligent, and "watchful" in prayer. *The Perseverance of Prayer.* We hold on and hold out "with all perseverance." *The Purpose of Prayer.* "... for all saints." Always is in the plural. Jesus taught us to pray, not My Father, but Our Father.

Aren't you grateful when you make someone's prayer list? Who's on yours? Whoever it is, don't forget we are already winners!

EVENING

Lord God of victory, not only have I been dressed for my battle, but I've taken my stand in it. I am a winner! There is no armor for my backside. It is because I will not retreat. I will lay down tonight in victory, and when I awake, victory will still be mine. Because You defeated the Enemy, I stand in prayer to do the same. It is a good fight and now I know why. . . it is because I win. In Jesus' name, Amen.

MORNING

Lord, all this week I have been learning and meditating on the beauty and the benefits of prayer. I know some days I don't say it like I mean it, or even like my heart wants to say it, but this morning I do want to say it: "Lord, I love You just because." Amen.

"I love the LORD, because He has heard my voice and my supplications. Because He has inclined His ear to me, therefore I will call upon Him as long as I live."
PSALM 116:1, 2

The opening statement of this psalm is a good way to begin a song, a day, a marriage, or even a new life. When we make a bold confession of our love for the Lord, it declares to others and our own heart that our spiritual walk comes from a place of deep emotion.

"I love the Lord because . . ." For Hezekiah, the psalmist, it was because God had heard his voice. God heard your voice this week, and today He still has inclined His ear to your tears, your thoughts, and even to your trials. I love the Lord because . . . He has saved me, given me a beautiful family, placed me in a wonderful ministry, given me a host of friends, a wonderful church family, health, His Word, and His Spirit. And when I die, I will awake in my eternal home where there's a reunion no one this side of heaven has ever witnessed!

This whole love thing didn't even begin with me—it began with Him. John said, "We love Him because He first loved us" (1 John 4:19). He loved me—why? It is not what I am, but who He is that makes Him love me. We love Him because of His faithfulness and His forgiveness. Go ahead, you fill in the blank: I love Him because _____. No wonder Hezekiah said he would call upon Him as long as he lived. Me too, Hez, me too!

EVENING

Father, You are the love of my life. Help me to be bolder in expressing it, living it, and sharing it with others. May my love deepen for You. And Lord, may I "comprehend with all the saints what is the width and length and depth and height" of Your love for me (Eph. 3:18). In Jesus' wonderful, exalted name, Amen.

Father, today I will be confronted by the Enemy of my soul. He will attempt to make me afraid, rendering me ineffective in Your service. Help me to remember You are watching over me, keeping me by Your grace. Remind me that Your eyes are upon me. Cause me to reflect on the truth that You are enough for every situation and that You are bigger than any opposition I may encounter. Thank You for being my heavenly Father. Amen.

"For the eyes of the LORD are on the righteous, and his ears are open to their prayers; but the face of the LORD is against those who do evil."

1 PETER 3:12

Fear is one of the most effective weapons Satan uses against Christians. He is a beast who loves to bully and intimidate us. We cannot stop the devil from his onslaughts, but we can experience victory over them. Peter reminds us of three truths to remember when Satan tries to make us afraid. First, the Lord is always watching the righteous. As believers, the righteousness of Christ has been imputed to us. We stand before God covered in the righteousness of Jesus! As a loving Father, God is always watching us. He sees us and knows our situation. Even when we feel alone, we can be sure He sees us in love. Second, the Lord is always ready to hear our prayers. It does not bother Him when we pray. His ears are always open to us. He invites us to pray and delights in hearing and answering our prayers. Third, the Lord is against those who do evil. Our enemies are His enemies. They can do no more to us than He allows. They are mere tools in His hands to mold us into the image of His Son. Remember, "Fear not!"

EVENING

Father, thank You for being with me today. Your love strengthened me, and Your grace sustained me through every situation. Your presence encouraged me to live above the circumstances. Your provision adequately met all my needs. Your loving eyes watched over me as I took each step, and Your open ears heard me every time I breathed a prayer. Because of You no defeats were experienced and all day long I have known victory in Jesus. I love You and thank You for seeing me through the day. Amen.

MORNING

Father, thank You for another day in which to serve You. Today I will be faced with many opportunities and will have to make decisions that affect me and those around me. Give me the wisdom to seek Your will in evaluating those opportunities. I ask that You order my steps so that my walk will have a positive influence for Christ on those I meet. I ask that You guard my lips so that my words may minister grace to others. Show me Your will and enable me to live in it today. Amen.

"Now this is the confidence that we have in Him,
that if we ask anything according to His will, He hears us."
I JOHN 5:14

Many Christians have been deceived into believing that God is a heavenly jack-in-the-box who pops up at the turn of the crank ready to grant the slightest whim of the flesh that may be on their mind at the moment. However, this is not true. God hears and answers prayers that are according to His will. Fleshly desires and selfish wishes are not solid foundations for real prayer. Real prayer is praying according to the will of God. How can a believer know the will of God? First, realize that God wants to reveal His will to you. Second, understand that His will is usually revealed to His children as they study His Word. Third, the Holy Spirit within you will guide you in discerning the will of the Father. When in doubt, just ask the Holy Spirit for direction. When you know the will of God you can approach His throne in confidence. Confidence means freedom or boldness. When you know the will of God in a matter, you can freely and boldly come into His presence and be assured that He will hear you and answer you.

EVENING

Father, as this day comes to an end I want to praise You for giving me knowledge. Thank You that I did not have to slip through the shadows today—I walked in Your light. Through Your Word and by Your Spirit I was able to make good choices. When I was unsure, You provided direction. What a wonderful heavenly Father You are. I love You and appreciate Your love. My desire is to walk in Your will as long as You give me breath. Amen.

BOB PITMAN, MUSCLE SHOALS, AL

Morning

Father, thank You for giving me a sound mind and for opportunities in which to serve You. You know all things. Therefore, I trust You to see me through this day. For every situation that arises I ask You to control my thoughts and restrain my flesh. This is a day You have given me, and I desire to be a good representative of You. Give me Your grace as I live this day for Your glory. Amen.

"And He said to me, 'My grace is sufficient for you, for My strength is made perfect in weakness.' Therefore most gladly I will rather boast in my infirmities, that the power of Christ may rest upon me."
2 CORINTHIANS 12:9

God answers our prayers, but sometimes He answers them in ways we least expect. Paul was troubled by a thorn in the flesh (2 Cor. 12:7), and whatever it may have been, it caused him to ask the Lord to remove it. He asked the Lord three times to take it. God answered Paul's prayer, but not in the way Paul anticipated. God did not remove the thorn, but He promised Paul that His grace would be sufficient to see him through the difficulty caused by the thorn. If we can trust God enough to pray to Him, then we should also trust Him enough to answer us as He sees fit. There are two things to remember about God's answers to our prayers. First, He answers them to bring glory to Himself. Second, He answers them to produce the best benefit for His children. God answered Paul in a different way than Paul expected, but He also answered in a greater way than Paul expected. Sufficient grace is better than thorn removal. We might forget a removed thorn, but we never forget sufficient grace or the One who supplies it. God's grace is amazing. Ask God for it!

EVENING

Father, thank You for grace. There were times today that I would have messed up without it. My flesh and my human ingenuity wanted to intrude in situations that desperately needed Your touch. You were so faithful to provide sufficient grace. Thank You for allowing Your amazing grace to be in charge of my life today. I praise You for Your Son, Jesus Christ, through whom Your grace is bestowed. I love You and praise You for answering my prayers. Amen.

MORNING

Father, You show me Your love abundantly. One of the greatest ways is allowing me to come into Your presence unendingly. What a joy. I do not take that for granted. Thank You for letting me be a part of Your family. Thank You for so loving me that You would give Your only Son to die for me. Thank You for placing Your Holy Spirit within my heart. Because I love You today there will be some who oppose me. Give me the wisdom to watch and pray all day long. Amen.

> *"Now it came to pass in those days that He went out to the mountain to pray, and continued all night in prayer to God."*
> LUKE 6:12

Jesus was a man of prayer. He sometimes prayed in the presence of large groups, sometimes in the presence of His disciples, and sometimes He prayed alone. On this particular occasion, Jesus was facing sore opposition from those who hated Him. They were looking for any excuse to inflict harm or death upon Him.

It was "in those days" of extreme opposition that He retreated "to the mountain to pray." If Jesus needed to pray, how much more we need to pray! Do you have a place of prayer? Yes, you can meet God anywhere, but every child of God needs a specific place in which to spend time with God in prayer every day. It can be a bedroom, a breakfast nook, or a prayer closet. A prayer altar is not a piece of furniture, but it is a specific place.

Jesus was also persistent in prayer. He "continued all night in prayer." One of my favorite old hymns speaks of a "sweet hour of prayer." How long has it been since you spent an hour talking with God? It is not necessary for you to forfeit any peace or to bear needless pain. Take everything to God in prayer.

EVENING

Father, thank You for every blessing You have bestowed on me today. Thank You for standing beside my family and watching over them. Thank You for being patient with me today and for giving me second chances. Thank You for the blood-sprinkled path that led me to Your throne throughout the day. Thank You for never being too busy for me. You have been a wonderful Father to me today. Oh, how I love You! Amen.

Father, thank You for my health. Help me today to show my gratitude. May I be sensitive to those around me who do not enjoy good health. Help me to be a blessing to those who are physically handicapped and to those who are sick. Let someone cross my path today who needs a word of encouragement so I can share this prayer. I make this prayer in faith, believing that what I have asked will come about. Amen.

"And the prayer of faith will save the sick, and the Lord will raise him up."
JAMES 5:15A

M any pastors and theologians have wrestled with this text. No Christian would deny that God can heal the sick. However, it is wrong to conclude that perfect health is always a prayer away. There have been some believers who were healed of sickness after church leaders anointed them with oil and prayed. There have also been believers who were just as committed to Christ as those who were healed who died shortly after the leaders did the same. Outstanding Christian men and women die every year because of illness. It is the will of God for saints to go to heaven, and disease is often the vehicle He uses to transport us there. All physical healing that takes place on earth is temporary. Only in heaven will there be no more sickness. Nevertheless, God has extended to us an invitation to pray when we are sick.

The most important thing to remember is to pray a "prayer of faith." That means prayer is more than words. Real prayer comes from a heart that genuinely believes God. Jesus taught us to pray *believing*. When you ask, be sure to ask in faith. Prayer is never just religious verbiage; it is the verbal communion that stems from a relationship with God.

EVENING

Father, thank You for using me today to bless others. As I prepare for a night of sleep, bless those whose bodies are ravaged by pain to whom sleep will not come easily. Heal them by Your grace and power. Touch them according to Your tender mercies and make them well. Thank You for doctors, nurses, and other professionals. May I see them as Your servants that You use to care for us. Today You have walked by my side and kept me by Your power. Lord, I thank You. Amen.

Father, thank You that I can come into Your presence anytime. There is no problem that will come my way today that will be too big or too small for You. Thank You for allowing me the privilege of casting every care on You. Would You please fill me with Your Holy Spirit? May Your Son be seen by my words and deeds. May my disposition reflect the presence of Jesus in my heart. Thank You for this day. Amen.

"Be anxious for nothing, but in everything by prayer and supplication, with thanksgiving, let your requests be made known to God."
PHILIPPIANS 4:6

People who do not pray are usually great worriers. Without God there is certainly much to worry about. However, with God things take on a different slant. We are not the victims of fickle fate; we are the children of God. We have been adopted into His family. We are never out of His presence or His care. We do not have to live in fear. We do not have to fear circumstances. God encourages us to bring our circumstances before Him. He tells us to bring our "requests" to Him.

Requests are not general, but specific. Dr. Robert G. Lee, famed prince of preachers, used to talk of the uselessness of "Polly-want-a-cracker" praying. That kind of praying goes something like this: "God bless everybody, help everybody, and be with all the missionaries around the world." Be specific as you bring your requests to God. Also, be thankful as you pray. Be thankful that God has invited you into His presence. Be thankful that the blood of Jesus has provided you a way of access. Be thankful that God hears and answers your prayers. As the children's chorus says, "Why worry when you can pray?"

EVENING

Father, thank You for listening to me. Even those situations that may have seemed trivial to others were important to You. Thank You for never making me feel unwelcome. Thank You for being God of the little things as well as the big things. Thank You for allowing me to be in Your family. As I look forward to this Lord's Day, please prepare my heart to hear from You. There will be those who sit around me with needs of which I am unaware. Bless my brothers and sisters in Christ from Your Word. I love You. Amen.

BOB PITMAN, MUSCLE SHOALS, AL

Lord, help me to walk in a balance of grace and truth today. Strengthen my health so I may serve You. Give me this day my daily needs and prosper my finances so that I may serve You with the first fruits of all You have given me. Amen.

"Beloved, I pray that you may prosper in all things and be in health,
just as your soul prospers."

3 JOHN 2

In the Western world some are preaching an out-of-balance "health and wealth" theology. They say if you have faith, you will have the "blessings of God" visibly on your life. Well, there is one major problem—God has not seen fit to remove us from suffering, pain, and want, regardless of the amount of faith we exercise.

Does God care about your financial well-being? The answer is obviously yes. Jesus talked openly and practically about trusting God for physical needs (Matt. 6–7). Does God care about our health and physical condition? He does care and offers wisdom for wise choices in life. In this one verse, John links our physical and financial blessings to the prosperity of our souls.

Is your soul prospering? Are you growing in the knowledge of the Lord? Can you detect spiritual progress from this time last year? So often, if our bank account and our health prosper, we tend to the extreme of ignoring our souls. John says that our outward blessing is an outgrowth of our spiritual well-being. How does your soul prosper? Like solid financial and medical advice, let me suggest some disciplines that are necessary.

1. Daily, let God speak into your life by reading His Word.
2. Daily, spend time in close communion with the Lord.
3. Daily, take time to boldly ask for God to prosper your soul and use your blessings to fulfill His glorious purpose.

When your soul prospers, you will look at your health and wealth as gifts of God, undeserved but much appreciated and dedicated to His glory.

EVENING

Thank You for Your provision for this day. I rest trusting that Your provision for the next day is already in Your hand. You are good and awesome and worthy of my praise. Amen.

MORNING

In this certain place I meet You this morning with a grateful heart that You are faithful to meet me and hear my prayers. I want to be in close contact with You. I adore You and worship You, my God. Amen.

"Now it came to pass, as He was praying in a certain place, when He ceased, that one of His disciples said to Him, 'Lord, teach us to pray, as John also taught his disciples.'"
LUKE 11:1

Jesus had a certain place He went to pray. His disciples knew the place, but more importantly, they knew prayer was the priority of Jesus' life. Jesus modeled a life of consistent prayer. His disciples had to see the results of prayer in One who bore unbearable burdens, yet left that certain place uplifted, joyful, and peaceful.

Why did Jesus—God's one and only Son—pray? He prayed for communion with the Father in order to stay in close contact for direction and instructions. There was a childlike quality of boldness in Jesus' prayers. There was also a deep desire to please the Father (John 17:1). All of this and more lifts the burdens and floods the praying soul with peace and joy that truly transcends human comprehension (Phil. 4:7).

Our prayers need more than memorized words; they need hunger, desire, and intimacy. In order to pray like Jesus we must find a certain place—a place of desire to be with God no matter what and a place of praise. Praise puts our hearts in the proper frame. Then we make our requests plainly to God. But don't stop there. Go further by asking God to search your motives and help you understand why you ask what you ask. Be willing for the Lord to reveal sin in its smallest form, and then confess it. Above all, be honest with God. Real prayer is not trying to change the heart of God—it is letting God change your heart.

Jesus remains in a certain place of prayer for you, interceding on your behalf. Join Him now.

EVENING

As I prepare to rest from this day's events I ask You to search out my heart and help me to know my own thoughts. Help me to learn from this day that I may serve You better tomorrow. Change what needs to be changed in me. Amen.

Lord, I come to You at times with confused emotions. I trust that You are too good to ever be wrong. I ask for Your grace in this moment to endure during the hard things of this life. Amen.

"Trust in the LORD with all your heart, and lean not on your own understanding; in all your ways acknowledge Him, and He shall direct your paths."

PROVERBS 3:5, 6

Sometimes life is so hard that you can reasonably doubt the goodness of God. When my wife of twenty-five years died, I could not see anything good in life. The next morning I arose, still in shock and fighting my new reality as I went to my study, sat down, and began to meet with my God. I opened my Bible and cried out to God. In the passage I read that morning, God's Word revealed that He is good. It would take time for my damaged emotions, wounded heart, and aching soul to catch up with this truth.

The Hebrew word for "trust" used in this passage is *batach,* which means to lie down and stretch out. To trust God is to rest in God's powerful, loving provision of grace for our lives. What are you facing today? It may be that your greatest act of faith in this moment is to present yourself to the Lord in prayer and then rest in His goodness, especially with those things you cannot understand.

The next verse says that in all our ways we are to acknowledge Him. The word "acknowledge" means to know His nature and character, which helps you to see every trial, every difficulty, and every unfulfilled dream as an opportunity to discover Christ's rightful lordship over your life. Will you live this day aware of His presence in your life and trust in His love and care? As we do we will know His goodness, and He promises in this verse to direct our paths. This kind of direction speaks of a clearing away of obstacles. God promises that as you rest in His goodness, He will make a way where there seems to be no way.

EVENING

Lord, thank You for Your faithfulness throughout this day. I praise Your goodness and mercy toward me. In all my ways, even as I lay down to rest I am trusting in You. Amen.

MORNING

Thank You for going to the Garden on my behalf. Your struggle had eternal consequences for me. Thank You for surrendering to the Father's will. Help me to surrender to Your will today. Amen.

"He went a little farther and fell on His face, and prayed, saying, 'O My Father, if it is possible, let this cup pass from Me; nevertheless, not as I will, but as You will.'"
MATTHEW 26:39

What would cause Jesus, the bravest Man who ever lived, to shrink back in dread? In the Garden Jesus looked into the cup and saw something so horrific that He prayed, "If it is possible, let this cup pass." What was in the cup? Physical death? Yes. Evil? No doubt. Betrayal? Probably. The distilled combination of all of this, plus the separation from His Father, undoubtedly made up the dregs of this drink. The pollution of all my sin and your sin was in that cup (2 Cor. 5:21). This was far more horrific to Him who never knew sin than for us who are all too comfortable with it.

I cannot help but be moved for my Lord at this moment in the Garden—forsaken by disciples like me and bearing the weight of the world most literally upon His shoulders. Yet I am stunned by His submissive prayer. The word He spoke was "nevertheless." "Nevertheless" echoes throughout the pages of Scripture whenever God's children face life-threatening challenges. Yet all the saints of all the ages must have marveled on this dark night of Jesus' soul. God incarnate bowed, submitting to the Father's will in order to save us by exchanging the bitter contents of the cup we deserve for a sweet flowing cup of communion we could never deserve.

As you pray today, maybe in your own agony, lift up your requests and then add, "Nevertheless, not as I will, but as You will." The Father is glorified when we pray like Jesus.

EVENING

Jesus, I pray that You were glorified this day in my surrender to Your will. I ask for greater grace tomorrow to bring You honor. I am overwhelmed by the price You paid for my sin. You knew no sin, yet You were willing to be made sin for me. I worship and adore You, and I am not ashamed to call You my Lord and my God. Amen.

ED LITTON, NORTH MOBILE, AL

Good morning, Lord! I want to thank You for praying for me. I ask for grace to keep my focus on You and Your Word. Help me to obey You and do what You command, regardless of how I may or may not feel. Amen.

"And when He had sent them away, He departed to the mountain to pray."
MARK 6:46

Most pilots simply call it vertigo, though the technical term is "spatial disorientation." It is the powerful sensation that you are otherwise than you really are. Pilots have recorded feeling upside down when in fact they were right side up. Spatial disorientation is most often experienced in dark storms or foggy weather conditions. The eye cannot see anything that resembles reality, and an alarming uncertainty sets in. What are pilots trained to do in such conditions? They are trained to trust their instruments.

As a disciple of Jesus Christ, you will encounter turbulence in life, and you will at times feel a form of spiritual vertigo. Our best response to disorientation is to look to the instrument panel of God's Word. You may feel at times like He is distracted or burdened by "bigger" things. In truth nothing is "big" for God; He is ever praying and interceding on your behalf (Heb. 7:25). In spiritual vertigo we may conclude that Jesus is incapable of helping, but nothing is impossible with God (Matt. 14:27). The terminal fear is that Jesus will just never come to your rescue. That is why Jesus said in John 6:20, "It is I; do not be afraid."

Disciples will experience disorientation. If you are disoriented, trust Him; He is not distant or unconcerned—He lives to pray for you, and He will rescue. Andrew Murry said, "God is willing to assume the full responsibility for the life that is totally yielded to Him." Surrender to Jesus, who can walk on water and rescue you in the storm of your life.

EVENING

I just want to say that it was sweet to hear Your Word say, "Do not be afraid." I want to thank You for Your faithful love this day. I ask for strength to trust Your promise to assume the full responsibility for my life as I totally yield to You. Amen.

MORNING

Lord, I want to thank You for Your good, pleasing, and perfect will for my life. Thank You that today You have plans and purposes for me. There will be no accidents today—only divine appointments. I pray that Your Word will light my path. Amen.

"We also, since the day we heard it, do not cease to pray for you,
and to ask that you may be filled with the knowledge of
His will in all wisdom and spiritual understanding."
COLOSSIANS 1:9

The apostle Paul was never content to merely know people were justified and safe for eternity. He prayed for those who embrace the gospel to move forward into God's will for their lives. He prayed they would live in the awareness of their calling in Christ, which is to bring God glory and bring others to a knowledge of the Savior.

In his day, Paul battled an idea that crept into the hearts of some church leaders called Gnosticism. This word comes from the Greek word *epignosis*. The prefix *epi-* means "super." These guys believed they had a super-knowledge above that of the revealed Word of God. The gnostics were a serious threat to the early church because they were leading people to go deeper into themselves by trusting a mystical "knowledge." This would lead God's people to greater uncertainty and constant distraction from God's will.

What is God's will for your life? It takes spiritual wisdom and understanding to know the specific details of "who, what, and when." One thing remains clear in God's Word: the Lord saved you to surrender your life to His service. Since He came "to seek and to save that which was lost" (Luke 19:10), He is glorified when we seek the unsaved and then help them grow in knowledge of His will for them. How God uses you today will be a unique experience to your life. That God wants to use you is a fact. Pray the prayer of Paul for yourself and others, and don't stop: "Lord, please fill me with the knowledge of Your will through spiritual wisdom and understanding."

EVENING

Lord, help me gain spiritual wisdom and understanding from this day. Help me to find principles in Your Word to better understand Your ways and Your plan for my life. Amen.

ED LITTON, NORTH MOBILE, AL

Father, I thank You that I am Your child and that I can live in the security of this relationship. I pray that throughout this day You will direct my ways so that I will be a child who brings You honor by living in the power of Your holiness. In Jesus' precious name I pray, Amen.

"Our Father in heaven, hallowed be Your name."
LUKE 11:2A

This prayer was given by Christ in response to a direct request by His disciples, "Lord, teach us to pray" (Luke 11:1). In this opening line, Jesus transformed the relationship with God from a distant, corporate experience into an intimate, one-to-one bond. God is referred to as Father only fourteen times in the thirty-nine books of the Old Testament. When used it was done in reference to Israel as a nation and not to individuals. This would no longer be the case in the New Testament, because God desired the same relationship with those who believed in His Son as He had with His Son.

Christ was also teaching that the powerful would not be compromised for the personal. God wants to have an intimate relationship with us, but we must treat Him with proper respect. He is holy, and He deserves to be treated as such. Jesus emphasized the reverence of this relationship by drawing attention to the holiness of His Father's name. "Your name" represents all of God's character and attributes.

It is only when we recognize the power of God's holiness that we enjoy the intimacy of His presence and that we have an invitation to come boldly to His throne of grace as His child and heir.

EVENING

Father, as You have kept me through the day, please keep me through the night. Guard my mind as I sleep so that my dreams will be pleasing to You and I can rest in the security of Your protection and provision. In Jesus' name, Amen.

MORNING

Father, I choose to surrender my will so that I can live in Yours. I ask that You make Your will clear to me today so that I will be pleasing to You and be seen and known as a productive citizen of Your kingdom. In Jesus' name, Amen.

"Your kingdom come. Your will be done on earth as it is in heaven."
LUKE 11:2B, C

Today in heaven there is no election to see who will rule. Today in heaven, there are no lawyers or politicians debating interpretation of Scripture. In fact, there is no debate in heaven because God is on His throne and He is doing as He pleases.

Could it be that we live in such turmoil because we are often trying to serve the wrong king in the wrong kingdom? Philippians 3:20 says, "For our citizenship is in heaven, from which we also eagerly wait for the Savior, the Lord Jesus Christ." As believers our citizenship is in heaven, which means we should be living under the same authority that the inhabitants of heaven are living under right now.

Jesus wanted His disciples to start living under the authority of heaven in this world. Wouldn't it be great if we lived our life in such a way that heaven would not be a big change? This is why Jesus instructs us to pray this way; to surrender to the will of God on earth, just as we will do when we are in heaven. He is instructing us to live in this world with the heart and habits of our eternal home.

EVENING

Lord, I thank You for directing my steps throughout this day and for guarding my heart against my own desires. It is my desire that You be my desire. In Jesus' name, Amen.

Father, I thank You that You are concerned about the needs of my life today, and I trust You to provide me with all that I need to sustain me in the life You have given me to live this day. In Jesus' name, Amen.

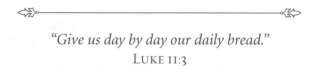

"Give us day by day our daily bread."
LUKE 11:3

It is significant that the initial thing Christ instructs us to pray for when we pray for ourselves is "our daily bread"—our material needs. Notice that we are invited to pray for bread, not dessert. We are not to use the latest and greatest shopping catalog as our daily devotional guide.

It is also significant that we are instructed to pray for the needs of today. There is nothing wrong with planning for future rainy days, but it is wrong to allow such a goal to consume us. God wants us to depend on Him daily.

It really is amazing that a God who sees the universe as a whole is also so concerned with our lives that are lived out daily. If He is aware of every sparrow that falls from the sky, every star in the sky, and every grain of sand, why would He not be concerned with the daily needs of our life? Don't be so consumed by tomorrow's request that you don't seek God for today's requirement. Matthew 6:34 says, "Do not worry about tomorrow, for tomorrow will worry about its own things. Sufficient for the day is its own trouble."

EVENING

Father, You have shown me great love throughout this day by providing me with all that I need, and I praise You for the security and sufficiency of Your love for me. In Jesus' name, Amen.

Week 30, Thursday

Father, give me a heart of forgiveness that does not hold a grudge or look to be offended. As an act of my will, I choose to forgive those that would cause me offense or harm just as You have forgiven me for the harm and offense I have done against You. In Jesus' name, Amen.

"And forgive us our sins, for we also forgive everyone who is indebted to us."
LUKE 11:4A

Corrie ten Boom, author of *The Hiding Place*, tells the story of how she, after being taken captive during World War II, was interned in a concentration camp and there humiliated and degraded, especially in the delousing shower where the women were ogled by the leering guards. By God's grace, she survived and made it out of that hell.

Eventually she felt she had forgiven, by grace, even those fiends who guarded the shower stalls, so she preached forgiveness, for individuals and for all of Europe. She preached it in Bloemendaal, in the United States, and, one Sunday, in Munich. After the sermon, while greeting people, she saw a man come toward her, hand outstretched: "Ja, Fräulein, it is wonderful that Jesus forgives us all our sins, just as you say." She remembered his face; it was the leering, lecherous, mocking face of one of the SS guards from the shower stall.

Her hand froze by her side. She could not forgive. She thought she had forgiven all, but she could not forgive when she met a guard, standing in solid flesh in front of her. Ashamed and horrified at herself, she prayed, "Lord, forgive me, I cannot forgive." As she prayed she felt forgiven and accepted, in spite of her shabby performance as a famous forgiver.

Her hand was suddenly unfrozen. The ice of hate melted. Her hand went out. She forgave as she was forgiven.

EVENING

Father, I thank You for the freedom of forgiveness and for the peace that it brings as I rest in Your love and grace. In Jesus' name, Amen.

Father, I will trust in Your faithfulness that I will not be tempted beyond what I am able and that by Your grace, You will make a way of escape (1 Cor. 10:13). In Jesus' name, Amen.

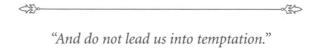

"And do not lead us into temptation."
LUKE 11:4B

The conjunction "and" ties the previous petition about forgiveness with this one. The Greek word used here can mean temptation (enticement to engage in sin) or trial (testing). Here in Luke 11:4 the meaning is temptation that, if yielded to, will lead us into sin.

An unforgiving heart is the pathway to an overwhelmed saint. If we aren't careful, God's test of forgiveness can turn out to be our temptation to sin because Scripture teaches us in James 1:13 that God does not tempt anyone, and verse 14 says, "But each one is tempted when he is drawn away by his own desires and enticed."

I believe the best interpretation of this petition in today's verse is this: "Please don't let me be overwhelmed by temptation." Satan tempted Jesus in the wilderness, but He was not overwhelmed. We live in a fallen world where temptation is inevitable, but we also serve a risen Savior who tells us that we are not helpless victims to the inevitable temptation of sin. By His grace, we are overcomers to the inevitable.

First John 5:4 says, "For whatever is born of God overcomes the world. And this is the victory that has overcome the world—our faith."

EVENING

Father, I thank You for Your protection and guidance throughout this day. Thank You for making me aware of the snares of the Enemy by giving me the hope and help of victory. In Jesus' name, Amen.

MORNING

Father, I thank You that I can live in victory today because You defeated the devil at Calvary, and he no longer has authority over my life because I belong to You. I claim deliverance from anything that would keep me from living in the victory of the Cross. In Jesus' name, Amen.

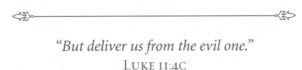

"But deliver us from the evil one."
LUKE 11:4C

As believers, we need to face the reality that we have an Enemy whose name is Satan, and he has a plan to try to put us in bondage so that we will be ineffective and immobile in our faith. This petition for deliverance in today's verse is based on the truth that Satan is defeated and that as believers we are fighting from victory and not for victory.

Satan is defeated strategically. As a creation, he is forced to depend on God for his existence. Any power he exercises is subject to God's will and decrees. Whatever Satan is allowed to do is appointed by God for the ultimate service and benefit of the saints.

He is defeated spiritually. The devil could have never predicted the outcome of the Cross. The death and resurrection of Christ guaranteed that at least part of fallen humanity would be purchased out of the kingdom of darkness back into the kingdom of light. The fact that those who were once owned by Satan will one day be exalted to rule over him drives him crazy.

He is defeated eternally. He will be forever cast away from the divine presence. His humiliation will be public, painful, and endless. He is a hapless player in a scheme that he himself set in motion, and he can do nothing to change the outcome.

Your deliverance has already been won, so don't be bound by a loser when Christ has made you a winner.

EVENING

Father, I thank You for a victorious day and for giving me the heart of a champion and the life of a conqueror. In Jesus' name, Amen.

Father, deepen the magnitude of my spiritual intimacy, intensity, and influence upon my world around me by guiding my life and growing my faith through Your Word. I yield my life to You for that end. Amen.

"Now faith is the substance of things hoped for, the evidence of things not seen."
HEBREWS 11:1

The word *faith* flows easily from our lips as followers of Christ. Downloading it into the details of life is the challenge. Understanding what it is and how it functions will help flesh faith out before a world that is hopeless without Christ.

Dissecting spiritual faith reveals it is more than an assumption based on wishful thinking. Faith is an assurance convinced that God's promises are so trustworthy that we can base our lives upon them. It does not depend upon the circumstances one can see, but upon the certainty of God's truth one believes. It gives the present tense grind of life a future and security to hold onto—and a reason to remain steadfast.

True faith believes and receives. It saves and satisfies because: Faith has *confidence* that every promise of God will be fulfilled. Faith has *courage* that despite what we suffer in this world, we can remain faithful because we will be glorified forever in the next. Faith has a *conviction* of spiritual things becoming reality even though there is no visible verification. Faith has a *comprehension* of an invisible, spiritual world that is more real than the visible, natural world. Faith has a *commitment* that continuously learns and conspicuously lives in light of Christ's lordship. Faith has a *contentment* that the future God has promised is so sure, we can patiently rest in the present.

Every believer wants to experience and enjoy spiritual vitality and victory. All of the spiritual blessings in the Lord Jesus flow from the dynamic of a supernatural faith that trusts in and relies on God. True faith renounces self-dependence, embraces God, and enjoys a fulfilling fellowship with a loving God who is pleased with those who live by faith.

EVENING

Father, thank You for the gift of saving faith. Enlighten and enable me through Your Spirit to function and flourish in complete reliance and trust. Help me express an intense and influential faith that reflects Your life, for Your glory. Amen.

MORNING

Father, help me to hear what You are saying through Your Word. Help me to respond to Your Word with faith and faithfulness. Impart to me a greater understanding of what it means to trust and obey. Amen.

"So then faith comes by hearing, and hearing by the word of God."
ROMANS 10:17

It was one of those defining moments. I was a ministerial student in college and had gone home with a friend for the weekend. His dad, a great evangelist, poured truth into our lives that weekend. It deeply shaped my spiritual thinking about living by faith. This evangelist said, "Faith is saying a thing is so, even though it is not so, in order for it to be so, because God said it was so." He made it clear that faith was not positive thinking or moving in accordance to subjective feelings. Faith was hearing from God, believing what was said, and then acting upon it as truth. What Manley Beasley taught that weekend long ago has miraculously been confirmed as truth in my own life.

I was not prepared for the report from the doctor in November 2007. "You have pancreatic cancer," he said. I knew this disease was no respecter of persons and had a nasty reputation for being lethal. I also knew I needed to hear from my Great Physician.

That following morning, I read Psalm 118:17, 18. The words jumped off the page and into my heart. "I shall not die, but live, and declare the works of the Lord. The Lord has chastened me severely, but He has not given me over to death." That written word became a personal and living word in my heart that I claimed and confessed.

Through the journey of surgery and chemo/radiation treatments, the Word of God sustained and strengthened my faith. Every report since has come back the same: "There is no evidence of any cancer in your body." And the miracle continues!

Do you want a strong faith? Learn to listen to God's voice through His Word. Hear it. Believe it. Act on it. And watch that truth miraculously become reality!

EVENING

Father, I bless Your name for Your faithfulness in fulfilling every promise. Empower me to act in steadfast obedience to Your Word. Enlarge my faith through Your Word, and let Your truth become reality for me. Amen.

KEITH THOMAS, MOBILE, AL

Father, I rejoice that nothing is impossible with You. Empower me to be disciplined in developing a mountain-moving faith that meets needs around me. Amen.

"So Jesus said to them, 'Because of your unbelief; for assuredly, I say to you,
if you have faith as a mustard seed, you will say to this mountain,
"Move from here to there," and it will move; and nothing will be impossible for you.'"
MATTHEW 17:20

The disciples were stumped and shamed. They knew they had spiritual authority to meet spiritual needs, but they were unable to appropriate it. Helpless and powerless to make a difference where they should have been able to, Jesus revealed why: unbelief. Faith is our spiritual and moral response to the trustworthy character of God. Unbelief dishonors God because it expresses God is not worthy of our trust. This sin, more than any other, short-circuits the supernatural from being experienced and enjoyed—in salvation and in sanctification.

The disciples' faith had either been misplaced—trusting in their fleshly abilities and authority rather than Christ's—or malnourished—being weak and unprepared for the spiritual challenge they faced.

Jesus used the mustard seed to teach a spiritual principle. The least amount of faith is greater than the greatest amount of difficulty. God will honor even a little faith. The mustard seed also implies a spiritual pattern. A mustard seed will grow if nurtured. Faith will grow if it is cultivated. A healthy, growing faith will see the miraculous grace of God bringing deliverance to the spiritually shackled and sick.

Let me suggest three key basics for developing a vibrant, victorious faith that overcomes the domain of darkness. (1) *Refocus your heart through self-denial and surrender.* (2) *Renew your mind through Scripture.* (3) *Release your faith through prayer.* These three things will help you develop a faith that sees the invisible, believes the incredible, and experiences the impossible.

EVENING

Father, forgive my unbelief. Grow and guide my faith to become an instrument of Your righteousness that makes a difference in this hurting and helpless world. Amen.

MORNING

Lord, I rejoice in Your great grace that was expressed at Calvary so that I might know the fullness of Your life. I rejoice in Your great gift of eternal life that has given me right-eousness I could never gain on my own. Empower me through Your Spirit to show and share this gift with others this day. Amen.

"For in it the righteousness of God is revealed from faith to faith; as it is written, 'The just shall live by faith.'"
ROMANS 1:17

When saving faith is expressed from the heart, the power of God in salvation is experienced. Our lives are altered for time and eternity by this faith trans action because we receive a righteousness that is not our own. Righteous-ness is that which God is, has, and gives when individuals receive Jesus Christ as Savior by faith. In this transforming transaction we gain a likeness to God—we become "just." We also receive a lifestyle for godliness—we "live by faith."

What a great salvation! When you believe in Christ, the righteousness of God is *re-vealed* to you, convincing and convicting you of your sin. Righteousness is *received* by you, imparted by the Holy Spirit. Then, righteousness is *reproduced* through you as you live by faith—trusting and obeying. What a great Savior! Having no capacity to be right-eous on my own, God gave me His righteousness. Jesus, having taken my sin and dying my death upon the Cross, exchanges it in salvation and gives me His righteousness. In other words, He became as I am so that I might become as He is. Now I can enjoy the reality that God accepts me through Christ. I no longer have to be shamed by guilt or shackled by doubts regarding my righteousness. I have His righteousness! Motivated by that one thought, the saved soul lives in full surrender to His lordship, expressing and extending His righteousness to a world that is in need of the power of the gospel.

EVENING

Father, it is my heart and hope that Your righteousness would be so conspicuous in my life that others would sense Your presence in my life. I desire for it to be so contagious in my life that others would begin to desire the incredible gift of salvation You have given me. Amen.

KEITH THOMAS, MOBILE, AL

Father, we rejoice that You are sovereign and sufficient to handle all our needs. Enable us to see beyond the present and focus on the invisible, trusting and resting in Your promises. Amen.

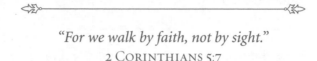

"For we walk by faith, not by sight."
2 CORINTHIANS 5:7

We need a faith that is powerful and practical if we are to consistently tap into the blessings of God. Living a life of faith not only opens the door of the heart of Jesus but also the door of heaven's riches. All of God's blessings come to us through faith. But we have a major vulnerability. We are so sight oriented. If we can touch it or see it or prove it, then we think we have faith. God, however, is pleased with true faith. It is when we have nothing to fall upon but Him that God does His best work in us.

There are two kinds of people who live in the realm of faith. (1) *Those who walk in faith*—they surrender their life to the lordship of Christ, trusting in His sovereign providence within their circumstances. (2) *Those who wander from faith*—they choose to take matters into their own hands.

Walking by faith involves *focusing confidently on the Word of God.* You receive, remember, rehearse, and rely on God's promises and precepts. You count on God's faithfulness to fulfill His Word. Walking by faith involves *living obediently to the will of God.* Since you know the will of God is best, you obey from a surrendered heart, regardless of the costs. Walking by faith involves *enduring patiently while waiting upon God.* You persist in believing. You remain steadfast under adverse circumstances. You do not doubt in the dark what God has shown you in the light. You understand that to God, timing is more important than time. Above all, you faithfully wait with joyful expectation.

EVENING

Lord, thank You for the joy of this day. Thank You for the truth of Your Word that lives and abides forever. Help us remember, recognize, and rejoice that You are always trustworthy and there. Amen.

MORNING

Lord, I am grateful that despite the pull of this world, I can walk in overcoming faith. Teach me how to live in this victory and share it with my world. Amen.

"For whatever is born of God overcomes the world.
And this is the victory that has overcome the world—our faith."
1 JOHN 5:4

In life, we can be a victim or a victor. The difference between the two is the activation and appropriation of faith. Victory over the world is not achieved by fighting—it is achieved by faith. If we place our faith in Christ, we are born again into a victorious life to be a super-conqueror. This overcoming faith wholeheartedly accepts everything that is implied in the claims of Christ and commits one's whole life to serving Him as Lord. Though Satan goes around as a roaring lion, seeking whom he may devour, the ultimate battle has already been won by Christ at Calvary. Positionally, you are already a conqueror over the domain of darkness because of Christ! Practically, you exercise that victory in life by embracing and exerting the spiritual authority you have in Christ over the world system that is manipulated by the pervasive hand of Satan and his demons. You are a conqueror who can daily walk in triumph!

No longer do you have to be victimized by death and condemnation. Immediately upon receiving salvation, the believer overcomes death. "Death is swallowed up in victory" through Christ's resurrection (1 Cor. 15:54). You are a conqueror who is destined for heaven! No longer do you have to be victimized by the subtle and seductive pull of the mindset and morality of the invisible, spiritual system of evil that operates in the unregenerate world and opposes the work of Christ on earth. You can resist the cosmos mentality and live in daily victory by having your mind stayed on God—full of God's Word and led by the Holy Spirit. So stay in the battle! We have absolute assurance and complete certainty about the ultimate victory. It is eternal life with Jesus Christ!

EVENING

I praise Your name, Lord Jesus, for the victory You have given to me as Your child. I bless You that whatever is over my head is under Your feet. You have already conquered it. Help me appropriate moment by moment the victory that is mine in You. Amen.

KEITH THOMAS, MOBILE, AL

Father, I love You. Thank You for being faithful and true. Help me to live this day in faith, not fear. In Jesus' name, Amen.

"God is faithful, by whom you were called
into the fellowship of his Son, Jesus Christ our Lord."
1 CORINTHIANS 1:9

Believe it or not, we have something in common. Even though we may not know each other, I am certain that we share uncertainties. Every life is full of uncertainties. We don't know the future. We can't accurately predict what will happen tomorrow or even in the next few minutes. No one has a crystal ball, and no one can read the stars to see what the future holds. None of us has enough power today to control every part of tomorrow. It may sound strange, but that is actually okay. Because even though the future is uncertain, from our vantage point it is not out of control.

As believers, one of the great things about our fellowship with Jesus Christ is that we know our future is in God's hands. We don't fear what we don't know because we have faith in the One who owns the past, the present, and the future. The Bible teaches that the future is not uncertain to God. He not only knows the future but also controls it. The life of Jesus reveals the greatness of God's compassion for us. Through His life, death, and resurrection He has secured a future in heaven for all those who trust in Him for forgiveness and salvation.

For believers many of the details of our future are still unknown, but our destiny is secure because God is faithful. God's Word reassures us that what God has begun in us, He will bring to completion (Phil. 1:6). His promises are true, and our ultimate future is certain because we are secure in Christ.

God is faithful, so faith in Him is always best.

EVENING

Father, I love You. My faith is in You for all of my tomorrows. Thank You for Your faithfulness. In Jesus' name, Amen.

MORNING

Father, I love You. Thank You for sharing Your love with us through sending Jesus. He is our life and our hope. Help me to live today with eyes for eternity. In Jesus' name, Amen.

"We do not look at the things which are seen, but at the things which are not seen. For the things which are seen are temporary, but the things which are not seen are eternal."
2 CORINTHIANS 4:18

Several years ago, my wife and I had the opportunity to attend a World Series Game. To say the least, I was excited about this once-in-a-lifetime experience. Before the teams emerged from the dugouts to start the game, I scanned the field with my binoculars to check out the majestically manicured field and all the incredible artwork that accompanies such a game. Once the game started, I passed the binoculars to my wife so I could get the full, natural view of the action and she could get a closer look at the stars of the game. In the heat of the battle during the middle innings, I looked over at my wife, and she had the binoculars pointed in the stands. She had become more intrigued by the stars at the game than the stars in the game.

It is so easy for us to get caught up in the same game spiritually. We need to be careful not to get so intrigued by the "stars" in this world that we neglect to see and live for the real, eternal world. Paul makes it clear that if there is nothing after this life then we (believers) should be pitied more than anyone else, because everything we are and do is for the eternal life yet to come. I believe one of the great devices the devil uses to get us off track and miss the eternal is distractions—or to put it another way, the attractions of the present life. The differences between the eternal and temporal, earthly and heavenly, visible and invisible are immeasurable; so watch your eyes, your heart, and your life . . . and live for what really matters.

EVENING

Father, I love You. I want to live for what really matters, so protect me from earthly distractions. In Jesus' name, Amen.

TIM DOWDY, MCDONOUGH, GA

Father, I love You. It is my desire to walk through this day completely trusting in You. As challenges come, help me to trust the sufficiency of Your grace and the strength of Your might to carry me through each struggle. In Jesus' name, Amen.

> *"And immediately Jesus stretched out His hand and caught him, and said to him, 'O you of little faith, why did you doubt?' And when they got into the boat, the wind ceased."*
> MATTHEW 14:31, 32

Want to hear something remarkable? A man named Peter walked on water. Want to hear something unremarkable? Peter sank. This story is remarkable because people don't walk on water (Jesus is the only other Person who has walked on water), and it is unremarkable because people sink. The focus of the story, believe it or not, is on the unremarkable. We have all been there; one step is faith and the next step is doubt. One minute we are walking, and the next minute we are drowning.

Jesus asked a simple question in that kind of a situation, "Why did you doubt?" At least part of the answer can be found in the definition of the word *doubt*. The word conveys the idea of attempting to travel in two directions at the same time or following two masters simultaneously. Impossible? Yes. This kind of living always results in failure. Peter did not sink because he quit believing in Jesus' ability to keep him afloat. Rather, he began to sink by trusting his own ability.

Faith isn't about our ability; it is complete trust in Jesus. When our faith is divided, our failure is certain. So when the winds of challenge blow, trust in Jesus alone.

EVENING

Father, I love You. Thank You for walking with me through another day. I realize that even in the storms of life I can trust You to see me through. Thank You for being my strength and my life. In Jesus' name, Amen.

MORNING

Father, I love You. Thank You for loving me. I pray that today my faith would be evident. Help me to be Your hands and feet. I pray Matthew 5:14–16 will be real in my life. I pray I would be the light of the world, visible for all to see. And I pray that my obedience and loyalty to You would cause others to glorify Your name. In Jesus' name, Amen.

"What does it profit, my brethren, if someone says
he has faith but does not have works? Can faith save him?"

JAMES 2:14

Have you ever tried to describe something invisible? Something that you cannot see, hear, taste, touch, or smell is almost impossible to describe and even more difficult to defend. Such is the case with faith. James is not making the argument for salvation through or by good works, but he is making a case for faith that is visible. You may not be able to see its essence, but you can definitely see its presence when faith is real.

"Seeing is believing" is a catchy phrase, but it's not a good description of what causes or motivates real faith. When the resurrected Jesus appeared to Thomas to give proof that He was alive, Thomas responded with this confession of faith: "My Lord and my God!" (John 20:28). Then Jesus replied, "Because you have seen Me, you have believed. Blessed are those who have not seen and yet have believed" (v. 29).

When you have genuinely placed your faith in Jesus, that invisible faith should be visible in life. The powerful transformation of the new birth through saving faith is so radical that a new life will result. That new life will be visible for all to see. A life rescued from the mire of sin and brought to life by the grace of God through the salvation supplied in Jesus is a changed life. That change is indeed personal, but it is not invisible. An invisible faith is really no faith at all.

EVENING

Father, I love You. Thank You for Your gift of eternal life in Jesus Christ. I pray today You have been honored by my life and that You have been made known to the world around me by the way I have lived. Jesus, have Your way in my life and be glorified! Thank You for loving me. Amen.

TIM DOWDY, McDONOUGH, GA

Father, I love You. Thank You for giving me the strength this day to live for You. I give myself to You and depend on the strength of Your might for each moment. Be glorified in me today. In Jesus' name, Amen.

"Therefore we also pray always for you that our God would count you worthy of this calling, and fulfill all the good pleasure of His goodness and the work of faith with power."

2 THESSALONIANS 1:11

How much can you bench press? Unfair question? Okay. How strong of a person are you? Being strong is equated with being tough. If someone is emotionless, business-like, resolved, or self-assertive, we call him or her "strong." But how strong are the strongest of the strong? Can they carry any amount of pressure? Is there nothing in life that can make them crack? Is there nothing that can touch the sensitive side of their heart? Is there any temptation that can win against the warrior inside of them?

No matter how tough you may be or how strong you think you are, the strength of any person can quickly fade to weakness when the pressures and battles are spiritual. For believers, that is where the field of battle really is.

Listen to what the Bible says about our battles: "For we do not wrestle against flesh and blood, but against principalities, against powers, against the rulers of the darkness of this age, against spiritual hosts of wickedness in the heavenly places" (Eph. 6:12). None of us is strong enough to stand up to that kind of battle. Don't fear the battle, though. God never meant for us to be strong on our own. We are the strongest when we rely on Him! As believers, we are never alone. "Finally, my brethren, be strong in the Lord and in the power of His might" (Eph. 6:10).

EVENING

Father, I love You. Thank You for giving me the strength to live for You today. Forgive me for those times when my faith is weak, and please strengthen my faith. Thank You for the comfort of Your love. In Jesus' name, Amen.

Father, I love You. Help me to live this day completely dependent on You. Keep pride and arrogance from entering my heart. With a humble, thankful heart I place my life in Your hands. Use my life for Your glory. In Jesus' name, Amen.

"Behold the proud, his soul is not upright in him; but the just shall live by his faith."
HABAKKUK 2:4

The life of the Christian is different. At one point in the Scriptures we are called "special," and some translations use the word "peculiar" (1 Pet. 2:9). The secular world probably would not disagree with that assessment! The reason believers are different is not because we are perfect or because we think we are better than other people in the world. That kind of perspective is rooted in pride, and the Bible makes it clear that there is no room in a Christian's life for pride.

Faith is the real reason we are different. The believer is called a believer because of the distinctive of faith. Paul describes the Christian's life this way: "I have been crucified with Christ; it is no longer I who live, but Christ lives in me; and the life which I now live in the flesh I live by faith in the Son of God, who loved me and gave Himself for me" (Gal. 2:20).

In one sense, Christians have died. That is, our sin and self have been crucified with Christ. God sees us that way. But we also die daily to anything that would entice us to be unfaithful to Christ. Because we have died, we have a new life. Christ is our life. We no longer live this life alone. God gives us the power to live, and it is in Him that we place our complete faith and trust. Everyone lives a life of faith—some place their faith in themselves and others in their jobs or bank accounts, but as believers our reliance is in Jesus Christ.

EVENING

Father, I love You. Thank You for carrying me through this week. I pray my life has been pleasing to You. Prepare my heart for worship with Your people. Bless my pastor and small group leaders with wisdom in Your Word. Continue to strengthen my faith and use my life to share Your love with the world. In Jesus' name, Amen.

Father, Your magnificence is indescribable, Your glory is incomparable, and the depth of Your love is inconceivable. You are a great God, and You deserve my greatest praise. You are the object of my faith; You are steadfast and unchanging, the same throughout the ages. In Jesus' name, Amen.

"Though now you do not see Him, yet believing,
you rejoice with joy inexpressible and full of glory."
1 PETER 1:8

Followers of Christ are called to walk by faith, not by sight. Scripture defines faith as the "substance of things hoped for, the evidence of things not seen" (Heb. 11:1). Why did first-century Christians continue their allegiance to Christ when swift and fierce persecution, including unspeakable tortures or even death, were almost inevitable? How could they stare in the face of such fierce difficulties with such a godly stature? What was their secret? Faith.

Faith has the power to propel believers through the bleakest days imaginable. Faith is what kept Abraham going through the years while he awaited the arrival of God's promised heir. Faith kept Noah working 120 years without a convert, without a single reason to keep working except the promise of God. Faith keeps us looking forward. Faith keeps fresh the conviction that our best days are not reserved for this world—our best days lie ahead. Faith creates an atmosphere in which hope thrives.

Faith is the fuel that drives believers through the circumstances of life. Peter told his audience of believers in today's verse that someday they would see Jesus. This confidence became their driving force. Their motivating persuasion propelled them past their circumstance with unwavering hope in an unseen reality. Those believers' perseverance, according to Peter, was an expression of the genuineness of their faith. This type of faith ultimately brings praise, honor, and glory to Jesus Christ.

EVENING

Father, Your faithfulness overwhelms me. Your constant companionship comforts me, and Your grace sustains me. Thank You for every blessing, for You are the author of them all. In Jesus' name, Amen.

MORNING

Father, it is with a grateful heart that I wish to say thank You for Your grace. Lord, Your heart beats to the tune of grace, and I worship You for that truth. You deserve my best today, because You gave Your best on the Cross. Amen.

"That no one is justified by the law in the sight of God is evident, for 'the just shall live by faith.' Yet the law is not of faith, but 'the man who does them shall live by them.'"

GALATIANS 3:11, 12

When Paul wrote these words, he was dealing with a group of people known as Judaizers, whose theology held that one becomes right with God not by faith in Christ alone but also through keeping the Mosaic Law. Very simply, they were teaching a faith plus works method to salvation. Paul said it best in Romans 8:3, "For what the law could not do in that it was weak through the flesh, God did by sending His own Son in the likeness of sinful flesh."

You see the problem was not the Law; as a matter of fact, the Law was perfect. The problem was that we are not. The Law was capable; however, we are incapable of keeping it because of our sinful natures. Therefore, if salvation could come through the Law only, we would be forever hopeless.

Thankfully, our gracious God intervened by sending Christ, who knew no sin to be sin for us, that we might become the righteousness of God in Him. On the Cross God treated Jesus as if He had lived our sinful lives so that by faith in Christ, His righteousness could be credited to our account. This results in God now treating us as if we had lived Christ's perfect life. Therefore, our faith must rest solely upon Christ, because He alone did what the Law could never do—bring someone into a rightful standing with a holy God. The wonderful truth of salvation is that by faith alone, through grace alone, in Christ alone.

EVENING

Father, how sweet it is to rest in the fact that our relationship is not based on my works, but rather on the finished work of Your dear Son. I take comfort in the sufficiency of Jesus Christ. I glorify You, God, for the peace and joy that result from knowing You. Amen.

TREVOR BARTON, LONDON, KY

Week 33, Wednesday

MORNING

Father, My heart is to worship You in spirit and truth. I want not only my words to glorify You but my very life itself to bring You glory. Lord, You are the creator of life, the author of salvation, the sustainer of all that is, and You are my Savior. I love You and desire to serve You. Amen.

"For in Christ Jesus neither circumcision nor uncircumcision avails anything, but faith working through love."
GALATIANS 5:6

Salvation is not static; it is a reality, a force, and a life transformation that works from the inside out. That's how an authentic relationship with God works. Mere religion attempts to work only from the outside in, attempting to modify behaviors and sinful tendencies through the observance of certain rules and regulations. Such was the case concerning circumcision.

For Jews, circumcision was an outward sign of their covenant relationship with God. Scripture's first mention of circumcision occurred when God instructed Abraham (who was previously justified by God) to circumcise every male child of his household (Gen. 17:10ff). This rite was to be observed the eighth day after birth. Over the centuries, especially in Christ's day, there was strong sentiment among the religious crowd that salvation required circumcision. Circumcision created an element of drama in the first-century church. In Acts 15, a special counsel convened to resolve the issue; the debate ended with the apostles and elders affirming that salvation is by faith alone. Once again religion had attempted to make individuals right with God from the outside in. When this happens people often tend to use works as a substitute for faith, rather than seeing works as a product of their faith. Believers in Christ do not perform good works in order to be saved; we perform good works because we are saved. Very simply, our works are a reflection of our faith. Genuine faith always produces results—always produces action. Faith and good works are inextricably connected in Scripture.

EVENING

Father, You are my everything! You are my stronghold, my help, my strength, and my friend. Everything that I need, Lord, You are! With all my soul I bless Your name. Amen.

MORNING

Dear God, Your Word teaches that faith is the catalyst of a life well lived; with that in mind, I ask You to strengthen my faith. Amen.

"Therefore we conclude that a man is justified
by faith apart from the deeds of the law."
ROMANS 3:28

Thousands of years ago, Job asked the question, "How then can man be righteous before God?" (Job 25:4). Paul makes very clear the answer to the question: faith. Apart from faith, biblical salvation becomes an impossibility. Possibly the greatest deception ever spoken is the lie that men and women are capable of making themselves acceptable to God. In one verse Paul eliminates good works, good intentions, rituals, religious exercises, or anything else that man can think to do in hopes of bringing himself to God. Essentially Paul makes clear that salvation is of the Lord, and humanity has no contribution in a genuine salvation experience. To put it another way:

- Salvation is not by man's merit—it is by God's mercy.
- Salvation is not by man's goodness—it is by God's grace.
- Salvation is not a result of human religion—it is a result of divine relationship.
- Salvation is not the result of religious exercise—it is the result of a relational encounter with Jesus Christ founded on faith.

God views our faith as righteousness. Paul taught that when Abraham acted in faith, God credited him with righteousness (Rom. 4:9). However, it is also important to note that faith is not a human work—it is a divine gift. It is God's grace that makes faith possible. Faith has the power to move mountains, heal the sick, or be a catalyst for good works; but the most profound power of faith is seen in justification. Justification very simply is the act whereby faith gives a guilty sinner a righteous standing before a holy God. God took justification, something that was and is a human impossibility, and made it not only possible but also simple because of faith.

EVENING

Father, all day my work is my focus. I struggle to live in Your mercy and grace. Thanks for saving me, even from myself. Amen.

TREVOR BARTON, LONDON, KY   197 ✳

You, God, are worthy of praise. You are seated on Your throne in power, glory, splendor, and majesty. Even now the angels are declaring Your holiness; those around the throne sing Your praise. I bless You for Your mercy that endures and Your Spirit that empowers. Be glorified in my life, oh God. Amen.

"So Jesus answered and said to them, 'Have faith in God.'"
MARK 11:22

Faith in and of itself will never be as important as the object of our faith. We live in a world where faith is prevalent, but sadly, faith is placed in all the wrong places. Faith is only as valuable as the value of its object.

The words of Jesus in Mark 11 have an interesting context. Immediately after Jesus spoke these words, He proceeded to teach the disciples about the power of faith. According to Jesus, faith has the power to remove mountains and toss them into the sea. Faith also has the power to capture God's attention in our prayers. Jesus said, "Therefore I say to you, whatever things you ask when you pray, believe that you receive them, and you will have them" (Mark 11:24). I don't think we appropriately appreciate the profundity of Jesus' words. It should lead us to ask this question: "How much faith do we really have?" When we consider the incredible potential of living life with faith, why would we settle for anything else? What would cause us to pray such little prayers to such a big God? Why are our dreams so small when the Lord of heaven and earth has unlimited resources?

In Jesus' words we find a challenge to be a people of audacious, radical, extraordinary faith. Faith is the drawing board on which we sketch our dreams. Faith believes when there is no sight. Faith stimulates obedience when it is contrary to our will. Faith perseveres even when confronted with fatigue and discouragement. Faith forgives wrongs. Faith allows us to step out of the boat. Faith lifts us after failure. Faith opens our hearts to people. Faith has the power to do all these things only when it is faith founded on God and God alone.

EVENING

Father, I thank You for being a God in whom my complete trust can rest. You have never disappointed me; You are faithful in every way. Amen.

Dear God, I want my life to count. My heart's deepest desire is to live a life that makes an eternal difference in the lives of those around me. Father, I want Jesus Christ on the inside to be what the world witnesses on the outside. Amen

"But do you want to know, O foolish man, that faith without works is dead?"
JAMES 2:20

Our works are a visible manifestation of our faith. Faith itself is invisible, but genuine faith will always ultimately reveal itself. Our good works paint the portrait of our faith. In Scripture faith and good works always go together. However, while faith plus works do not save us, we are saved by a faith that works.

True faith in God will never be invisible. Faith always surfaces and becomes the catalyst for fruit in the Christian's life. When Jesus taught about the vine and branches in John 15, He made it clear that when the branch is connected to the vine, the internal life of the vine will be expressed outwardly through the fruit of the branch. The same is true in the context of faith. Faith on the inside produces fruit (good works) on the outside. Faith always incites action! For example, we see the faith of:

- Abel in his more excellent sacrifice (Heb. 11:4).
- Joseph in his perseverance and forgiveness of his brothers (Gen. 39—48).
- David slinging a stone, fully expecting God to slay a giant (1 Sam. 17:45–50).
- Daniel at peace in the lions' den (Dan. 6:22, 23).
- Isaiah saying, "Here am I! Send me" (Is. 6:8).
- Nehemiah leaving his job to go join God in rebuilding the wall (Neh. 2ff).
- A nameless woman as she presses through the crowd to grab the hem of Jesus' garment (Matt. 9:20).

The point is this: good works uncover our faith. Faith produces results, and those visible results lead people to glorify God (Matt. 7:15–20). Now the question is, what type of faith do others see in you?

EVENING

Dear Lord, every good and perfect thing comes from You. God, You have been more gracious to me today than I deserve, and for that I am grateful. Amen.

TREVOR BARTON, LONDON, KY

Father, at the start of my day, before I begin running this day's race, I want to set my eyes on the prize of Your upward call. Let me see in my mind and sense in my heart the joy of being with You, so that I will run well today. Grant me grace so that I will not turn to the right or the left, to the distractions of the world or to pride, and in so doing stumble in sin. I confess my utter dependence on Your infinite strength. Let me run in You and unto You, for Your glory and my delight. In Jesus' name, Amen.

"Looking unto Jesus, the author and the finisher of our faith,
who for the joy that was set before Him endured the cross, despising
the shame, and has sat down at the right hand of the throne of God."
HEBREWS 12:2

In running a marathon, as with any sport, what you focus your attention on is critical. It is the difference between winning and losing, finishing well and not finishing at all. In the Isthmian games in ancient Greece, a pedestal stood at the finish line. On that pedestal, most likely, was a laurel wreath to be worn by the winner. A wreath that would fade, become brittle, and crumble in time. The writer of Hebrews tells us that we are to fix our attention on Jesus as we run this race called the Christian life. Too often we get our focus on the wrong things. We may focus on the person in the stand or maybe even our own feet as we run, but our focus should be Jesus. He is our goal. His goal was the joy that was set before Him, our salvation. He not only is our example, He is our focus.

EVENING

Gracious God, today had unexpected twists and turns, hard places and difficulties, yet all along the way Your grace was sufficient, Your mercies were new. Reviewing my race today, I see where I failed You or missed opportunities. Yet I see also how You moved me forward toward Yourself and how You carried me, encouraged me, and strengthened me. Thank You for pouring Your goodness on me all through the day. Now, grant me rest and refresh me with sleep for our run tomorrow. I love You. In Christ's name, Amen.

MORNING

Blessed Savior, crucified Lord, risen King, I live because You live in me. This life You grant me is a gift, the result of Your glorious salvation plan. You have drawn me into Your triune circle of love and allow me, by Christ and Your Spirit, to revel in the marvelous wonder that You are. May the light of Your love and glory empower me today to live in a manner worthy of the God who loved me and gave Himself for me. Amen!

"I have been crucified with Christ; it is no longer I who live,
but Christ lives in me; and the life which I now live in the flesh I
live by faith in the Son of God, who loved me and gave Himself for me."
GALATIANS 2:20

One of the great mysteries of the ages is the lost tomb of the great Mongol warrior Genghis Khan who died in 1227. According to legend, he was buried in an unknown location under heavy guard. The funeral escort killed anyone who crossed their path. Once Khan was buried, the soldiers who attended his interment massacred the slaves who built the tomb. Then those soldiers who killed them were also killed in an attempt to absolutely conceal the burial place of the man who ruled the largest contiguous empire in history. Some say that a river was diverted to flow over the tomb of Khan, but no one knows with certainty. Marco Polo wrote that by the thirteenth century the Mongols had no idea where the grave of Genghis Khan was located.

While we as the people of faith do not know exactly where the tomb of Christ was, we do know where He lives . . . Christ lives in me. Hallelujah!

EVENING

Father, Jesus said that in the world I would have tribulation, but to be of good cheer, for He has "overcome the world" (John 16:33). I experience that tribulation every day—in the world and in my own heart. O, God, I long for You. I thank You, God, that Christ will deliver me into Your very presence, where He is now seated! O, glad news is mine. Christ is mine. I am His. Take joy my soul. "He who is in you is greater than he who is in the world" (1 John 4:4). Praise God . . . praise God . . . praise God! Amen.

Father, crouching at the door is the Enemy of all that is holy, righteous, and good. He waits for me, seeking to devour me. By Your strength deliver him a mighty blow today through my life. I am no match for him. But he is no match for You. Steel my nerves, quicken my mind, strengthen my shield of faith, and guide my arms to wield the sword of Your Word. May the gospel go forth from my lips today. May Your victory be heralded in the earth and in the heavens once again—through me—this day. In the mighty name of Jesus I pray, Amen.

"Fight the good fight of faith, lay hold on eternal life, to which you were also called and have confessed the good confession in the presence of many witnesses."
1 TIMOTHY 6:12

Paul comes to the end of 1 Timothy and calls the believer to fight the good fight of faith. By the end of 2 Timothy 4:7 Paul says of himself, as he faces execution, that he fought the good fight. Not long ago, a championship boxer stood to apologize for fighting such a poor fight. The fans had chanted, "Boring!" through the entire match, and the boxer was embarrassed. Paul challenges us to live the life of faith in such a way that we will not have to apologize to a watching world. Then we will be able to say, like Paul, when we come to the end of the way, "We fought the good fight." Our prize will be the words of our Lord: "Well done, good and faithful servant" (Matt. 25:21).

EVENING

"The LORD is my helper; I will not fear. What can man do to me?" (Heb. 13:6). God, because You are my helper, I fight against sin, the world, and the principalities and powers that You now allow to reign in it. Because Jesus said, "All authority has been given to Me . . . and lo, I am with you always, even to the end of the age" (Matt. 28:18, 20), I fight, and I am assured of ultimate victory in Christ. Because nothing can separate me from the love of Christ, tonight I rest in Him, placing all my care upon Him, for He cares for me (1 Pet. 5:7). Thank You, Father. Thank You, Jesus. Thank You, Holy Spirit. Amen.

Lord, this day I desire, above all else, to love You with my whole heart. Therefore, cover it with the breastplate of Your righteousness, so that Satan's accusations cannot condemn me. Enlarge and uphold my faith so that it shields me against all the flaming arrows launched against me. Bring to my mind the remembrance of Your great salvation, and thus sustain my hope in You. Make Your love flow over the brim of my life into the lives of others, that they may believe. In Jesus' mighty name I pray, Amen.

"But let us who are of the day be sober, putting on the breastplate of faith and love, and as a helmet the hope of salvation."
I THESSALONIANS 5:8

Recently I stood on a mountain and looked over into the most famous battlefield in the world, the Valley of Jezreel. We know it as the Valley of Armageddon. The first recorded battle in history took place there, and the last battle fought on earth will take place there. Everyone from pharaohs, Romans, Crusaders, Napoleon, Germans, and Brits have fought in that valley. While it is the most famous valley, the most common battlefield is the human heart and mind. That is why Paul instructs us to cover our hearts with the breastplate of faith and love and our minds with the helmet of salvation. Faith brings the righteousness of Christ to our lives, and love expresses that righteousness to men. The hope of salvation protects the mind and encourages us as well. Every day Satan battles for control of your thoughts and your heart. The only way to have victory is by staying on the alert and being ready. Suit up.

EVENING

"And now abide faith, hope, [and] love" (1 Cor. 13:13). Precious Father, thank You that by Your Spirit I have faith to believe on Jesus Christ; that by Your Word I have hope in Your steadfast love; that by Your love I have love for You, which grows from glory to glory. Thank You that no one can pluck me from Your mighty hand and nothing can separate me from Your love because I am in Christ. You are before me, behind me, and all around me, overwhelming me in Your love. Such knowledge is too wonderful. I cannot contain its fullness. With all that is in me, I bless Your holy name! Amen.

God, You are life. Before the beginning, You were. You spoke a word and life sprang into being, into the reality of time and space, so that we could know You. You became flesh in order that we might more fully know You. Your Spirit is in the world today pouring forth rivers of life and calling people to faith, that they might eternally know You. Cause my life today to exude Your life, so that others may believe and receive life in Christ. Amen.

"Therefore He who supplies the Spirit to you and works miracles among you, does He do it by the works of the law, or by the hearing of faith?"
GALATIANS 3:5

The law of biogenesis states that there can be no life without antecedent life. In his lectures, the great scientist Louis Pasteur would hold up a thoroughly sterilized and hermetically sealed flask and would say that it was devoid of life. "I can keep it for a hundred years, and it will still be devoid of life." Why is that? Because the truth is, life begets life.

That was the entire issue with the law. Paul wanted the Galatians to see that the law did not produce spiritual life in them—faith did. Do you recall the rich young ruler in Matthew 19? He told Jesus that he had kept the law from his youth, but he knew he was still lacking something. Legalism cannot give life. No amount of keeping the law and rules or doing this, that, and the other will bring spiritual life. Jesus told Nicodemus, "That which is born of the flesh is flesh" (John 3:6). If you take the law of biogenesis and apply it to the spiritual dimension, the truth is still there—the law cannot produce life. Life comes by the Spirit, and the Spirit is received by faith.

EVENING

Jesus came that we might have life and have it more abundantly (John 10:10). God, in Christ You have set me free from the law of sin and death and have secured for me eternal life in Your presence. I will see You, face to face, and know You, even as I am known. This is a certainty more certain than life itself, for it has been secured by the One who is life. Thank You for saving my soul and giving me life through Christ! Amen.

MORNING

Lord, the Enemy rushes at me in the morning with the cares of the day, hanging them about my neck, cluttering my heart, disturbing my mind, and seeking to steal my peace. But You instruct me not to be anxious about anything, but by prayer to bring all my requests to You (Phil. 4:6). And You promise that, when I do, Your peace will secure my heart and mind (v. 7). This morning, God, I am casting all my cares on You, knowing that You are infinitely able to carry them. Thank You for caring for me. Make Your peace reign in me through Christ. Amen.

"Therefore, having been justified by faith,
we have peace with God through our Lord Jesus Christ."
ROMANS 5:1

T he twentieth century was the bloodiest in human history. In *Humanity: A Moral History of the 20th Century,* Jonathan Glover estimates that eighty-six million people died in wars fought from 1900 to 1989. That means that twenty-five hundred people every day or one hundred people every hour died in war for ninety straight years. All through that time, man was seeking peace through one means or another. The sad legacy of the twentieth century is that man cannot broker peace between himself and other humans, nor can man achieve peace with God apart from faith in Jesus Christ.

Paul states that we have been justified by faith. Man likes to think he can do something to bring about peace, but the truth is he cannot. The last century is proof of that. Man also thinks he has to do something to gain peace with God. The truth is, before justification, we were enemies of God. We were at war with Him. We have been justified by faith, Paul says, and now we have not only the peace of God (Phil. 4:7) but also peace *with* God (Rom. 5:1).

EVENING

As "It is finished!" was declared from Calvary's Cross, the peace accord between my rebel heart and Your holy heart was made through the exchange of the life of Your Son for the atrocities of my sin. He was made sin. I was made righteous. He was forsaken by You. I was accepted by You. O mighty God, what unfathomable lengths You have gone to in the securing of peace for all who love You. Praise to my crucified and risen Savior! Amen.

MAC BRUNSON, JACKSONVILLE, FL

Lord, I thank You for the church. I thank You for my local church. Teach me today to love the church as You love it. You made the greatest sacrifice for the church. Show me how to do the same. God, You gave Your Son for the church. Give me courage to give obediently to my church. Lord, give me grace to love the members of my church and cherish them as You do. In Jesus' name, Amen.

"For no one ever hated his own flesh, but nourishes and cherishes it, just as the Lord does the church."

EPHESIANS 5:29

Jesus loves the church. It is His body on earth today. He made the supreme sacrifice on the Cross to purchase the church. By the "washing of water by the word" (Eph. 5:26), He sanctifies the church. Jesus' goal for the church is to present herself spotless, holy, and blameless! Today He will nourish and cherish the church, and that includes you if you are a follower of Christ.

Jesus loves and cares for His church as a husband should his wife. The church is the bride of Christ. Today He will protect you, desire good for you, and pay attention to you. He will help you, feed your soul, and give you strength for the journey. The church is central in the mind of Christ, the first love of His life and the object of His sovereign work.

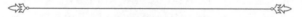

EVENING

Lord, as I conclude this day, I rest and rejoice in the fact that You have been watching over Your church. I am grateful that includes me. Thank You for nourishing and cherishing me today. I confess I need Your love. Forgive me when I take it for granted and neglect to tell You. I acknowledge You as the caretaker of the church. I love You. In Your name, Amen.

Week 35, Tuesday

MORNING

Lord, as I begin the day, prepare me for tough things that may come my way. I am not too good to know affliction. Lord, You suffered for me—thank You. Great Christians in history have paid a harsh price. Thank You for my heritage. Teach me today to be strong for the sake of Your body, the church. In Jesus' name, Amen.

"I now rejoice in my sufferings for you, and fill up in my flesh what is lacking in the afflictions of Christ, for the sake of His body, which is the church."
COLOSSIANS 1:24

The sufferings of Christ are understood from two standpoints. The first is that Christ's suffering was atoning. Romans 5:10 says, "For if when we were enemies we were reconciled to God through the death of His Son, much more, having been reconciled, we shall be saved by His life."

The other standpoint is that the suffering of Christ was exemplary to His followers, who were taught they would enter the kingdom by way of tribulation and endurance. It is this kind of suffering in which Paul rejoices. And he does it on behalf of the body of Christ, the church.

Perseverance is needed in the church. Peter tells us in 1 Peter 5:10 that the God of all grace will "perfect, establish, strengthen, and settle" us after we have suffered for a little while. As with Paul, we are to welcome the chance to partake of Christ's suffering. Persist!

EVENING

Thank You, Lord Jesus, that You never leave me to myself. Today You have walked with me through the valley. Today we walked with endurance. Continue, I ask, to bring me to maturity when I am tested. Refine me as gold in the fires of tribulation. Give me grace to rejoice when I am counted worthy to suffer for Your sake. In Jesus' name, Amen.

Father, I begin this day with confession. Jesus is the Christ, the Son of the living God. Thank You, Lord, that You are eternal. I know I can count on You today. Even when I am weak, You are strong. Jesus, thank You for being my Rock today. In Your holy name I pray, Amen.

"And I also say to you that you are Peter, and on this rock I will build My church, and the gates of Hades shall not prevail against it."
MATTHEW 16:18

There are various opinions about who or what Jesus is. Some see Him as a good teacher, a godly prophet, or a social radical. Peter's confession was the correct identification of Jesus. He is the promised Messiah, the Son of the living God. That is the bedrock upon which the church is built. Peter became a foundational rock in the church, because he stood on the confession in Matthew 16:16: "You are the Christ, the Son of the living God."

The church is built one stone upon another, as each of us becomes a living stone placed on the foundation stone of Christ. The word "church" is found twice in the Gospels. It is in today's verse and in Matthew 18:17. As Jesus builds His church, the gates of hell will not prevail against it. We shall overcome sin, sorrow, and death. The destination of the church is not to end up in the possession of hell, but rather to break forth in victory.

EVENING

Lord, thank You that the church stood today. It was not defeated. I rejoice to be a living stone in the structure that Jesus is building. Thank You for surrounding me with others who are part of the church. Teach us to stimulate one another to love, faith, and good works. I rest tonight in the eternal security of the Rock of Ages. In Jesus' name, Amen.

Good morning, Lord! Thank You for being the exalted One. You are the head of the church. I pledge to follow You fully today. Help me understand my place in the body of Christ. I pledge to keep You in first place in all things today. Forgive me when I have moved second place things into first place. You alone are adequate to be Lord. I crown You King of my life as I begin the day. In Jesus' name, Amen.

"And He is the head of the body, the church, who is the beginning,
the firstborn from the dead, that in all things He may have the preeminence."

COLOSSIANS 1:18

Jesus is the only One sufficient to be Lord. He is the only One who deserves prominence and preeminence in all things. Jesus is sufficient because God made Him the head of the church. Ephesians 1:22, 23 says, "And He put all things under His feet, and gave Him to be head over all things to the church, which is His body, the fullness of Him who fills all in all."

Jesus is sufficient because He is eternal. Jesus is the word of finality. Jesus is the "Amen." John 1:1, 2 says, "In the beginning was the Word, and the Word was with God, and the Word was God. He was in the beginning with God."

Finally, Jesus is sufficient because He was raised from the dead. First Corinthians 15:20 says, "Christ is risen from the dead, and has become the firstfruits of those who have fallen asleep."

Allow Jesus to have first place in your life today. He is sufficient for anything you will face. The fullness of deity dwells in Him, and He dwells in you.

EVENING

King Jesus, I confess You as Lord. Thank You for being my Victor. You lived, died, and rose to demonstrate You are the only true God. Forgive me where I have enthroned less than sufficient things on the throne of my life. I bow before You and crown You Lord of all. In Jesus' name, Amen.

Father, I acknowledge You as the One who is able to keep me from stumbling and make me to stand in Your presence blameless and with great joy. To You be all glory, majesty, dominion, and authority in my life today and forever. In Jesus' name, Amen.

"To Him be glory in the church by Christ Jesus
to all generations, forever and ever. Amen."
EPHESIANS 3:21

God deserves all the glory in our lives and in the church. This glory is to be His in every generation forever and ever. Why does God deserve all the glory? First, He deserves it because He can do all things. Paul tells us in Ephesians 3:20 that God "is able to do exceedingly abundantly above all that we ask or think, according to the power that works in us." The God of heaven can go over and above what we can even mentally comprehend. Whatever you face today, God can handle it. No matter what challenge comes to your church, the Father is adequate beyond all you can imagine.

Second, He deserves all glory because He has all power. That power works in you. The Greek word for "power" used in Ephesians 3:20 is the same word for "dynamite." Jesus promised that He would not leave us as orphans, but would send a Helper who would be with us forever. That Helper is the Person of the Holy Spirit, who lives in every follower of Christ and is a conduit of God's power directly into our lives and into our churches. Do not grieve or quench Him today. He desires to teach us God's mind (Rom. 8:27), His love (15:30), and His will (1 Cor. 12:11).

Allow Jesus to have all the glory in your church. Exalt His name. He purchased the church. He builds the church. And Jesus deserves all the glory for the church.

EVENING

Lord, I pray for my church. Forgive us when we have stolen the glory from Your name. Forgive us for trusting in our own strength rather than Your power. Lead us to include all generations and all races that desire to follow You. Bless my pastor today. Lead him to shepherd us in ways that will give glory to Your name. Thank You for the church. Amen.

MORNING

Father, thank You for the body of Christ. I rejoice today in the way You created and crafted the church. I thank You for all the people and gifts You place in it. As the day of corporate worship approaches, I pray for my church leaders. Bless my pastor with a relevant Bible message. Anoint my small group teacher to challenge me and motivate me to be a better disciple. Open the windows of heaven and provide for all the needs of our church. Amen.

"For as we have many members in one body, but all the members do not have the same functions, so we, being many, are one body in Christ, and individually members of one another."

ROMANS 12:4, 5

The church is an amazing, multifarious thing. The church includes people from all over the globe from every tribe and tongue, yet they have this in common: Jesus is their Savior and Lord! He is the wonderful common denominator of the church. While the church includes many individuals, it is built one member at a time.

To be part of the body of Christ, one must be saved. Regenerate church membership is a cornerstone of the body of Christ. Not everyone is a member. The prerequisite for membership is salvation in Christ alone. We are one body in Christ. Unity is essential for the church. It was Jesus' prayer for us. His desire was for the Father to make us one (John 17:20–23). Are you walking in fellowship with other members of your church? Seek oneness and be willing to repent and work toward unity.

You have been given a function in the church and spiritual giftedness to carry out the task. The church needs you and every other member in the body. Find your spiritual gift (Rom. 12:6–8) and develop it. Make certain that you are walking in full obedience with a God-honoring function in the local church.

EVENING

You have gifted me, O Lord, to bring honor to You. Thank You for blessing me with the mind to recognize and the desire to carry out an earthly mission designed by You. Help me to encourage those with different spiritual gifts to use them to reflect Your nature. Remind me to have a spirit of gratitude for how You created me. I love You. Amen.

TED TRAYLOR, PENSACOLA, FL

Lord, You are the Head of the church, and I surrender this day to You. In Jesus' name, Amen.

"And He put all things under His feet, and gave Him to be head over all things to the church, which is His body, the fullness of Him who fills all in all."
EPHESIANS 1:22, 23

During the financial crisis of 2008-2009, most Americans were disappointed or angry to learn that some CEOs took massive bonuses for themselves, while investors and employees lost their savings, their retirement, and their jobs. CEO bonuses for the Fortune 1000 companies topped four hundred million dollars, while many of their companies suffered record losses. Sometimes, corporate heads are less than generous with the people they lead.

Thank God it is not that way in the body of Christ. Jesus is the Head of the church, but He is different than the head of any other organization. The New Testament uses the word "head" in much the same way we use it today when we refer to the "head of the house" or the "head of state." The Head of the church is the Lord of the church!

While the church is His body and submissive to His lordship, it shares in everything He has and is. As the Head of the church, Jesus never depletes the church or robs it of its blessings. Instead, Jesus fills the church with His characteristics, His power, and His life. He shares everything with us and fills the church with all His fullness, so that everything He enjoys as the Head, He shares for the benefit of the body.

EVENING

Thank You, Lord, for blessing us with all of Your fullness. In Jesus' name, Amen.

MORNING

Lord, thank You for the Word of God. Today it will be the foundation of my life. In Jesus' name, Amen.

"Having been built on the foundation of the apostles and prophets, Jesus Christ Himself being the chief cornerstone, in whom the whole building, being fitted together, grows into a holy temple in the Lord."

EPHESIANS 2:20, 21

If you open the Yellow Pages to the word "church," the variety of options may be the first thing you notice. We use numerous words to describe the church. We hear about the Catholic Church, the Orthodox Church, the Reformed Church, the Mega Church, the Traditional Church, the Liturgical Church, and the Contemporary Church. To that list, we add denominational names like Pentecostal Church, Baptist Church, Presbyterian Church, and the list goes on. Defining the church can be a big job!

The apostle Paul also used a variety of words to describe the church. He called it a body, a bride, and a building. Using the building metaphor, the Scripture teaches that the foundation upon which the church is built is, in part, the Word of God. In today's verse, Paul called that foundation the "apostles and prophets," in other words, the Old and New Testament teachers who gave the church the bedrock message of truth found in Scripture. In addition, the church is built on the chief cornerstone—the most important foundation piece of all. Jesus is the cornerstone. He is the standard by which the growing church is aligned and made secure. You might say the church is built upon the Word of God and the God of the Word!

At the dedication of a new sanctuary, a pastor friend of mine told his young congregation, "Today we have finished the church building, but building the church has just begun." Undergirded by the teaching of Scripture and supported by the Lord Jesus, the people of God—His church—are being built into a holy people and "a holy temple in the Lord" (Eph. 2:21)!

EVENING

Lord Jesus, I praise You, the cornerstone of the church and of my life. In Jesus' precious name, Amen.

KIE BOWMAN, AUSTIN, TX

Lord, today use my spiritual gifts as I serve You as a member of Your body. In Jesus' name, Amen.

"Now you are the body of Christ, and members individually."
I CORINTHIANS 12:27

The church is the body of Christ. Jesus lives in us and uses us like His feet, His hands, and His voice. Every believer is individually gifted and positioned in the church to help fulfill God's purpose for the church. Today's passage is found in the context of Paul's explanation of spiritual gifts. When he calls us "members" of the body, the word refers not to church membership rolls, but to the "limbs" or "members" of a body.

I visited a church recently where thousands of people attend every week. The pastor is a gifted teacher and is one of the most well-known Christian leaders in America. The music ministry is known everywhere. Giftedness is obvious on the public platform.

After the service, I noticed an army of volunteers take brooms and garbage bags, and they started cleaning the worship center. Their smiles and fellowship seemed to indicate that they were serving in the joy of the Lord! That is a picture of the body functioning as the Lord intends. Some teach and preach and minister with beautiful songs, but others are gifted to clean up and prepare the physical surroundings for worship. Others cook, administrate, or care for babies. Every member is needed in the body!

In the physical body, hands, eyes, feet, and arms all function differently, but they are all important parts of a healthy body. In the church, every believer's spiritual gift is an important part of Christ's body. Together, every Christian is a gifted member of the body of Christ!

EVENING

Father, thank You for including me in the body of Christ. In Jesus' name, Amen.

Lord, You have placed leaders in Your church. Help me to love and respect the leaders at my church and around my community for Your sake. In Jesus' name, Amen.

"And we urge you, brethren, to recognize those who labor among you,
and are over you in the Lord and admonish you, and to esteem them
very highly in love for their work's sake. Be at peace among yourselves."
1 THESSALONIANS 5:12, 13

In the Gospels, Jesus warned His followers not to adopt the brutal style of leadership common in the kingdoms of their day. Leadership in the church is based upon a different model, but leaders do exist in the church. To the church at Thessalonica, Paul referred to the leaders, not by title, but by function. In today's verse, he says that leaders "labor among you." That word "labor" literally means "to be exhausted from effort." He also says they "are over you in the Lord." That phrase refers to a position of authority, having been previously established or literally "set in place." He hints at the nature of their work when he writes that they "admonish you," which suggests a teaching or preaching role.

The recognized church leaders are those hardworking teachers of the Word with a spiritual responsibility for the lives of others in the church. How are we to treat these leaders? Paul says to "esteem" them, a word that has a root meaning related to leadership or command over a military unit. To esteem them, therefore, means to follow their lead. In the church, we esteem or follow our leaders in two specific ways. We esteem them "very highly" by following them without reluctance or measured compliance. We follow our leaders "in love" because of the nature of their work. The end result of this kind of relationship between hardworking leaders and loving followers is "peace among yourselves."

Church leaders everywhere would welcome the kind of love and respect Paul talks about in today's verse. So strive to follow Paul's suggestions, and you'll be sure to set a great example for your fellow brothers and sisters in Christ!

EVENING

Father, give us peace in the body of Christ as we lead and serve Your people. In Jesus' name, Amen.

Week 36, Friday

Thank You, Lord, for the leaders who equip me to serve You. In Jesus' name, Amen.

*"And He Himself gave some to be apostles, some prophets,
some evangelists, and some pastors and teachers, for the equipping
of the saints for the work of ministry, for the edifying of the body of Christ."*
EPHESIANS 4:11, 12

The right tools make any job a lot easier. I have used dimes for screwdrivers and almost anything heavy for hammers. Nothing, however, ever takes the place of the right equipment. It is the same in the body of Christ. The members are equipped to serve Christ and witness to the world.

While it is common to refer to pastors as ministers, and they are, it is also biblical to think of every member as a minister. Imagine waking up every morning headed to the boardroom, the classroom, or the living room, knowing that you are on call as a minister of Jesus Christ! How would your approach to life be different? Would you be more encouraged to pray for the Spirit's guidance? Would you seek God in prayer with a little more faith?

Pastors and teachers, along with evangelists, youth ministers, and the other spiritual leaders of your church, have been gifted and called to help you discover, develop, and deploy your spiritual gifts. D. L. Moody, the nineteenth-century evangelist, once said, "I don't want to do the work of one thousand men. I want one thousand men to do my work." He understood the need to equip every believer to serve Christ and witness to the lost. Our cities would be affected overnight if the millions of Christians around the nation realized how God wants to use all of us in some form of ministry.

Today's scripture promises that when every member of the body becomes a minister, the body of Christ is edified, or built up. If you are a believer, God is already equipping you as a minister and will use you to accomplish His will.

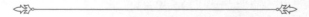

EVENING

Lord, thank You for allowing me to serve You. In Jesus' name, Amen.

MORNING

Lord, You created the church in the power of the Spirit. Bless Your church today with that same power, and help us appropriate Your power to do Your will. In Jesus' name, Amen.

"So continuing daily with one accord in the temple, and breaking bread from house to house, they ate their food with gladness and simplicity of heart, praising God and having favor with all the people. And the Lord added to the church daily those who were being saved."

ACTS 2:46, 47

For my wife's birthday, I put together a DVD of her life including her childhood, our life together, and our children's lives. I sneaked photographs out of her albums for weeks to assemble the story of her life. I looked at hundreds of pictures, and great memories flooded my mind as I reviewed photographs of our adult children when they were babies. The old saying is true: "A picture is worth a thousand words."

In New Testament times, the biblical writers used words to paint pictures. In Acts 2, the church was born in a Spirit-empowered prayer meeting in the city of Jerusalem. As a result, thousands of people were swept into the kingdom. The story of the early church could not be more vivid or more packed with fast-paced action. The story reads like the script of an action movie until the author slows to a snapshot pace at the conclusion of the chapter. There we find a synopsis of events, as if we are seeing the Lord's photo album—the scrapbook of His church in its infancy. What a picture it is! It still stands as God's personal description of a healthy church. In its infancy, the church was full of fellowship and praise to God, the favor of the community, and new people daily coming to faith in Jesus. The picture God saved of His infant church should look like the picture of our church today. Stop and compare the two. How are we doing? A picture is worth a thousand words.

EVENING

Lord, I love Your church. Help me to continue building up your people and your church so that the body of Christ resembles the snapshot of the first-century church in Acts 2. In Jesus' name, Amen.

KIE BOWMAN, AUSTIN, TX

Father, thank You for my spiritual family. Open my eyes to the hurts and needs of those I love. Help me to not be a burden, but rather a blessing, to everyone I come in contact with today. Help me to love even those who seem so determined to be unlovable. May I live my life today in such a way that I bring Your great heart pleasure. In the strong name of Jesus, Amen.

"Behold, how good and how pleasant it is for brethren to dwell together in unity!"
PSALM 133:1

Have you ever been on a trip with a group when one person in the group complained about everything and was generally disagreeable? If one person is out of step, it tends to ruin the trip for everyone. On the other hand, nothing is more enjoyable than sharing the adventures of life with friends of a like mind and kindred spirit. God expects us to live in unity with other believers. That does not mean that we are all to be "cookie cutter" Christians who agree on everything. There is a vast difference between uniformity and unity. Someone has said that you can tie two cats' tails together and have union, but you sure won't have unity.

Maybe the best illustration of dwelling in unity is a loving family. Each family member is different in his or her temperaments, talents, and perhaps even tastes. Yet, as family, we share a common heritage and values. We are to relate to other Christians as family, not only because we share the same parentage and heritage but also the same hope for the future.

For a family to function the way God intends, we have to be willing to yield our rights on occasion and to be quick to give and receive forgiveness. The same is true for our spiritual family—the church. God loves it when His kids "dwell together in unity!"

EVENING

Father, it is so easy to get tangled in the cares of the world. Keep my heart centered upon You. I give You my worries, frustrations, and petty irritations. Let me live with a higher priority—Your kingdom and Your righteousness. I rest tonight in Your unchanging and matchless grace. In Jesus' name, Amen.

Father, make me sensitive today to the needs of others around me. Use me as a channel for demonstrating Your great love to hurting people. Give me an opportunity to show the world Your mercy and grace. In Jesus' name, Amen.

"I in them, and You in Me; that they may be made perfect in one, and that the world may know that You have sent Me, and have loved them as You have loved Me."
JOHN 17:23

Alexander the Great sought to unite humanity through conquest, but after his death, his empire disintegrated. Jesus, on the other hand, united people not through conquest, but by love. After His death and resurrection, His message has continued to change lives and unite His followers.

When our hearts are tuned to Christ, we find ourselves drawn in unity to His followers. It is impossible to tune several pianos on a stage to one another. However, if each piano is tuned to the same tuning fork, then they will automatically be in tune with each other. Being one as Jesus prayed does not mean that we give up precious doctrinal distinctives. Augustine reportedly said, "In essentials unity, in nonessentials liberty, in all things love." It is easy to say that we love one another; however, love is measured in how we treat those around us who are imperfect or even those who fail us. Someone once cleverly said, "To dwell with saints above will be glory, but to dwell here below with saints I know, that's another story."

Sometimes Christians have a deep love for sinners but are not as loving toward other believers. Maybe that is because we expect more from one another and are often disappointed. If you struggle with extending grace to your brothers and sisters in Christ, ask God to help you see them through His eyes. The world is watching and waiting to see if Jesus is real and if He really makes a difference in the lives of His followers.

Father, help me to love others as You love me. Help me to be slower to criticize and quicker to encourage. Help me to be less judgmental and more accepting. Help me to contend for the faith without being contentious. Help me to be uncompromising in my convictions, yet be considerate to all. Make me like You. In Jesus' name, Amen.

ROGER SPRADLIN, BAKERSFIELD, CA

Father, draw my heart away from the pull of the world and the whispers of the flesh, and let me delight in You and You alone. In the busyness of this day, let me not forget You. Let me hear Your sweet voice above the clutter and chatter of life on earth. Keep me from becoming so bogged down in trivial pursuits that I forget that I am Your child, destined to live with You forever. In Jesus' name, Amen.

"One thing I have desired of the LORD, that will I seek: that I may dwell in the house of the LORD all the days of my life, to behold the beauty of the LORD, and to inquire in His temple."
PSALM 27:4

The psalmist declared, "One thing I have desired." Our problem is not always the lack of desire for an intimate relationship with God, but rather that we have numerous competing desires. God is reduced to an item on our to-do list or a line on our daily calendar. One of the keys to spiritual contentment is reducing and focusing our desires.

One Saturday I was bored. I must have been, because I watched a British TV program about growing giant vegetables for a county fair. I was amazed by a five-hundred-pound pumpkin and a nine-pound tomato. One farmer explained that the key to growing such large vegetables was to remove all of the vegetables on a plant but one. That way, one vegetable received all of the nutrients, allowing it to grow to enormous size. If we are willing to trim our desires to a singular focus upon God and doing His will, we will grow in our spiritual stature.

We are constantly pulled in different directions. As Christians, our lives are not necessarily filled with bad things, but rather many good things. The good can become the enemy of the best. Desiring God and taking time to worship Him along with other believers must remain a top priority for those who would be content in such a hectic world.

EVENING

Father, I acknowledge my utter dependence upon You. In Your mercy You have forgiven me, and through Your grace You have changed me. You are the basis of my hope for the future and my strength for today. I bless Your holy name. In Jesus' name, Amen.

MORNING

Father, help me not to be distracted by the petty demands of the day. Help me to focus on the eternal rather than the temporal. May Your agenda for this day become mine. In Jesus' powerful name, Amen.

"According to the grace of God which was given to me, as a wise master builder I have laid the foundation, and another builds on it. But let each one take heed how he builds on it. For no other foundation can anyone lay than that which is laid, which is Jesus Christ."

I CORINTHIANS 3:10, 11

When Paul arrived in Corinth, he found it to be like a modern day Las Vegas or "sin city." He was determined that the only thing that could penetrate the spiritual darkness of the city was the gospel message in its purest form—Jesus Christ and Him crucified. That singular message became the focus of his preaching.

Each generation must learn to contextualize its evangelistic methods to its time and culture. The message, however, is timeless and must not change. The world can out-build us, out-advertise us, out-spend us, and at times, out-think us. What we have as Christians that is unique is our message of Good News. That message of Jesus' death and resurrection is the foundation of the church.

Jesus is the foundation of the church and of an individual's life as well. Foundation work is hidden work. No one looks at the architecture of a beautiful building and becomes enamored with the foundation. If we are not careful, we will invest our whole life in the outward and visible. We can become consumed with maintaining our reputation but neglect our character, which is hidden and foundational. One of my seminary professors used to say that some folks have more in the showcase than in the warehouse. The private, foundational aspect of life is not visible and cannot easily be measured, but it is where real worship takes place and is the wellspring of both joy and contentment.

EVENING

Father, keep my heart from sin and my spirit from discouragement. Keep my mind focused upon Your Word, and may my will be submitted to Your plan for my life and for the ages. In Jesus' name, Amen.

ROGER SPRADLIN, BAKERSFIELD, CA

Father, I bow before You today, not only as the sovereign Creator of heaven and earth but also as the One who rescued my soul from darkness. Thank You for so great a salvation. I am humbled by Your mercy and grace and the thought that You might use me today in Your kingdom's work. In the name of our Savior, Jesus, Amen.

"But now indeed there are many members, yet one body. And the eye cannot say to the hand, 'I have no need of you'; nor again the head to the feet, 'I have no need of you.'"
I CORINTHIANS 12:20, 21

The New Testament gives us a number of images and metaphors concerning the church. The church is often depicted as a family. A family is a wonderful picture of love and nurture. At times the church is described as a house, representing stability. Perhaps Paul's favorite analogy for the church is that of a body.

A body is not an organization, but a living organism. There are different aspects of a body, such as eyes, hands, and feet. Someone who is athletic is said to be coordinated, that is, each member of his or her body fulfills its specific function and works in harmony with the other members.

A church is not simply an organization. It is made up of members who have different backgrounds, talents, and gifts. Some are like eyes or feet. Everyone is important. When one member of the body hurts, we should all enter into that pain. When one member refuses to use their unique abilities, the whole body suffers and is weakened. A wise man once said that no man is an island. It is especially true in the church. We are connected not only as family but in function as well. In order to be useful to God, we must not only recognize our dependence upon Him but also accept and nurture our interdependence upon one another.

EVENING

Father, You alone are holy. I am unworthy of Your affection, let alone Your favor. I come to You with nothing to commend myself except the righteousness of Your own beloved Son whom I love. Forgive my failures and restore a right spirit within me. Let me experience anew the pleasures of Your presence. In the sweet name of Jesus, Amen.

MORNING

Father, You have promised that if we ask for wisdom, it will be given. Grant me wisdom today regarding decisions that I will make. Grant me wisdom in discerning both the needs and motives of those I will encounter. Grant me the wisdom to recognize my own spiritual blind spots and the discernment to avoid unnecessary temptation. May my actions and attitudes please You today. In Jesus' strong name, Amen.

"But if I am delayed, I write so that you may know how you ought to conduct yourself in the house of God, which is the church of the living God, the pillar and ground of the truth."
1 TIMOTHY 3:15

As Christians, we are the sons of God, which implies privilege. However, we are also the servants of God, which implies responsibility. And we are called as God's children to embrace and balance both of those roles.

At times we emphasize character over conduct, not wanting to highlight good works. The fact is, character is shaped and reflected by our conduct. Did your mother ever instruct you to "mind your manners"? Such an admonition was not related as much to character as to conduct. Paul declares a similar intention in his instructions for Timothy. Who we are as Christians is important. We are God's children, not because of our good works, but because of His grace and mercy. However, as God's children, He expects us to mind our manners.

The context of Paul's admonition regarding our conduct is the church. It is easy to start thinking that piety is only measured vertically in our devotion and worship of God. There is a horizontal aspect of our faith that is lived out in our relationships to others. The way we conduct ourselves with others in the nitty-gritty of life is perhaps the most accurate measure of how deeply the grace of God has penetrated and shaped our character.

EVENING

Master, I submit myself to You. Allow in my life whatever is necessary to make me like Jesus. Help me not to waste my sorrows. Use even my failures and Your forgiveness to conform me into Your image. Let me be but a tool in Your hand. In Jesus' precious name, Amen.

ROGER SPRADLIN, BAKERSFIELD, CA

Week 38, Monday

Father, I stand in awe today of the wonderful truth that You have made me Your child, placed me in Your family, and given me a unique role to serve. I know that I bring nothing of value into the body of Christ, but in You I have been given value. I acknowledge by faith today that, in Christ, I am valuable to the body. I acknowledge my dependence on You to live out that value. Amen.

"But one and the same Spirit works all these things, distributing to each one individually as He wills. For as the body is one and has many members, but all the members of that one body, being many, are one body, so also is Christ."
1 CORINTHIANS 12:11, 12

In 1990 a brand new "all-in-one" soap was released on the market called Lever 2000. The slogan simply said, "For all your 2000 body parts." As human beings, God created our bodies with a great degree of complexity. Eyes, ears, fingernails, liver, spleen, ribs, nose, uvula, tonsils, larynx, elbows, fingers, toes—one body, but many parts. And every part is important to the health of the body. What would it be like to live without a finger or a kidney or a brain or a heart? Could you do it? Yes, depending on the body part. Assuming it wasn't a vital organ, your body would adapt, but would you want to live this way? No. You'd be incomplete.

Often in the church, we fail to acknowledge what our culture considers the "less important" parts of the body. We celebrate teaching, for instance, and may look down upon the hospitality that creates a warm and loving environment for visitors. We highlight the missionary without praising the faithful giving that allows him to be sent. The Bible reminds us that each part is uniquely assigned by the Holy Spirit and equally significant to the health of the body.

EVENING

Lord Jesus, thank You for Your marvelous grace that works in and through my life. Thank You for the opportunities to serve, and continue to make me sensitive to needs in the body that You desire to meet through my life. As Your life is pressed out in my life, I, too, will live not to be served, but to serve. Thank You for giving me life and giving life through me! In Jesus' name, Amen.

MORNING

O God, I will never comprehend the depth of what took place on the Cross! I stand amazed at the unfathomable love You poured out for me to experience forgiveness. May I never forget the suffering You endured on my behalf, and may I live today in light of the Cross. Thank You, Jesus, for saving me and giving me life abundantly. Use me today to share this life-changing message with others. Amen.

"The cup of blessing which we bless, is it not the communion of the blood of Christ? The bread which we break, is it not the communion of the body of Christ? For we, though many, are one bread and one body; for we all partake of that one bread."
I CORINTHIANS 10:16, 17

On the night before He was crucified to atone for the sins of the world, Jesus gathered His ragtag band of followers in a small, dimly lit Upper Room. The accommodations would have been modest at best, and the scene would have resembled a group of friends lounging around a campfire. In this unlikely setting, Jesus introduced a practice to those men that has traveled down through all the generations. We simply refer to it as the "Lord's Supper." At this table, we are invited to intimate fellowship with the Lord Himself and with our fellow believers in Christ in order to remember, celebrate, and proclaim all that His death, burial, and resurrection accomplished on our behalf. The practice itself is not the focus—the sacrifice it represents is. This practice is an anchor to ensure that we never drift too far from the glorious gospel.

With all our attempts at creativity and relevance, may we never be ashamed of the blood of Jesus Christ and the wonderful redemption that He purchased for us. For in this truth alone is found the power of God for salvation to all who believe.

EVENING

Lord Jesus, thank You for the amazing practice that You gave to Your church to remember Your death, burial, and resurrection. Prepare my heart for those moments of fellowship with Your family around Your table. May we sit at Your feet, listen to Your Word, and celebrate the glory of the Cross. May we faithfully proclaim that without the blood of Jesus there is no forgiveness of sins. We do all this in remembrance of You. Amen.

VANCE PITMAN, LAS VEGAS, NV

Father, I thank You today that there is nothing I must do to earn Your favor. I am accepted in the beloved because of Jesus and His finished work on the Cross. Thank You for the freedom that is found in knowing Jesus. What a wonderful truth that nothing can separate me from the love of God that is found in Christ Jesus. I love You, oh God, and am grateful to be a part of Your family. In Jesus' name, Amen.

"I was glad when they said to me, 'Let us go into the house of the LORD.'"
PSALM 122:1

Why church? Some people consider church attendance an offering to God to try and gain His approval. They think God will be disappointed in them if they don't go to church. But nothing could be further from the teaching of Jesus. My relationship with the Father is not based on my performance, but on my position in Christ. God loves me unconditionally. I don't have to go to church! Wait a minute . . . what did I just say? That's right—I don't have to go to church. I *get* to go to church. Worship with other believers is not a ritual I must perform; it is a privilege I am allowed to enjoy.

Therein lies the freedom we have in Christ. He said, "You shall know the truth, and the truth shall make you free" (John 8:32). There is no freedom in believing I must measure up on my own. There is freedom in the truth that I belong, that I am a part of God's family. In worship I am inspired to love God in richer and deeper ways. In fellowship with others God reveals Himself to me in ways I could not experience alone. No wonder David said, "I was glad when they said to me, 'Let's go to church!'"

EVENING

Father, You deserve my worship. You have brought me into a relationship with You on the basis of Your grace, and You are worthy of my praise. I long to worship You both privately and with others. Thank You for the privilege of worshiping with brothers and sisters in the body of Christ. May we worship You in spirit and in truth. May we worship You with hearts full of rejoicing and gratitude. May we worship You in the freedom of Christ. Amen.

MORNING

Lord Jesus, I realize that You want to live Your life in and through me. Thank You for inviting me to love others out of the overflow of my love relationship with You. Help me today to live in dependence upon You, so that You might make Your life known in and through me. Love others through me today that the world may know You. Amen.

"And let the peace of God rule in your hearts, to which also
you were called in one body; and be thankful."
COLOSSIANS 3:15

Paul's life message could be summed up in one phrase: "Christ . . . is our life" (Colossians 3:4). He was consumed with the life of Christ being manifested in his life and the life of those he discipled. He devoted the entire third chapter of his letter to the community of faith at Colossae to this principle. It is in this marvelous context that we read about our calling into the body of Christ. We are His body. Think about what that means. The way people know that I am a real person is that they can see my body. My physical presence provides a concrete reality that I am alive.

How does the world know that Jesus is alive? They can see His body—us! As brothers and sisters in Christ, we are the body of Christ. As He lives His life in and through us, together we are the physical manifestation of Jesus Christ in the world. We provide concrete reality to the truth that Jesus is alive. The apostle John said it like this: "No one has seen God at any time. If we love one another, God abides in us, and His love has been perfected in us" (1 John 4:12).

EVENING

Father, I pray today for my brothers and sisters in Christ. I thank You for the fellowship You have given us. May You use us to share Your love and light with a lost and dying world. May You manifest through us Your life that our city may experience life. May we be a church filled with changed lives and a place that changes lives. Unite us in Christ so that the world may see in us the difference Jesus makes in a life and be drawn to Him. For Your glory, Amen.

VANCE PITMAN, LAS VEGAS, NV

Father, thank You for the relationship You have given me through Your Son, Jesus. I know that I was not created to enjoy a relationship with You apart from fellowship with Your family. Help me to stay connected in community and experience life-changing relationships with others. May my life be an inspiration to others to love You more. Make me mindful throughout this day to pray for my brothers and sisters in Christ. Amen.

"Not forsaking the assembling of ourselves together, as is the manner of some, but exhorting one another, and so much the more as you see the Day approaching."
HEBREWS 10:25

We are commanded to gather together with other believers. Why? Not because we have to go to church to go to heaven. We are commanded to gather because following Jesus is all about relationships. First and foremost being a Christian is about a relationship with God. If we miss this, we miss everything about following Jesus. But second, following Jesus is about a relationship with others. It is my relationship with others that deepens my relationship with God. It is my relationship with God that enables me to rightly relate with others. These relationships are interdependent.

Today's verse says that when we gather, we are "exhorting" one another. This word literally means "to invite to come along." As we gather together with other believers, God uses that experience to invite us to deeper levels of intimacy with Himself. We don't go to church to go to heaven, but in one sense our involvement in a church family is preparing us for heaven. Eternity is simply enjoying our relationship with God in fellowship with God's family at a deeper level of intimacy. As you and I gather together on earth, we are getting a taste of what is to come.

EVENING

Lord Jesus, thank You for the family of God. I rejoice that in eternity past You designed that my relationship with You would be strengthened through my fellowship with others. I acknowledge my need for community and that the Enemy would love for me to be disconnected. I ask You by Your grace to grant me faithfulness to Your family. Give me the wisdom to seek relationships of accountability in my life and the transparency to enjoy them. In Your name, Amen.

MORNING

Lord Jesus, You have invited me on a mission to make Your life known. This mission begins in my family and reaches the ends of the earth. Help me to so love Jesus that those closest to me are drawn into intimate fellowship with Him. Help me to touch the generations to come by making a difference in this generation. Lord, use me that my family may know You. Lord, use me that the nations may know You. In Jesus' name, Amen.

"Only take heed to yourself, and diligently keep yourself, lest you forget the things your eyes have seen, and lest they depart from your heart all the days of your life. And teach them to your children and your grandchildren."

DEUTERONOMY 4:9

The church is on a mission! Jesus said, "Go into all the world and preach the gospel" (Mark 16:15). We understand that this mission has geographical implications, but has it ever occurred to you that this mission also has generational implications? Did you hear the challenge from Moses in today's verse? Through discipling your family, you are reaching future generations.

A great example is the life of Jonathan Edwards. Born in 1703, he loved God and became a preacher of the gospel, and ultimately president of Princeton University. He married a godly woman named Sarah, and together they had 11 children. It is widely reported that by 1874 they had 1400 descendants: 13 were college presidents; 65 were college professors; 100 were attorneys; 32 were state judges; 186 were preachers; 85 authored classic books; 66 were physicians; and 80 held political offices, including 3 governors, 3 state senators, and 1 vice president of the United States. William James once said, "The great use of life is to spend it for something that will outlast it." By pouring the life of Christ into your family, you can impact the generations to come.

EVENING

Father, I understand that Your work in the world is not just getting on a plane and going to another country, but it is also sitting at the breakfast table in my house. May You plant my family as a godly seed in this world to bear fruit for You. Lord, may our church understand both the geographical and generational implications of the mission. To You be the glory. Amen.

VANCE PITMAN, LAS VEGAS, NV

Lord, I want to start this day with You! Before the rush of the day starts, I want to tell You that I love You and that I want to walk closely with You today. Help me today to not be overcome by any evil but to overcome evil with good. Help me today to be compassionate! Help me to show love even to the unlovely, knowing that will make You smile. In Jesus' name, Amen.

"If your enemy is hungry, give him bread to eat; and if he is thirsty, give him water to drink; for so you will heap coals of fire on his head, and the LORD will reward you."
PROVERBS 25:21, 22

I heard it said once that when we harbor resentment and unforgiveness in our hearts toward our enemies, we're simply drinking the poison of bitterness and waiting for the other person to die. The bad news is the poison is only killing us, and the other person is quite possibly going merrily along with their lives. Sadly, that is the way many of us deal with those that have in some way offended us.

Jesus offers us a completely different way of dealing with our enemies. He says to loan to your enemies and not even expect to be paid back, to love your enemies even though quite often they may be hard to love, and to do good to them even though they have done and may still be doing bad things to you.

His way is a tougher way, but it is a better way, because it comes with a spiritual promise from God. He will reward us, and as a bonus has thrown in some abundant life (John 10:10). To respond to our enemies with love is truly one of the most selfless things we can do, and it carries with it the stamp and character of God on our lives.

EVENING

Lord, it has been a great day in You. Great is Your faithfulness! Please help me to be more like You every day. It is my heart's desire to die unto self and to love unconditionally as You do. Help me to love those who love me and even more importantly, to love those who don't. In Jesus' name, Amen.

ONE YEAR DEVOTIONAL PRAYER BOOK

MORNING

Lord, this is the day You have made, and I'm going to rejoice and be glad in it. I have reason to rejoice, because You have taken me out of darkness into Your marvelous light. Help me today to extend the same forgiveness to others as You have so freely given me, and please guard me from anything that might become a root of bitterness in my life. In Jesus' name, Amen.

"As far as the east is from the west, so far has He removed our transgressions from us."
PSALM 103:12

I have received a few rude and hurtful emails over the years. My first tendency is to read them over and over again and save them for later use, in case the writer of the e-mail ever tries to deny the hurtful things he or she said. I also want to keep them to prove to others just how right I am and just how wrong the other person is.

Turns out, that is a perfect recipe for bitterness and unforgiveness. Thankfully that is not how God treats us. He forgives and forgets. Today's verse says our merciful God has removed our sins "as far as the east is from the west," an infinite distance that makes our sins as though they never even existed. We need to delete our e-mails, talk to the other person, and love them no matter how they respond to us. We have been forgiven of much and have no right to keep record of others' mistakes. Extend the same mercy and grace to others that you have received.

My friend and songwriter for Casting Crowns, Mark Hall, poses a question in his song "East to West." Mark asks, "Just how far is the east from the west?" And the answer he gives is, "From one scarred hand to the other." We are to forgive others even as Christ has forgiven us.

EVENING

Lord, I don't want to end this day without telling You how much I love You. I want to thank You for being with me all day long. Please cover me with a forgiving and forgetful attitude. I want to learn to give grace as freely and as extravagantly as You have given it to me. In Jesus' name, Amen.

Week 39, Wednesday

Thank You, Lord, for another amazing day. With eyes wide open, help me to see this world of wonders You have created. I pray that the gifts You have entrusted to me will be received with wonder because they are stamped with Your touch. Amen.

"But You are God, ready to pardon, gracious and merciful,
slow to anger, abundant in kindness, and did not forsake them."
NEHEMIAH 9:17C

When I think of the wonders of God, my mind quickly races to things like the sun, moon, oceans, and other such awe-inspiring things. God has definitely created a wonder-filled world that keeps us totally amazed. But when I really dwell on God's wonders, I think about the gifts He gives to each of us. I like to refer to them as "wonder gifts." They are the special abilities we have that enable us to supernaturally encourage the family of God.

The "wonder gift" God has given me is writing songs. Since I have no real training for songwriting, it is a wonder that only God's power can explain. Songwriting is one of the most enjoyable and fulfilling things I do. However, it is also extremely frightening to be out on this long limb alone with God, fully aware of my own inabilities, yet confident of His abilities. He has brought me so far that I cannot go back and climb down off that limb, so I keep moving forward and trusting Him. At the end of the day, I hope the songs are special and He gets all the credit.

This process causes me to be very mindful of God's wonders. It reminds me that He has brought me out of darkness into His marvelous light, and it makes me want to spend time with Him and follow Him. God has given you a "wonder gift" as well. It may be in your ability to be a mother or father, in your selfless service to others, in the art you paint, or in the work that you love to do. If you're a believer, then God's power is working in and through you to encourage and edify others. You are a work of wonder that brings God great glory.

EVENING

Lord, it has been a wonders-filled day. Thank You for strengthening me and allowing me to participate in Your work with the gifts You have entrusted to me. Amen.

Lord, today is going to be a great day because I am starting it with You. Thank You for being interested in everything going on in my life. Help me today to be ready to give and to forgive, because there is no room in my heart for anything else. Help me, Lord, to be on mission for You today. Amen.

"But love your enemies, do good, and lend, hoping for nothing
in return; and your reward will be great, and you will be sons
of the Most High. For He is kind to the unthankful and evil."
LUKE 6:35

A few years after Dr. Martin Luther King Jr. was assassinated in Memphis, TN, the *Atlanta Journal Constitution* did a very interesting interview with his dad, Martin Luther King Sr. Toward the end of the article the interviewer asked Mr. King about the obvious bitterness and hatred he must have in his heart toward the person responsible for his son's death. Mr. King responded with an amazing answer that I am relatively certain the interviewer was not expecting. Here is what he said, and I am paraphrasing: "I have no room in my heart for bitterness, hatred, and unforgiveness. I am a Christian, and Jesus Christ lives in my heart and fills it. He leaves no room for anything else." That amazing statement speaks volumes about Mr. King's walk with the Lord! He obviously had spent years of daily devotion and alone time with the Savior learning God's great lesson of how to love your enemies. In reference to probably the most painful event of his life, Mr. King exhibited his closeness to the Savior and testified to the world of the abundant life in Christ.

There are many ways we can show the world the love of God. We can pay a struggling family's rent, help the homeless, care for orphans, and many other kind acts. But one of the greatest proofs that the love of God is in us is shown when we the hurting love and forgive the hurtful!

EVENING

Lord, what confidence it gave me today knowing You were with me every step of the way. Thank You for filling my heart to overflowing so that there is no room in my heart for anything else. Please help me to guard my heart. Amen.

EDDIE CARSWELL, WOODSTOCK, GA

Lord, I woke up excited because You are in complete control of my life. In this crazy world we live in, I know You will never leave me or forsake me. Please walk with me today and give Your strength to be Your ambassador. Amen.

"For the LORD God is a sun and shield; the LORD will give grace and glory;
no good thing will He withhold from those who walk uprightly."

PSALM 84:11

I recently made an amazing trip to St. Thomas with my wife, Terrie, for our anniversary. Our hotel advertised free Wi-Fi, so I brought my computer along. When we got to our beautiful room and turned on my computer, the screen that appeared was one I had never seen before. It said, "Welcome to Mac" and then asked me what country I was from. Everything else that would normally appear on my screen was completely gone. I filled out all the information I was asked in hopes of reviving my ailing computer. Once I clicked the submit button, my computer said again, "Welcome to Mac" and asked me what country I was from. All I knew to do was quickly turn it off and put it away before it exploded. I was frustrated to say the least.

I'm sure glad that God is not like my computer. The psalmist David says that our God is a sun and a shield. When I think of the sun, the words "constant" and "dependent" come to mind. It is always there, shining brightly and giving life. The writer of Hebrews says that God is upholding all things by the word of His power (1:3). One of His "upholding" jobs is to control the power of the sun and keep it suspended in the air. You know, I've never had to rush to the window to see if the sun would come up in the morning or go down at night. God is doing that. He is reliable; He is constant. Rejoice and be encouraged today that there is no need to worry that God might break or short circuit like a faulty computer. He is the same yesterday, today, and forever!

EVENING

Lord, it has been an amazing day. Thank You for the confidence I had today that You were there with me. In this ever-changing world, thank You for never changing. Amen.

Lord, I thank You that I can begin this weekend by coming boldly before You. Thank You for understanding my daily struggles and needs. You are my Father, and I am Your child, so speak to me and give me ears to hear as I spend time with You and in Your Word. Amen.

"Let us therefore come boldly to the throne of grace,
that we may obtain mercy and find grace to help in time of need."
HEBREWS 4:16

What a wonderful and amazing truth that Jesus Christ, the Son of God, came to this earth and was tempted as we are tempted. He understands our daily struggles and is intimately familiar with all of our problems. Therefore, we can come boldly to Him as His child, knowing that He understands in all ways what we are going through. I do believe a great key to coming boldly comes by coming daily and establishing a history with Him, getting to know His voice and learning to be still and listen. I don't know about you, but it seems I'm in great need constantly. Therefore, I make it a priority to come boldly to Him every day in prayer, so that when that seemingly overwhelming need does arise, I'm ready to talk to the Father and ask for His grace, mercy, and help. One of my best friends and Newsong's road pastor, Bobby Joiner, explains this idea in a simple, but very memorable way. He calls it "going steady with EDDY."

Early—If possible get up early in the morning before the demands of the day overtake you and give the first thirty minutes or so to God in prayer.

Daily—We need daily food from the Father. Have a daily plan to feast on the Word of God. It provides us with nutrition for our spirits.

Diligently—You get out of your prayer time with God what you put into it. Put forth maximum effort to diligently focus on God and Him alone.

Yielding—Be ready to say yes to God. Don't let any fine print be in the contract of your obedience to God.

EVENING

Lord, what a great day it has been. Thank You for caring about my every need. Thank You that I can come boldly to You every day. In Jesus' name, Amen.

Father, I thank You for a new day. While I do not know the challenges or struggles this day may bring, I choose now to trust in You. I may encounter people who need encouragement, projects that need attention, or problems that need to be solved. Use me to interject the joy of Jesus into each situation. Amen.

"Rejoice and be exceedingly glad, for great is your reward in heaven, for so they persecuted the prophets who were before you."
MATTHEW 5:12

Many people who were raised in church remember singing this song as a child: "I've got the joy, joy, joy, joy down in my heart . . . and if the devil doesn't like it, he can sit on a tack!" Another song says, "This joy that I have, the world didn't give it to me; the world didn't give it, and the world can't take it away." Can we really have a supernatural joy that the world, with all its pressures, can't take away? How can Jesus expect joy in the face of persecution (Matt. 5:12)?

Real joy is only possible in a personal relationship with Jesus Christ. In fact, we can think of joy as the by-product of faith in One who will never fail us, disappoint us, or forsake us. As we rest in His care, we can "rejoice and be exceedingly glad"—no matter what. In *Jesus, Man of Joy,* Sherwood Wirt wrote, "We have learned that joy is more than earthly pleasure, and to the believer even more than what we call happiness. Joy is the enjoyment of God and the good things that come from the hand of God. If our freedom in Christ is a piece of angel food cake, joy is the frosting. If the Bible gives us the wonderful words of life, joy supplies the music. If the way to heaven turns out to be a difficult steep climb, joy sets up the chair lift."[4]

EVENING

Lord, what a joy it is to know You! When I think of all the precious things You have given me and all the good things You have planned for me, my joy overflows. Keep me from the folly of thinking that I can ever find true joy apart from You. I pray this may be clearer to me tomorrow than it has been today. In Jesus' name, Amen.

MORNING

Father, I rise with gratitude in my heart and thanksgiving on my lips, for You have been so good to me. Before the day slips away, I want to stop and say, "I love You." What a wonderful Savior You are! May the words I speak today be seasoned with Your love and grace. May I love others as You have loved me. Amen.

"You will show me the path of life; in Your presence is fullness of joy;
at Your right hand are pleasures forevermore."
PSALM 16:11

There is truly joy in the presence of God. Christians can experience joy at all times, for we are always in the presence of God, who lives within us. Joy is not like happiness. Happiness is a very fragile emotion. It is dependent on what happens. It is temporary, lasting only as long as the circumstances are favorable. Joy is different. Joy is independent of circumstances. It rises above whatever happens.

Think of joy as a perspective, not an emotion. Joy is a deep sense of pleasure and well-being based on God's character, promises, and ability. With the joy perspective, any circumstance is a reason to rejoice. Consider Habakkuk's perspective: "Though the fig tree may not blossom, nor fruit be on the vines; though the labor of the olive may fail, and the fields yield no food; though the flock may be cut off from the fold, and there be no herd in the stalls—yet I will rejoice in the LORD, I will joy in the God of my salvation" (3:17, 18). Choose the joy perspective today.

EVENING

Lord, what a comfort to know that I was never alone today. You were present in every situation and every conversation. As a loving heavenly Father, You directed my path and protected my soul. Thank You for giving me joy for my journey. I love You, Lord. In Jesus' name, Amen.

Week 40, Wednesday

Good morning, Father. I look forward to another day of walking with You. Because You are Lord of my life, I will follow You wherever You lead me. Sometimes You have led me through difficult places and painful experiences, but You have never let me down. Lead on, O King Eternal!

"Judge not, and you shall not be judged. Condemn not, and you shall not be condemned. Forgive, and you will be forgiven. Give, and it will be given to you: good measure, pressed down, shaken together, and running over will be put into your bosom. For with the same measure that you use, it will be measured back to you."

LUKE 6:37, 38

Followers of Jesus are not to judge. That means we are not to be critical, faultfinding, unmerciful, and judgmental. This does not forbid upholding biblical standards. The light of God's Word is painful to the eyes of a darkened culture, but Christians must shine it nonetheless. We must hold high the standard of God's Word and speak "the truth in love" (Eph. 4:15). But we are to do this without "judging."

The fact is that judging others, pointing out their faults, and "straightening them out" comes naturally to the flesh. We have all been guilty of that. A wise person once said, "Nothing is easier than faultfinding: no talent, no brains, and no character is required to set up in the judging business." Judging comes naturally, but followers of Jesus are not slaves to what comes naturally. As He transforms us, we develop a desire to do what comes *supernaturally*! The tragedy is that when we judge others, we reject God's command to "love your neighbor as yourself" (Lev. 19:18), and we neglect our responsibility to restore those who are fallen. Galatians 6:1 says, "If a man is overtaken in any trespass, you who are spiritual restore such a one in a spirit of gentleness."

When we are busy trying to figure out why someone fell, forming our hypotheses, and magnifying their failure, we are out of place. Jesus does the judging; our job is to do the loving.

EVENING

Lord, I thank You for the mercy You have shown me today. Teach me to be merciful to others so that I may reflect Your righteousness. In Jesus' name, Amen.

MORNING

Father, thank You for saving me. What a joy to know that I belong to You! Your love amazes me. I thank You for using someone else to get the gospel to me. Help me to see myself as a link in Your chain of grace. Help me pass the faith along today. Amen.

"Now he who plants and he who waters are one, and each one will receive his own reward according to his own labor."
I CORINTHIANS 3:8

Jesus called us to approach the task of evangelism like a farmer approaches the task of raising a crop. In this verse, which refers to Paul and Apollos, Paul advocated the partnership approach to this task. Paul knew that the harvest is better when we work together. Paul started the church in Corinth by sowing many gospel seeds as a missionary-evangelist. Apollos was an "eloquent man and mighty in the Scriptures" (Acts 18:24), which means that he was a very effective preacher. Here is how they partnered: Paul planted the seeds (sharing the Good News), Apollos watered the seeds (explaining the truth, encouraging receptiveness to the gospel), and then God made the seeds grow. What a great partnership! As Paul and Apollos worked together, each man doing his part, God did the saving.

The problem in Corinth was that the people took their eyes off of God and started looking to God's servants. The church became divided, with some following Paul and others following Apollos. Paul was quick to set the record straight, asserting in today's verse that "he who plants and he who waters are one." God wants us to work together in that way. The harvest is better when we work together! As we plant and water, we are working for the same goal: to see people come to Jesus. An old witnessing song says, "You win the one next to you; and I'll win the one next to me; and we'll work together, in all kinds of weather, to win them—win them one by one!"

EVENING

Lord, thank You for the Good News that Jesus Christ died on the Cross and rose from the dead. Thank You for the salvation that He offers to whoever believes. And thank You for the privilege of partnering with other witnesses. Teach me to be faithful, cooperative, and unselfish like Paul and Apollos. In Jesus' name, Amen.

DAN SPENCER, THOMASVILLE, GA

Good morning, Father. I rise today with gratitude that You have loved me, chosen me, and saved me. When I think that the God of the universe knows my name and calls me His own, I am overwhelmed. As I talk to others, do my work, and go about the business of life, cause me to be mindful of that fact. May that realization guide my thoughts, my words, and my actions. May today be a day of uncommon devotion to You. Amen.

*"Being confident of this very thing, that He who has begun a good
work in you will complete it until the day of Jesus Christ."*
PHILIPPIANS 1:6

Today's verse encapsulates the whole Christian experience. It outlines the entire story of our salvation from beginning to end. God begins the work of salvation with the miracle of "justification," which means the forgiveness of sins and the giving of new life that puts a person in right standing with Him. This origin of salvation is thrilling and glorious, but it is only the beginning.

Salvation starts there, but it does not stop there. God continues the work of salvation with the process of "sanctification," or making us holy. God is committed to that process, even when we are not. Even when we dig in our heels and rebel, He will complete what He began. So committed is He to our sanctification that He will discipline us, allowing perfecting problems to come into our lives.

God promises to complete His saving work. This completion is the final outcome of our salvation, eternal life in heaven. The Bible's word for this is "glorification," which refers to the time when we will be taken up to heaven. We will enjoy a new body, no longer feeling any effects of sin and our fallen nature. There will be no more dying, no more crying, and no more pain. There will be unspeakable joy in the presence of Jesus forever. Thank God for what He has done, what He is doing, and what He will do.

EVENING

Lord, I give You praise for what You have done for me, for what You are doing in me, and for what You have promised to me. In Jesus' name, Amen.

MORNING

Father, I humble myself before You. You are God and I am not. You are the Master; I am the servant. You are the Father; I am the child. I surrender all. Amen.

"For the law was given through Moses, but grace
and truth came through Jesus Christ."
John 1:17

Of all the great men of history, Jesus stands alone. Alexander the Great, Herod the Great, Catherine the Great, and others took the title "great," but each of them had a dark side to their character that mocked the title.

While others have done important things, Jesus alone brought us grace and truth. Jesus stands alone. Plato was a great philosopher, but Socrates was just as great. Demosthenes was a great orator, but so was Cicero. Michelangelo was a great artist, but so was da Vinci. Beethoven was a great composer, but Bach is remembered for similar greatness. George Washington was a great president, but beside his name, you can also put Abraham Lincoln and Thomas Jefferson. Florence Nightingale was a compassionate woman, but so was Mother Teresa. Tiger Woods is a remarkable golfer, but so was Bobby Jones.

For every great and powerful person who has ever lived, there is someone whom we can argue was just as great. But Jesus stands alone. The name of Jesus stands alone in its prominence and position because He is the One who brought us grace and truth. Praise His name!

EVENING

"Now may the God of peace who brought up our Lord Jesus from the dead, that great Shepherd of the sheep, through the blood of the everlasting covenant, make you complete in every good work to do His will, working in you what is well pleasing in His sight, through Jesus Christ, to whom be glory forever and ever. Amen" (Heb. 13:20, 21).

DAN SPENCER, THOMASVILLE, GA

Father, I thank You for the glorious grace that rescues sinners. I pray that I might live in the abundant life You have prepared for me through Jesus Christ. Amen.

"Eye has not seen, nor ear heard, nor have entered into the heart of man the things which God has prepared for those who love Him."

1 CORINTHIANS 2:9

Dwelling in the deep darkness, we search for the beautiful life. Surrounded by the stench of death's decay, the tunes of sorrow saturate our senses. We look for the light to break into the darkness. The tormenting mystery of abundant life sends us on a quest for the answers. Running to bookshelves packed with self-help sagas, we unpack the finite philosophies of our day. Our eyes keep searching, our ears keep straining, and our hearts keep longing.

So God's Spirit invades the darkness to unveil our blindness with the transforming truth that Jesus came to make us whole. He unplugs our ears with the song of God's salvation brought to sinners. He fills our heart with God's limitless love brilliantly displayed through Christ's death and resurrection. And we believe!

Sin's icy grip thaws, and death's darkness is defeated. The shattered heart and battered soul are made whole. Lyrics of despair are transformed into a song of joy. The dreary landscape of a drab life succumbs to the dazzling display of hope on the horizon. Like a radiant light coursing through the night, ancient anticipation invades the darkness and fills even the corners of our world with vivid, vibrant colors.

The celebration of God's wondrous work ignites our soul with hope, knowing that He will accomplish great things for those who fear Him. And the lights shine brighter, the laughter becomes more contagious, the songs sound more joyous. We live in the radiant light of victorious salvation under the banner of God's grace. Our eyes can see. Our ears can hear. Our hearts are full. For God has unleashed His desire upon those whom Christ came to save, and we live!

EVENING

Lord, as You have unveiled Your grace, may I sleep with certain confidence that You will prepare me for a new day filled with majestic opportunities to bring You pleasure. Amen.

MORNING

O Father, may I be captured once again by the grandeur of Your grace that has rescued me from the guilt of my sin. I pray that I might remember the forgiveness You have given through the death of Christ. I pray that I might live in the abundance of that forgiving grace today. In Jesus' name, Amen.

"In Him we have redemption through His blood,
the forgiveness of sins, according to the riches of His grace."
EPHESIANS 1:7

The prison camp personified death's unrelenting carnage. Nothing escaped the ravages of the enemy's ultimate goal. Every morning brought only the promise of more despair. Every night was filled with the howling cries of mourning. Thoughts of escape were like the morning dew long since erased by the burning sun. All were captives without hope or strength to help themselves.

Captured by the guilt of sin, we are captive to despair. Dead and dying, we long to find escape and life. Each morning we chew our breakfast of tears. Each night we taste the bitterness of our weakness. We are prisoners, locked in the cell of sin and swirling in the shame of guilt's chain. Unable to escape and unworthy of pardon, we long for a way out of our prison. Then we see Jesus. Faith is sparked in our hearts by God's power. Jesus has come with our salvation in His grip.

We hear of the awful and awe-filling transaction of grace. Jesus paid the ransom for our forgiveness through His death on the Cross. He took the place of sinners on the chopping block of sin. He is the Rescuer sent on mission to set the captives free. Through His death, the cell of sin has been shattered and the shackles of shame have been destroyed. Because of my faith in Jesus who died for me, I have been set free! I have tasted God's grace through faith in Christ, and now I live!

EVENING

Lord, I have been set free from the shackles of sin through faith in Christ. I once was living in the death-throes of darkness, but today I sing in celebration of Your grace through Jesus Christ. In His name I pray, Amen.

ERIC THOMAS, NORFOLK, VA

Week 41, Wednesday

Lord God, I pray that all of my moments might be given for Your glory and fame today. I pray that You would grant me the courage and wisdom to honor You with every word, every thought, and every action. Amen.

"Commit your works to the LORD, and your thoughts will be established."
PROVERBS 16:3

The heat-robbing wind whips across the knee-deep snow, and the arctic chill bites his nose, but the little boy is unconcerned. His thoughts aren't fettered to the icy chains of the wind or cold, but they are stretching adventurously to his next step. Mustering strength and unfrozen hope, he coils like a spring and soars from his spot. Landing his two feet into the one footprint left in the snow by his father, his squeals of delight and contagious laughter fill the air, drowning out the howl of the wind. Sheer joy fills his heart, for he has followed in his daddy's footstep.

Our delight is not found in the balmy weather, nor is it lost in the frozen seasons. Unfettered joy comes when we walk the path God has made for us. When we commit our works to Him, He will add His richest blessing to our future. These are the roots that produce a life of joyful abundance. Our life flourishes when our roots grow deep into the soil of God's powerful purpose. Like the antelope in the Serengeti searching for water's life, we dive into the depths of God's desire, feasting on His promises each day. Like fingers groping for a handhold, fighting against gravity's pull, we wrap our souls around His design, finding strength to stand against the fierce winds that will certainly come.

Without deep roots, sagging limbs, lifeless leaves, and a fruitless future await in the season of drought. In the season of the storm, broken branches and tree-toppling terror pen the plot of rootless living. Our security and future flourishing depend upon deep roots plunging purposefully into the purposes of God. When we give Him our today, He will create a glorious future for us in the grip of His grace and glory.

EVENING

Father, I praise You for the compassion that You continually show me. I thank You for the love that continually strengthens me. I rest in the grip of Your grace, surrendered fully in dependence upon You. Amen.

Lord Jesus, the mission continues, and I pray that You might grant me the grace to be Your faithful missionary today, as I live by the power of Your Spirit for Your glory and the profit of all. In Jesus' name, Amen.

"But the manifestation of the Spirit is given to each one for the profit of all."
1 CORINTHIANS 12:7

Rumbling and tumbling through the defense, he knows the pain is on its way. Running across the middle of the field, he sees the ball spiraling through the wind, just above the fingertips of the defensive line. Even as he leaves his feet, stretching for the catch, his mind knows what's coming next. Padding from head to foot will not deflect the piercing, impending pain, but his focus is on the ball. The team needs him to make the catch and take the hit to move one step closer to the game's victory.

From heaven's throne to humanity's cradle, Jesus knew that the pain was on its way. Living in the midst of sin-soaked souls, He moved fearlessly for the fulfillment of God's mission. Jesus stretched out His arms upon a Cross, knowing what was coming next. Nothing would deflect the piercing pain He was to face, but His focus was on God's glory. He became the sacrifice for God's glory and humanity's rescue.

As we step up to the scrimmage line, we stand with every member of Christ's missionary team. From the blocking back to the tackle, from the center to the tight end, we have a wondrous purpose to fulfill. There are no spotlights resting on any of the team, save the Captain of our salvation, Jesus Christ.

God has called together His people to fulfill His mission. As missionary followers of Christ, God has filled us with His Spirit, energizing us with gifts, service, and activities to display His glorious grace. The Spirit supremely equips us for the wondrous task of honoring God and bringing His rescue to humanity.

EVENING

My Lord and my King, I yield to the Spirit so that He might press me onward toward the fulfillment of Your mission. I humble myself today, knowing that I exist to shine the spotlight on Christ. I set my hands and feet to work, playing my part, so that God's rescue of sinners might be fulfilled! In Jesus' name, Amen.

ERIC THOMAS, NORFOLK, VA

Week 41, Friday

Father, I exist for Your pleasure and at Your pleasure. I pray that my life might bring honor to Your name and spread Your fame. Amen.

"And we know that all things work together for good to those who love God, to those who are the called according to His purpose."

ROMANS 8:28

The seas give way to the force of the storm, felling towering oaks of water across the bow. The skies are darkened with a blanket of doom as the sadistic squall swallows hope and spits out despair. The soaring winds steer the vessel to the ravenous reef, drowning dreams and devouring delight.

Many storms develop from the atmosphere of circumstance, but we need not run away, cowering. We run toward the strong embrace of the Lord of the storm who will lift us above the ravaging winds toward victory. The storms that erupt within the atmosphere of our souls pelt our hearts with fear, guilt, and shame, and there is no escape in hiding from the pain it inflicts. We must run toward the Lord, seeking His favor through repentance and faith, depending upon His grace to restore the wholeness of peace in our lives.

In the face of the terrifying tempest, hopeless hearts can give way to courage. When the ravaging rage of the storm pillages our strength, fear-filled souls are buoyed by faith. Even as despair's darkness shrouds our thoughts, the shimmering rays of peace pierce our anxiety-saturated spirit. For we are not alone. We follow the wave-walking, wind-taming, shadow-shattering, death-destroying, rock-rolling Rescuer, and when He speaks the raging storm is silenced, the tempest trembles, and tumultuous seas are stilled.

Abundant life is dependent neither upon calamities averted nor upon the favorable winds of circumstance. Abundant life is found through the glorious work of God's grace invading our every moment. In the grip of His grace, we sing in the storm the song of His goodness with unfettered faith. In the grip of His grace, we live courageously in the confidence of His good pleasure being worked in us and His glory being revealed through us.

EVENING

Lord, I pray that You would deliver Your peace to my mind that I may remain fixed upon Your pleasure. May my heart sing of my absolute dependence upon You. Amen.

Lord, You are my King, and I live each moment fixed firmly in Your grip. You have all of me. I pray that I would continue to submit myself fully to Your will and purpose. Amen.

"For the grace of God that brings salvation has appeared to all men."
TITUS 2:11

The dawn breaks, and we begin our race through the day. Meticulously we mark the moments with red lines of monotonous movement through the completed tasks of the day. From dawn to dusk the surround sound of anxious thoughts offers no solitude in our frenzied world.

The whipping force and whistling wind of worry and confusion whirl us around. Our hearts become the playground for every fear that haunts midnight moments. The dizzying nausea of uncontrollable chaos clouds our mind's insecurity. Swept away in the race of restless living, we grasp at the slippery vapors of victory with the elusive, shrinking power of our will. The specter of surreptitious circumstances steals our hope and joy. We are powerless to escape the twirling torment of an empty, meaningless life. But God's grace has invaded the ruined world, erasing the chaos of sin's consequence and delivering abundant life. Terror and horror bow before the victorious invasion of God's grace. Death succumbs to the majestic power of life, as Jesus crushes sin and delivers rescue to sinners held captive. The brilliant rays of grace highlight the Cross of Christ, the empty tomb, and heaven's home. We who are dead in sin can now live by God's grace through faith in Christ.

Grace unveils the vibrant colors of life-giving victory and power. It is His favor and fidelity to those who have not earned either. With the notes of God's love song floating through time's passage, we rehearse the glorious song of God's grace written in the red ink of Christ's sacrifice. Our hearts find courage and strength because we remember God's unfailing favor written in the pages of history and on the tablet of our life. And as we rehearse God's great grace, our life is transformed into victorious voyage for His pleasure.

EVENING

God, I confess my failure in serving Your glory. I am thankful for Your forgiveness and pray You would once again adjust my heart so that I might honor the grace You delivered to me for salvation. Amen.

ERIC THOMAS, NORFOLK, VA

Week 42, Monday

Heavenly Father, thank You. Thank You for the blood of Jesus. By it You have forgiven me of all my sin. By it You have purchased my freedom from sin and made me Your very own. Your blood has set me free from the power of sin and darkness and now empowers me to live righteously as a citizen of Your kingdom of light. Thank You, Lord. Amen.

"He has delivered us from the power of darkness and conveyed us into the kingdom of the Son of His love, in whom we have redemption through His blood, the forgiveness of sins."
COLOSSIANS 1:13, 14

Have you ever heard someone say, "I am simply grateful to be here"? This expression of gratitude is often born out of deliverance from past difficulty. Christian, are you grateful you are where you are today? Don't think about your physical location, per say, but consider the spiritual position you enjoy because you have been delivered, conveyed, redeemed, and forgiven through the blood of Jesus.

One of the keys to living the abundant life promised to all believers in John 10:10 is the realization of the blessings in today's text. Christian, you are no longer controlled by the power of darkness—you have been delivered from it, and it has no authority over you. The Lord Jesus has paid your ransom note with His own blood, redeeming you from the power of darkness and conveying you into His kingdom. That is where you are now. Jesus is your King! He has jurisdiction over you and has given you authority over the power of sin. Confess this truth with gratitude today. Be convicted of the triumph you now experience over the power of darkness because you have been delivered from its power to God's.

EVENING

Heavenly Father, like a prisoner of war rescued from the concentration camp of his enemy, You have delivered me from the power of darkness and brought me into the kingdom of Your Son. Thank You that You rescued me. I am even more grateful that I now belong to You. Thank You for redeeming me through the blood of Jesus and for forgiving me for all my sins. Amen.

MORNING

Heavenly Father, I begin my day knowing I am not alone. You desire fellowship with me and made our relationship possible through the Cross of Your Son, Jesus Christ. I am humbled at the thought of Your presence. I am thankful that You will never leave me or forsake me. I will live today consciously aware of Your presence in my life and in every situation I encounter. Thank You for the assurance of everlasting life in heaven, where I will enjoy Your presence forever. Amen.

"In My Father's house are many mansions; if it were not so, I would have told you. I go to prepare a place for you. And if I go and prepare a place for you, I will come again and receive you to Myself; that where I am, there you may be also."
JOHN 14:2, 3

A few days ago a friend of mind described how he was awaken from sleep and reminded of the words of Jesus in this text, in particular, "If it were not so, I would have told you." I had no idea when he relayed what the Holy Spirit had recalled from the Scripture memory bank of his heart that he would a few days later leave this world and be present with the Lord. It is obvious now that my friend was comforted with this assurance, and so are we. These words of Jesus were meant for comfort.

The disciples were reeling at the revelation that their Lord was leaving. Had it not been for hearing His purpose for leaving, the disciples would have been distraught. He was going to prepare a place, a real place, for them so they could be with Him forever.

Christian, be comforted today—Jesus is preparing a place for you so that where He is you can be also. Living with Jesus in heaven is our future reality, but His presence with us is our present reality. Therefore, live today in full assurance of His never ceasing presence. You are never alone.

EVENING

Heavenly Father, I thank You that You are here and will not leave. I will rest peacefully tonight because You are here. I have nothing to fear or dread, and there is no need to pace the floor or lose sleep for worry. Father, I pray that when I awake I will again remember Your presence. I pray that my awareness of You will motivate me to make others aware of heaven for Your glory. Amen.

SCOTT YIRKA, ORANGE PARK, FL

Heavenly Father, You are so forgiving. Thank You that You put my sin away and do not bring it up again. You have said You will cast my sins into the depth of the sea (Mic. 7:19). Thank You for dealing with me in Your love and compassion. Grant me grace to do the same for others today for Your glory. In Jesus' name, Amen.

"See that no one renders evil for evil to anyone,
but always pursue what is good both for yourselves and for all."
1 THESSALONIANS 5:15

This is the motto for some: "I don't get mad; I get even." The truth is, it is natural to want to get mad and seek retribution. There is something about anger that is enjoyable for a season. Like all sin, however, anger also becomes regrettable. There should be no surprise that we suffer evil treatment. Paul expected it, Jesus warned us of it (Luke 6:22), and we will experience it.

When we are treated poorly, we may be tempted to retaliate or to slink into passive-aggressive behavior. This is contrary to Scripture, Christ, and our new nature. So are we just to internalize our feelings and bottle up our anger? No, not at all; instead, we are to respond. We are to respond with good and not with evil.

Do you like this command? Sure you do. You like that God does not give you what you deserve. You may have someone in mind right now that does not deserve even the time of day from you. What does God say? See to it that you pursue good for that person; it is good for you and good for all. Christian, we never have the right to be unkind to anyone—no matter what.

EVENING

Father, You are good. As I reflect on Your kindness today, I am so appreciative of Your care for me. I do not deserve Your care, but I thank You that You do care for me more than I can know. You told me I can cast all my burdens on You because You care for me. Thank You that You pursue good for me, even when I feel so undeserving. I can rest well tonight, knowing You have planned my tomorrow with great care. In Jesus' name, Amen.

MORNING

Heavenly Father, I am what I am by Your grace. I am saved because of Your grace and can live for Your glory because of Your grace. I shudder to think where I would be apart from Your grace. Today I need Your grace to strengthen and to guard me. Let my speech be seasoned with grace, my attitude motivated by grace, and my actions directed by grace alone. I pray that I would extend Your grace to others, as You have been so gracious to me. Amen.

"But He gives more grace. Therefore He says:
'God resists the proud, but gives grace to the humble.'"
JAMES 4:6

Our salvation is by grace alone (Eph. 2:8, 9). No one in heaven is boasting about how they got there. No, there's no bragging in heaven—only humble, grateful praise directed to the Father and the Lamb. That is God's will in heaven, and may it be done on earth. God saves us and fits us for heaven by grace and then requires we live by that grace here. Therefore, we are promised more grace as we humble ourselves.

We are also told God resists, or opposes, the proud. What do we have to be proud of anyway? All we have is from God by His grace. Have we learned anything without being taught by someone? Can we think fast, run fast, or throw fast without God endowing that ability? He resists the proud, but He gives more grace to the humble. The one dependent on God will not be disappointed. The one who thinks life can be lived independently of God will be humiliated. Which would you rather be? Humble or humiliated? A humble man seeks the Lord in prayer, submits to the Lord's will found in His Word, and gives glory to the Father for everything.

EVENING

Heavenly Father, I am learning more each day of my need for You in every situation I find myself in. My outer man is growing weaker, but I know You desire to strengthen me inwardly. So Lord, make my desire for worldly status and success diminish and my craving for inward holiness and outward witness increase by Your grace. I cannot accomplish this on my own. Without You, I can do nothing. In Jesus' name, Amen.

Week 42, Friday

MORNING

Heavenly Father, thank You for choosing me before the foundation of the world. You have made me holy by making "Him who knew no sin" to be sin for me, that I might "become the righteousness of God in Him" (2 Cor. 5:21). Make me more assured of my present relationship with You through the power of Your Word today. In Jesus' name, Amen.

"He chose us in Him before the foundation of the world,
that we should be holy and without blame before Him in love."
EPHESIANS 1:4

Do you see yourself as holy and without blame before Him in love? Assurance of our life in Christ is another key to the abundant life. How can a Christian walk in the assurance of Christ? By seeing yourself as He sees you. Too many Christians fail to see who they are in Christ. They succeed, however, in focusing on their failures and sins. As a result, they believe the lie spewed from the devil when he tells them, "Because you sinned, you are still in your sin; because you failed, you are a failure."

Christian, you are not to believe those lies for a millisecond. Believe God; believe the truth. God chose you and has made you holy, and you are without blame before Him. Believe it and confess it today. If you know that He has made you holy, then you will be motivated to live a holy life. We will fail at times to live in complete holiness. That does not change our position *in Christ.* Just because we have failed does not mean that He has failed. He has placed you in Christ, and He considers you without blame. Today, focus on His success—not your failure.

EVENING

Heavenly Father, today I have been reminded of what You have accomplished in my life. You have made me right before You. You are continuing the process of conforming me into the image of Your Son through sanctification. You have made me holy in Your sight, and You are enabling me to practice holiness as a result. I agree with You about my sin today. My choosing to sin is not in keeping with my new life in You. I desire to live a holy life for You because You so love me and are coming back for me. In Jesus' name, Amen.

Heavenly Father, thank You that I have not one sin greater than Your grace. Let grace reign in and through me today. You, Lord, are my Master, and sin is not. I desire You to master me today. Thank You for Your amazing, infinite grace. In Jesus' name, Amen.

"Moreover the law entered that the offense might abound. But where sin abounded, grace abounded much more, so that as sin reigned in death, even so grace might reign through righteousness to eternal life through Jesus Christ our Lord."

ROMANS 5:20, 21

Sin is strong, as strong as death. Adam's one sin plunged all mankind into death pursuant to the law of God. We need a sober view of the strength of sin. The wages of sin is still death. Look at its ravages upon our society. There is so much injustice, suffering, greed, hate, and hurt because of sin. Sin is strong, but praise Jesus, His grace is stronger. As our verse today says, "Where sin abounded, grace abounded much more." The grace of our Lord is stronger; it is stronger than sin and its wages.

Some may ask, "Why then am I still so tempted to sin?" Christian, we are still in a battle with indwelling sin. For us the temptation to sin is at times strong. But His grace is stronger. Let temptation serve you instead of being its servant. Allow temptation to drive you to Jesus Christ our Lord for grace to overcome temptation to sin.

It was the realization of our sin that first brought us to Christ by grace. Let the realization of indwelling sin continue to drive you to Christ for His abounding grace.

Evening

Father, I am what I am by Your grace. Everything I have and rejoice in has been provided by grace. You desire that I extend grace to others because it abounds in me. I was a great sinner, but You loved me and saved me when I did not deserve forgiveness. Lead me, Lord, to graciously forgive and give to others—especially when they do not deserve it. Make me an agent of Your grace, and let me abound more in my life of grace than I ever did in my life of sin before I met You. In Jesus' name, Amen.

Week 43, Monday

Father God, as I begin this new day I am reminded of how worthy You are of my praise. Thank You for clothing Yourself with humanity to come and dwell among us, to do for us what we could not do for ourselves. I bless You for experiencing life as I experience it to show me the way to a victorious life in You. Help me today to do the same thing for someone else. Open my eyes today to see an opportunity to extend Your love to others that they may come to know You as I have. Amen.

*"For though I am free from all men, I have made myself a servant to all,
that I might win the more; and to the Jews I became as a Jew, that I might win Jews."*
I CORINTHIANS 9:19, 20A

How long has it been since someone in the checkout line offered to let you skip to the front of the line? When was the last time someone saw you rushing to make the elevator and held it for you so you would not have to wait for the next one? How often does someone at a busy intersection motion for you to go first? Those are good questions, but not the best. When is the last time *you* did those things for others?

Each year the Salvation Army extends to one worthy person an award called the "Others Award." It is bestowed on an individual who exemplifies a life that is lived not for self, but for others. This award honors the Army's founder, William Booth. When it was time for him to send out his annual Christmas greeting to members all over the world, Booth discovered that there was not enough money to send the normal message by telegraph, which charged by the number of words sent. William Booth sent this one-word message: "Others." We would do well to remember his simple message as we live our lives each day.

EVENING

Lord, thank You for all the opportunities I had to extend Your love today. May those that have received that love acknowledge the fact that You are a loving and gracious Father. May I never take credit for what You do through me, and may I always seek Your strength to keep extending Your love to others. In Jesus' name I pray, Amen.

MORNING

Heavenly Father, I begin with praise and adoration to You. Without You life would be hopeless and aimless, but since You came to me when I couldn't get to You, life has been filled with great peace and anticipation and purpose. My voice will forever praise You for loving me enough to provide for my salvation through Your Son. Grant to me this day the vision to see opportunities to share that love with others. Because of Your strength, I will be successful in proclaiming Your love today. Amen.

"Therefore by Him let us continually offer the sacrifice of praise to God, that is, the fruit of our lips, giving thanks to His name. But do not forget to do good and to share, for with such sacrifices God is well pleased."
HEBREWS 13:15, 16

A young boy from the ghetto area of a large city wandered into a church one morning, heard the news that God loved him, and accepted Christ as his Savior. Not long afterward, someone tried to shake his newfound faith by asking him this: "If God really loves you, why doesn't someone take better care of you? Why doesn't He tell somebody to send you a new pair of shoes?" The boy thought for a moment. Then, with tears filling his eyes, he gave this wise answer: "I guess He does tell somebody, but somebody forgets!"

"Gossiping the gospel" is paramount as we seek to bring glory to our Lord. We cannot just rely on someone observing our worship, prayers, and praise and expect life change to occur. We must never forget to sacrifice our time, our love, and our resources if we are going to make a difference in the kingdom of God. Our lips should not only be used to praise the Lord but also to tell others of His greatness and of the difference He has made in our lives.

EVENING

Father, today has been a wonderful day of blessed opportunities to extend Your love to others. Thank You for Your gentle reminders to me throughout this day to demonstrate what a difference You have made in me. I know the results are in Your hands. May You be "well pleased" with me as I seek to continually be an effective witness. In Jesus' name, Amen.

MIKE WHITSON, INDIAN TRAIL, NC

This morning reminds me, Lord, of Your grace and mercy to allow me to experience a new day filled with incredible opportunities to love You and be loved by You. Thank You for extending to me salvation's wonderful forgiveness of my sin and the blessing of knowing You. The knowledge of that is too big for me to keep to myself. Plant someone in my life today who needs You, someone who will listen to the glorious way that You changed my life. Change them with Your power and grace. Amen.

"Go therefore and make disciples of all the nations, baptizing them in the name of the Father and of the Son and of the Holy Spirit, teaching them to observe all things that I have commanded you."
MATTHEW 28:19, 20A

Everyone is interested in what people say just before they die. On his deathbed, D.L. Moody said, "'Tis well." The last thing Jesus said before He ascended back to heaven was not about the Rapture of the church. It was not about His Second Coming. It was not about heaven. Jesus said to His followers that they should be witnesses. His imperative was so strong that there is no mistaking its importance or that it is optional for the believer. A witness is one who testifies of what he has seen and heard. Therefore, we are to tell others exactly what we have experienced as believers.

There are four kinds of witnesses: *the silent witness,* who expects people to come to Christ by watching his or her life; *the incidental witness,* who wants to casually talk to people about how God gave a beautiful day; *the public witness,* who has no trouble sharing the gospel before hundreds, but wouldn't dare share one-on-one; and *the authentic witness,* who lives life looking for open doors to proclaim his or her love for the Lord. Which one are you?

EVENING

Lord, forgive me for neglecting to seize opportunities to share Your love with others as I go about my day. Let my life be lived in constant awareness of others who need the life-changing experience of being born again. Help me "gossip the gospel" as I go through each day. In Jesus' name I pray, Amen.

MORNING

Father, You order the steps of a righteous person (Ps. 37:23), so may every move I make today be in the direction that Your Holy Spirit would have me walk. As I seek Your guidance, let me do so with the full confidence that You can be trusted to provide a more abundant life today than I could ever muster up in my flesh. "Let the words of my mouth and the meditation of my heart be acceptable in Your sight, O Lord" (Ps. 19:14). Amen.

"And you will seek Me and find Me, when you search for Me with all your heart. I will be found by you, says the LORD."
JEREMIAH 29:13, 14A

While listening to sermons on witnessing or sitting in a class about soul winning, have you ever asked why it is that you don't have the burden for the lost that deep in your heart you know should be there? Maybe you have asked the Lord to give you a burden for souls, and to date it hasn't come. Our flesh will never work up a burden for the souls of the lost on our own.

There is a direct correlation between our fellowship with the Lord and our burden for the lost. Wouldn't we be better servants of our Lord if we spent our time seeking after Him and getting to know Him? Remember when Isaiah was in such close communion with the Father and he encountered his own weaknesses (Is. 6)? After he fellowshipped and worshiped the Lord God, then he presented himself to be sent to meet the needs of the lost.

In order to maintain the Lord's passions in our own lives, we must commune with Him constantly and consistently in prayer, meditation, and fellowship. He promises us that we will find Him, and in finding Him, we will then carry the same burden He carries—to see lost souls find their way home.

EVENING

Blessed Father, the sweetness of Your presence is certainly real in my life right now. Today, as I have experienced Your nearness and close fellowship through Your Holy Spirit, my mind and heart have been more keenly in tune with the opportunity to share my faith with those You brought into my life. When I awake tomorrow, let my day begin with a desire to know You more! In Jesus' name, Amen.

MIKE WHITSON, INDIAN TRAIL, NC

Week 43, Friday

Father, today may my eyes be so lifted up that I will see the world as You see it. Your eyes of compassion constantly seek to save the lost, and it is my heart's desire to see with Your eyes. Deliver me from the mundane approach of this day, and grant me the honor of sharing my faith and Your Good News with people today. As You open my eyes to that opportunity, open their blinded eyes to see their need. I choose to live in that expectancy today. Amen.

"Lift up your eyes and look at the fields, for they are already white for harvest!"
JOHN 4:35B

Is your heart burdened today for someone who does not know the Lord as Savior? When you walk down the hall at school or your place of business or the mall, does it ever occur to you that people will spend eternity somewhere and that you have the directions to heaven? Are you cultivating a relationship with a lost person with the explicit purpose of seeing the door open to share the gospel with him or her? Have you thought about how heaven is going to be without having your earthly friends, neighbors, and loved ones there?

The mission of the gospel is simply not designated to the paid clergy. Yet we find it much easier to send a check to a missionary or cheer on the efforts of our pastor than we do to go across the fence to our neighbor's house or speak to that person at our office or convey our faith to the people we go to school with.

Today's verse says, "Lift up your eyes." It is a command, not a suggestion or a proposition. Let's show our love to our Savior through our obedience.

EVENING

Father, I bless Your holy and righteous name for coming to me when I could not come to You. Thank You for loving me in that while I was a sinner, Your Son died for me that I could have forgiveness of my sin and go to heaven when I die. Thank You for sending someone to me to teach me of Your saving grace. As I seek to pay it forward, give me the strength and power to be bold for You. In Jesus' name, Amen.

MORNING

Lord, yesterday I asked You to open my eyes to see what You see in our world. I am overwhelmed at the magnitude of the task before me. There are so many around me who are living aimless lives without hope and without Christ. My heart is heavy with the weight of responsibility that is laid on me for their souls. Raise up others with the burden to boldly proclaim the message of salvation through Jesus Christ. Amen.

"Then He said to His disciples, 'The harvest truly is plentiful, but the laborers are few. Therefore pray the Lord of the harvest to send out laborers into His harvest.'"
MATTHEW 9:37, 38

There are a couple of things we need to keep in mind when it comes to sharing our faith and seeing people saved. First, the harvest belongs to the Lord. We are just conduits of His grace and challenged to "gossip the gospel." It is God who gives the increase. Second, it is a supernatural force that raises up others to help us in the endeavor of reaching the lost. That is why today's scripture commands us to pray for others to come alongside us to go out and tell the Good News. The Lord, in response to our cry, will move toward those who need to be sharing, enabling the lost to hear the Good News.

A recent survey found that approximately 96 percent of the people born since 1970 do not have a personal relationship with Jesus Christ. That is only four percentage points away from having a pagan generation in America. Truly, the harvest is great. Pray that many will sense the burden to sow the seeds of the gospel for the world to hear and be saved.

EVENING

Father, I know that You are "not willing that any should perish but that all should come to repentance" (2 Pet. 3:9). Your Word invites "him who thirsts" to come to You and be saved (Rev. 22:17). Tonight, with great assurance, I pray back to You what You desire. Father, please raise up multitudes of witnesses to proclaim Your truth to a generation that has no understanding of what it means to be Your child. Let me model before others a lifestyle of obedience that might create a thirst in them for Your Water of Life. Amen.

MIKE WHITSON, INDIAN TRAIL, NC

Father in heaven, I praise You today for Your power, glory, and creation. Most of all, I praise You for sending Your Son, Jesus Christ, to die on the Cross for me. Help me to do what You have called me to do this day, and I trust You to do the rest. Amen.

"I planted, Apollos watered, but God gave the increase."

1 CORINTHIANS 3:6

God is at work. What task has He given you to do? Not everyone is gifted to plow and plant. Not everyone has the patience to water. Whether you plow, plant, or water, remember that no one can accomplish anything without God.

For the farmer, nothing is easier than planting and watering—it's all anyone can do. But then comes the mysterious part. The seed begins to germinate. Tiny roots go down into the moist soil. A green shoot begins to break the surface of the earth. A miracle has taken place with no explanation apart from God. The shoots become stems. The stems produce buds that blossom. The bees come, and in time the fruit appears. The miracle happens so often that we take it for granted.

In this passage, Paul planted the seed of the Word of God. Apollos came behind him and watered the Word. Anybody could have done what they did. It takes little skill to share a verse of Scripture with someone and encourage people to heed God's Word. But what miraculous process causes the seed that is planted in the heart to germinate? Salvation. Peter said believers have "been born again, not of corruptible seed but incorruptible, through the word of God which lives and abides forever" (1 Pet. 1:23). Only God gives the increase. The worker must focus on his work, trusting God to do His. This alone should be our focus.

EVENING

Jesus, thank You for allowing me another day to walk up and down the rows of Your redeeming work. Lord, keep me focused on Your work, and help me to have the spirit of cooperation with others as we labor with You. I ask You to allow the sun of Your glory to shine on the seeds that have been sown today. Please allow the rain of Your grace to fall on the soil of their hearts. Tonight, I trust that You will germinate Your Word into someone's life for eternity. Amen.

Week 44, Tuesday

MORNING

Heavenly Father, help me not to carry yesterday's burdens. I come before Your throne to receive Your mercy and grace. Help me to take Your mercy and grace with me and give it away to those I meet who are carrying the burdens of life. Amen.

"But I want you to know, brethren, that the things which happened to me have actually turned out for the furtherance of the gospel."
PHILIPPIANS 1:12

Do you remember how heavy a suitcase can get, especially without rollers? The longer you carry it, whether it is to the car or to the airport, the heavier it gets. Have you ever gone on a trip and returned with more things than you left with? Sure you have. Just as travelers pick up mementos like trinkets and magnets, we pick up memories and stuff them carefully inside the suitcase we carry through life.

Unfortunately, life does not always go according to plans. Even the apostle Paul had bad things happen to him (Acts 21:17—28:31). And those bad things tend to burden us down. We pack them into our life and say, "I can carry this" until there is no more room and not enough strength to hold them any longer. Some of you are so burdened that you can't take another step in life's journey.

But that's not what God intended. So what do you do? You set your suitcase of cares down at the feet of Jesus (1 Pet. 5:7). As you do, you'll notice there are other travelers around you burdened by the same things. Paul said in today's verse, "The things which happened to me have actually turned out for the furtherance of the gospel."

"Furtherance" is a military term that refers to engineers who go before the troops to open up the way. God can use your problems and burdens to open up the way for you to share the grace of Christ with others (2 Cor. 1:3, 4). So release your suitcase of cares and help another traveler let go and find freedom in Christ. Remember, God intends for you to travel light.

EVENING

Jesus, as I close this day, I pray for the people I shared with today, and I ask You to use my painful past to open the way for Your story of grace to set them free. Thank You for allowing me to travel light today. Amen.

RUSTY WOMACK, TUCKER, GA

Father, I come before You in the name of Jesus. I come with a heart of thanksgiving and praise because of Your power, presence, and purpose. I ask You now to fill me with the Holy Spirit that I might speak boldly about Your love and mercy today. God, replace my fear with faith in what You will do today through me. Please give me a window of opportunity to share Your story with someone today. Amen.

"Now therefore, go, and I will be with your mouth and teach you what you shall say."
EXODUS 4:12

What do you fear? In the United States, speaking in front of people is in the top ten of greatest fears. Is it true for you? What happens when you get an opportunity to say a few words for the Lord in front of a group of people, and the Holy Spirit nudges you, saying, "Go ahead"? Does your flesh just shrink at the thought of doing it? That is the way Moses felt. He lost his nerve and began to complain. He tried to convince the Lord that he simply lacked the necessary skills and experience, but in today's verse, God told him, "Go, and I will be with your mouth and teach you what you shall say."

God does not give you wisdom on credit—He will not give you timely statements to stick away for later. No, God gives you what you need to say the very moment when you need it. Why? Because it demands faith. When it comes to sharing your faith with someone else, understand that God is telling us the same thing He told Moses: "I will be with your mouth, I will guide your tongue, and I will give you the very words you need, exactly when you need them."

So when it comes to speaking up, why do we fear? We have fear because we are more concerned about how we are going to speak rather than what God wants to say through us. So when you are about to speak for God, will you get nervous? Probably. But ask God to replace your concern for yourself with the concern for what He is about to do through you.

EVENING

Jesus, thank You for replacing my fear with faith. Lord, use fear as an indicator that I am depending on myself rather than You. Thank You that I do not have to worry about what I should say, because You always give the right words at the right moment. I love You, Jesus. Amen.

MORNING

Father, only You know what is ahead of me today. I ask You, Lord, to fill me with the Holy Spirit so I can be the witness You desire me to be. I ask You to give me opportunities to share Your love with others. Amen.

"I urge you in the sight of God who gives life to all things, and before Christ Jesus who witnessed the good confession before Pontius Pilate, that you keep this commandment without spot, blameless until our Lord Jesus Christ's appearing."

1 TIMOTHY 6:13, 14

Your life is like a book that sits on the shelf of eternity, and each day is a new chapter God writes about you. How far are you in the story of God? God has a story that began with Adam and Eve and will end one day with the creation of the new heaven and new earth.

Somewhere in the middle of His story is your story, a story of redemption. While God has called us to evangelize the world, we all have to be careful to keep writing our story. The apostle Paul encouraged Timothy in today's verse to "keep this commandment." What commandment? There is no limiting context in this passage, so we would have to conclude that "this commandment" is meant in the broadest sense as the entire story of God. Wherever you find yourself in the story of God, your story should reflect His story.

Our encouragement to do this is found in "the sight of God" and "before Christ Jesus." In light of everything Jesus went through, He was able to give a good confession before Pontius Pilate. Jesus kept His story. And as Christ's storytellers on earth, our story must be completely beyond reproach, which means there should not be anything in our story to discredit His. We don't need to be perfect to share His story, but we do need to allow God to continue working on us so that our stories align perfectly with His.

EVENING

Jesus, thank You that the Holy Spirit helped me keep my story pure and clean today. Each day, Lord, as You write a new chapter of my life, I ask You to align my story more and more with Yours. As people see and hear me, may they see and hear You. With great anticipation, I look forward to tomorrow because I cannot wait to see how the story continues. Amen.

RUSTY WOMACK, TUCKER, GA

Father, as I begin this day, I ask You to help me fully believe in Jesus, to give me a growing understanding of Him, and to empower me through Your Holy Spirit to consciously submit to Him. This day give me opportunities to share my faith with others. Amen.

"He who believes in the Son of God has the witness in himself; he who does not believe God has made Him a liar, because he has not believed the testimony that God has given of His Son. And this is the testimony: that God has given us eternal life, and this life is in His Son."

1 JOHN 5:10, 11

Do you have a believable belief? What inspires other people to believe what you believe? The answer to that question is found in the word "belief" as it is used in 1 John. It is a powerful word that means intellectually understanding the gospel and submitting the heart. Simply put, as you understand who Jesus is in faith, God gives you an inner witness as you submit your whole life to Him. This inner witness comes from the Holy Spirit living inside of you. Furthermore, the witness of the Holy Spirit causes others to see through your actions that you have believed.

However, it is possible for you to believe and not receive the inner witness of the Spirit. James 2:19 teaches that demons understand the truth of Jesus but do not submit to Him. Those who do not fully believe in Jesus make God a liar because they do not have the inner witness of the Spirit. The key word in today's passage is "witness." What is a witness for? A witness simply testifies of what he or she has personally experienced. If a person has believed in Jesus, God gives him or her a personal experience with Him. As we share our personal experience with others, the Holy Spirit uses our faith as a witness to inspire them to believe that "God has given us eternal life, and this life is in His Son."

EVENING

Lord, through Your Holy Spirit, help those I shared with today believe in You. Help them to be inspired by what I have experienced by placing my faith in You. Help me each day to realize that my faith is both a growing knowledge of You and a consistent submission to You. Amen.

MORNING

Thank You, Lord, for helping me to understand that my witness is directly related to my life. Help me to be mindful that what You want to do in me is more important than what You want to do through me. Help me this day through the power of the Holy Spirit to abide in You as You abide in me. Amen.

"And we have seen and testify that the Father has sent the Son as Savior of the world. Whoever confesses that Jesus is the Son of God, God abides in him, and he in God."
1 JOHN 4:14, 15

L ove is the story of God. From Genesis to Revelation, the story is about God's love for us. We know that God loves us because Jesus demonstrated His love for us on the Cross. But the story of God goes deeper than Christ on the Cross. God desires His love to be in the believer. God is so in love with us that all He wants to do is abide in us. And when God abides in us, He reveals His love through us. The life of a believer who abides in God's love is a powerful witness for God in the world. People cannot see God, but they can see His love moving in us as we help others.

First John 4:13–15 describes three witnesses. Verse 15 explains the witness of the believer that Jesus is God's Son. Verse 13 explains the witness of the Holy Spirit in a believer's life. Verse 14 explains the witness of the believer that God is love and that He sent His Son to die on the Cross. These three witnesses cannot be separated. The people of the world will not believe that God loves them until they see His love at work in us. As the believer abides in God's love and spends time with Him, he comes to understand God and His love more and more. And unless we love those who are far from God, our verbal witness will be useless.

These two aspects of love cannot be separated—if we love God, we will love one another; and if we love one another, we will grow in our love for God.

EVENING

Father, thank You for opportunities to share with others about Your love. Your love motivates me to love You in return and to lead others in a growing relationship with You. Even though the world cannot see You, may they see Your love in me. Amen.

RUSTY WOMACK, TUCKER, GA

Thank You, Lord, for the gospel! Thank You, Lord, for giving Your life on a Cross and paying my debt so that I could be forgiven, set free, and know the joy and peace of salvation. Help me, Lord, this day to share the Good News with someone who needs to be set free, too! In Jesus' name, Amen.

"He has sent Me to heal the brokenhearted, to proclaim liberty to the captives, and the opening of the prison to those who are bound."
ISAIAH 61:1B

What a tremendous passage we have before us—a prophecy of the coming Messiah. Isaiah, under the inspiration of the Holy Spirit, tells us of the coming servant of the Lord (Is. 42:1), who will be the ultimate Preacher of all time, and describes the ministry that He will have.

He will be anointed to preach (proclaim) good tidings to the poor, to lead the brokenhearted, proclaim liberty to the captives, and open the prison doors for the prisoners. Sounds like the gospel to me! And that's exactly what it is! Note how this verse plays out in the New Testament. In Luke 4:18–21, Jesus returns to Nazareth and comes into the synagogue, where He sits down and reads this passage to the people. Note that He changes the words "good tidings" to "the gospel." In verse 21, Jesus says, "Today this Scripture is fulfilled in your hearing."

In Luke 24:46, 47, we as the church are commanded to preach repentance and the remission of sin (the gospel) to all nations. Paul says in Romans 1:16 that he is "not ashamed of the gospel of Christ." We must share it! The world hears enough bad news— today go share some Good News!

EVENING

Lord, help me to not be ashamed of the gospel. Help me to see the world the way You do, and help me to realize that people without Christ have no hope. Lord, set my heart on fire for souls, and give me a holy boldness to share the Good News with others. Thank You. In Jesus' name, Amen.

"This is the day the LORD has made; we will rejoice and be glad in it" (Ps. 118:24). It is a day that You have prepared for me. While I don't know everything I will face, You do. Give me grace to trust You for every event, every encounter I will make, and let my life be pleasing to You. In Jesus' name, Amen.

"By faith Abraham obeyed when he was called to go out to the place which he would receive as an inheritance. And he went out, not knowing where he was going."
HEBREWS 11:8

What is faith? As Manley Beasley used to teach, faith is calling those things which are not, as though they are! For whatsoever is not of faith is *sin*! Faith is dependence upon God, and this God-dependence only begins when self-dependence ends. Faith enables the believing soul to treat the future as present and the invisible as visible. Faith is as much at home in the realm of the impossible as it is in the possible. Faith is me trusting Jesus Christ to do what He said He would do in my life. Faith is certain of God's promise, confident of God's power, perceives divine design, and acts on God's Word.

By faith when God called Abraham, he obeyed. His call from God meant he had to leave home, family, and business—and yet he went! Why? Because he believed God and obeyed! We wonder sometimes what would happen to us if we took God at His Word and acted on His commands and promises. Abraham believed God, and so must we! Today, we face a greater responsibility, for ours is the greater revelation.

If faith does not involve risk, it is not faith—not from the divine side, but from the human standpoint. If faith can see every step of the way, it is not faith. It becomes necessary sometimes to do what God is calling you to do without knowing the consequences. Like Abraham, you have to go out into the unknown, trusting God. That's faith!

EVENING

Thank You, Lord, for Your love, grace, and goodness to me. Teach me to trust You, to walk with You, and to obey You. Help me to grow in my faith. In Jesus' name, Amen.

Week 45, Wednesday

MORNING

Father, today give me a loving and compassionate heart. Give me the ability to look into the lives of those who are hurting and sow the seeds of the gospel. Remind me, Lord, that Your heart is "to seek and to save" the lost (Luke 19:10). In Jesus' name, Amen.

"He who continually goes forth weeping, bearing seed for sowing,
shall doubtless come again with rejoicing, bringing his sheaves with him."
PSALM 126:6

As I think of this verse I am reminded of something Chuck Kelley, president of New Orleans Seminary, said years ago in an evangelism conference. He said, "Christians are a harvest-oriented people, living in an unseeded generation!"

Think about it—if the farmer plants no seed, how can there ever be a harvest? Truth be told, we live in the "ya'll come" generation. We send cards, letters, e-mails, and newspaper ads and basically say, "Ya'll come!" But have you ever noticed that there is no "Ya'll come" in Scripture? Instead, Jesus said, "You all go! And as you are going, make disciples" (Matt. 28:19, 20).

But notice here in our text how we are to go: we are to sow in tears, bearing seed for sowing. We are to go in the right spirit and with the right attitude to sow the seed of the gospel. We need to go in humility, broken-hearted over sin and pleading with God for the souls of men, women, boys, and girls.

Evangelism isn't as much a program as it is an attitude. Lost people know when we are genuine, when we care and really show the love of Christ. It's been said: "People don't care how much you know until they know how much you care!" If we will go with a right heart and sow the good seed, then the promise is we shall come with rejoicing, bearing our sheaves (harvest) with us. Remember what Jesus said, "The harvest is plentiful, but the laborers that are few" (Matt. 9:37). Let me ask you, are you sitting or are you sowing?

EVENING

Lord, help me to be sower of the Word. Let me see the harvest the way You do. If I need to be broken, give me the grace to be broken so that I can be a better servant of Christ. In His name, Amen.

ONE YEAR DEVOTIONAL PRAYER BOOK

MORNING

Father, as I begin this day, I choose to follow You. Fill me with Your Spirit, teach me Your truth, guide me onto Your path, and today, Lord, let my life shine for Jesus. In His wonderful name I pray, Amen.

"For God has not given us a spirit of fear,
but of power and of love and of a sound mind."
2 TIMOTHY 1:7

Paul is writing to Timothy, his son in the ministry. For Paul, the end is near, and knowing that, he writes to Timothy to encourage him to continue on—to be faithful and fight the good fight. In verse 6, Paul reminds Timothy to "stir up the gift of God which is in you." Timothy had a gift. Paul said, "Use it!"

Paul reminds Timothy he has been called to ministry; he has been set apart for ministry; he has been gifted for ministry; and he has been empowered for ministry. As Paul speaks to Timothy, he is also speaking to us. In Christ, we have all been gifted, and we have all been called to some kind of ministry. We are reminded in verse 7 that we have not been given a spirit of fear, timidity, or cowardliness. No, we have been given the Holy Spirit of God. And it is the Holy Spirit who enables us to serve God, and through Him we can overcome fear and weakness.

The Holy Spirit gives us power for witness and for service (Acts 1:8). He gives us power (*dunmus*), love (*agape*), and a sound mind (or discipline). We have all we need to live the victorious Christian life if we would learn to surrender and be filled with the Spirit of God. Let me remind you that the Father didn't give us the Holy Spirit for enjoyment, but for employment! Acts 1:8 says we are to be witnesses for Jesus to the end of the earth.

Timothy had every reason to be encouraged and to have spiritual enthusiasm in his ministry and so do you. If you are a believer in Christ, the question today is not, "Do you have the Holy Spirit?" The question is, "Does the Holy Spirit have you?"

EVENING

Father, fill me with Your Spirit; fill me with Your love, grace, and peace; and be glorified in me. In Jesus' name I pray, Amen.

ROB ZINN, HIGHLAND, CA

Heavenly Father, thank You for life. Lord, I pray that I would not take my life for granted, but rather reflect on how precious it really is. I give You this day, so use my life for Your glory, and may someone be blessed as they see You in me. In Jesus' name, Amen.

"I shall not die, but live, and declare the works of the LORD."
PSALM 118:17

A s you read Psalm 118, you will notice there is no author, and you'll also quickly realize that whoever wrote this psalm had been through a lot in life. He had been through the sifting process and had grown in his faith. Have you ever noticed that no one ever volunteers to be sifted—or to be broken? And yet, the truth is, we do most of our growing through times of trial. It is in our distress that we learn to call upon the Lord and to trust and follow Him (Ps. 188:5).

I have learned that God loves me so much that even if I don't volunteer, He knows exactly what I need and gives me the privilege to grow in His grace and love through it. If we never had trials, we would never learn to trust God, and we would never see how He brings us through them. Romans 5:3–5 has become a favorite passage of mine because I have learned that if I will keep my attitude right when trials come, then I will grow. Verses 3 and 4 say, "We also glory in tribulations, knowing that tribulation produces perseverance; and perseverance, character; and character, hope."

Our God is a great God, and there is so much He has done. Tell someone! Declare His love, His grace, His joy, His forgiveness, His mercy, His compassion, and His salvation. People need the Lord, and we as God's people have the responsibility and privilege to make Him known.

Jesus is so wonderful—how can you keep Him to yourself? What has the Lord done for you? Who else knows?

EVENING

Thank You, Father, for a mind to think, eyes to see, ears to hear, and a mouth to speak. Give me the grace to be a good steward of all You have given me. Thank You, Lord. In Jesus' name, Amen.

Week 45, Weekend

Lord, today give me the ability to see You in a whole new way. Give me insight into Your glory, and open my eyes and my heart to all that You are. In Jesus' name, Amen.

"For since the creation of the world His invisible attributes are clearly seen, being understood by the things that are made, even His eternal power and Godhead, so that they are without excuse."

ROMANS 1:20

Revelation is one reason God reveals His wrath against men. Men have been given the truth of God, regardless of who they are or where they live. If man is "without God" (Eph. 2:12), it is not because God has not revealed Himself to man, but because man has rejected Him.

When Paul refers to God's revelation, he is not referring to God's spiritual revelation of His Word, but of a general revelation through nature. Paul says that all men can know there is a God, not because they have read the Bible or heard the gospel, but because God has revealed Himself to their conscience through His creation.

Mankind has known instinctively from the beginning that there is a God. All you have to do is look at the flowers, the birds, the animals, and the heavens to know God exists. You have to get educated to believe there is no God. In creation you see God's power, God's goodness, God's mercy, and God's abundance.

Psalm 19:1 says, "The heavens declare the glory of God; and the firmament shows His handiwork." To look at creation and not acknowledge God is utter sin. And it is without excuse.

EVENING

Lord, thank You for all You have made and for the beauty of Your creation. Give me the grace and boldness to witness for the truth and to declare Your greatness to all who will listen. In a world of darkness, let me be light as I declare the truth of Your Word. Thank You Lord. In Jesus' name, Amen.

Week 46, Monday

Lord, I praise You, for You alone are God. I thank You for this new day that You have made. Today is filled with opportunities to talk to people about Jesus. Help me to be sensitive to Your Spirit as I rub shoulders with people in the world who need to know about the Savior of the world. Give me boldness to open my mouth and witness for You. I am Your servant who has been bought with a price . . . and I am reporting for duty. Amen.

"And I fell at his feet to worship him. But He said to me, 'See that you do not do that! I am your fellow servant, and of your brethren who have the testimony of Jesus. Worship God! For the testimony of Jesus is the spirit of prophecy.'"
REVELATION 19:10

The apostle John had just been given the most unfathomable vision in Revelation 19. He actually saw the marriage supper of the Lamb, that great feast that the bride of Christ and the Old Testament saints will experience with the Lord Jesus Christ. John was overcome with awe, and he bowed to worship the angel who showed him these wonderful things. He was rebuked immediately because the only One to be worshiped is God.

What a great verse to show us that Jesus Christ is truly Jehovah God! Jesus received worship on several occasions (Matt. 14:33; 28:17; John 9:38). If He were not God, He would be the worst of the worst, a blasphemer who promotes idolatry among His followers. But Jesus is God, the One who created it all and deserves all your love, praise, worship, and devotion. He is the One we are to tell others about because there is salvation in no one else. Today's verse says we have been given "the testimony of Jesus," the greatest story ever told. Will you share His story today with someone who is lost and desperately needs to hear of His love and grace?

EVENING

Lord, I thank You for all the things You blessed me with today, the good things as well as the trying things. Let the seed that was sown through the witness of my life and my lips bear fruit for the kingdom of God. I love You, Lord, and I worship You. You alone are worthy of all praise. In Jesus' name, Amen.

MORNING

Lord, I thank You that Your mercies are new every morning. I thank You that You love me, even when I feel unlovable, and that You have a wonderful plan for me, even when it is hard for me to see it. I praise You for this gift called "today." I know there is much You want to do in my life today. Help my heart to be sensitive to Your voice and open to receive from You. May Your name be glorified in me. In Jesus' name, Amen.

"And the things that you have heard from me among many witnesses, commit these to faithful men who will be able to teach others also."
2 TIMOTHY 2:2

When I was in college, I was told that the Lord is looking for FAT disciples. What?! Yes, but it's not what you're thinking. FAT is an acronym for **F**aithful, **A**vailable, and **T**eachable. We are to be faithful to the Lord and the life-changing message He has entrusted to us. A person who is **faithful** will not shirk his responsibilities—he will not go AWOL when the going gets tough. This person will stand up and be counted, regardless of the circumstances. Are you faithful? Are you **available**? Are you ready in season and out of season for the Lord? When God asks you to do something, to go out of your way to talk to someone about Jesus, are you available to do His will, or does your agenda trump His? And how about **teachable**? A teachable person is open to correction and rebuke. A teachable person says, "I don't have this all figured out. I have lots of room to learn and grow. Teach me, Lord!"

Without a doubt, we are to be FAT disciples and invest our lives helping others become FAT disciples so that together we can reach the world for Jesus, one heart at a time.

EVENING

Father, today had its share of ups and downs. Thank You that You were with me through it all. Lord, I want You to make me more like Jesus. I want to take seriously the call to be a FAT disciple who invests his life in making disciples and helping people come to know You and grow in You. Have Your way in me, Lord. I surrender all to You. Amen.

Lord, it is such a privilege to be able to call You Father. It is unfathomable that I am truly Your child, bought with a great price, the very blood of Jesus. I don't deserve one drop of Your mercy and grace, but thank You, Lord, for giving so richly to me. Help me to hear Your voice today and respond with swift obedience. You have a wonderful plan for me, and I choose Your ways over my ways. In Jesus' name, Amen.

"The word came to Jeremiah from the LORD, saying: 'Arise and go down to the potter's house, and there I will cause you to hear My words.'"

JEREMIAH 18:1, 2

Some years ago, I preached a sermon on this passage in Jeremiah on the potter and the clay. For my research, I went down to the potter's house (i.e., my friend, Catherine, who taught pottery). She taught me how to work the potter's wheel. After a couple of hours at the wheel, I learned two tremendous lessons: (1) Working on the wheel is *great* fun. (2) The clay must be soft and pliable for the potter to make what he desires. (Hard, stubborn clay is difficult to work with because it does not easily go in the direction the potter desires.)

God, our heavenly Potter, takes great delight in working on you and me, the earthly clay. We are not a chore and a burden to Him; we are His very own sons and daughters whom He loves to mold and shape. Our challenge as followers of Jesus is to be soft and pliable in the Lord's hands—to obey Him the instant He nudges us in a particular direction. Remember, the Lord's ways are always right. Yield to Him, even if it seems scary. He will make you into something beautiful if you will simply trust Him.

EVENING

Lord, I stand amazed that You, the great God of the universe, would love me, take delight in me, and sing over me (Zeph. 3:17). As hard as that is to believe, I do believe it. Lord, I thank You that You are working to make me like You. You are forming me and shaping me. May my life bring You great glory and bring people to You as I let You have Your way and shine through me. I love You, Jesus. Amen.

Lord, I praise You because You have done so much for me. You have forgiven me of all my sins and taken up residence in me. You have given me a story to tell of Your love and grace. May I not hide this story for fear of what people may think of me. May I open my mouth and take a stand for You this day as You give me opportunities. I want to be used for Your glory. In Jesus' name, Amen.

"I will deliver you from the Jewish people, as well as from the Gentiles, to whom I now send you, to open their eyes, in order to turn them from darkness to light."
ACTS 26:17, 18A

Prisoner Paul stood before King Agrippa, Governor Festus, and a host of other prominent men of the city of Caesarea. He was given the opportunity to speak, and before an unbelieving crowd, Paul gave a great witness for the Lord Jesus. What did Paul share? He simply shared what happened to him and what the Lord had done in his life.

Like Paul, Jesus Christ has called you and me to tell others about Him and be His witnesses. Now what exactly does a witness do? Does he have to know all the answers to all the hard questions about God and suffering children and the pagans in the remotest jungle who have never heard the name of Jesus? No! He simply tells what he saw, what he heard, and what he personally experienced. There are unsaved people in your life who may argue with you about the veracity of the Bible, but they can't really argue with you about your own personal testimony. They can't argue with what you have personally experienced with the Lord. Your witness has great power to influence people for Christ. Would you make a priority today of sharing your testimony with someone who is without Jesus?

EVENING

Lord, thank You for the person(s) I was privileged to share with today. May my witness make a difference. May the people in my life who do not have a personal relationship with You come to know You as they see Jesus in me. Give me a heart that longs for those who are lost and hurting to come to Jesus. In Your name I pray, Amen.

I bless Your name today, O Lord, for You alone are good. Thank You for Your goodness to me. I am excited about what You have in store for me today. I want to make the most out of every opportunity. You have called me to be salt and light in a lost and dying world. I am reporting for duty, my King and my God. In Jesus' name, Amen.

"And Elijah came to all the people, and said, 'How long will you falter between two opinions? If the LORD is God, follow Him; but if Baal, follow him.'"
1 KINGS 18:21

Have you ever tried to live with one foot in the church and one foot in the world? Have you ever tried to serve God and serve yourself at the same time . . . to have your cake and eat it, too? That kind of living is akin to straddling the fence. It is faltering and hesitating between following after God and following after your own selfish pursuits and the false gods of money, materialism, power, and pleasure. As Elijah challenged the people on Mount Carmel, God is challenging you today to make a decision. If God is truly God (and He is), you need to follow Him with all your heart. Half-hearted, fence-straddling devotion to Christ makes God sick (Rev. 3:16).

The time is now to get off the fence and serve the Lord with all that is within you. He has a job for you to do, and that job is to let Him have His way in you so that others would smell the sweet "fragrance of His knowledge in every place" (2 Cor. 2:14). Are you ready to decide? Fences make bad seats and have no place in the life of a Christian!

EVENING

Lord, I struggle with the false gods of this world. My heart is so easily led astray by lust, greed, and selfishness. Help me to live everyday sold out to You and You alone. I don't want to sit on the fence. I want my life to count for the King of kings. I want to see people come to know Christ as they see that You are real in me. Change me, Lord Jesus. I choose to follow You with all my heart. I pray all this in the matchless name of Jesus. Amen.

MORNING

Lord, I thank You for the weekend. I thank You for giving me unhurried time to simply unwind from the stresses of the week. Help me make time to rest in You, and please bless my time with You today, Lord. May I grow closer to You as I study Your Word and openly share my heart with You. You are the lover of my soul, and I put my trust in You. Amen.

"He who hears you hears Me, he who rejects you rejects Me,
and he who rejects Me rejects Him who sent Me."
LUKE 10:16

L et's face it, telling others about Jesus is something many Christians have a hard time doing. Often we fail to witness because we don't really know what to say or how to start a spiritual conversation. But the biggest reason so many of us are silent is because of *the fear of rejection.* The devil whispers in our ear, "If you talk to this person about Jesus, he may not want to hear it and will reject you as a result. It is probably better to just be quiet." Remember, the devil "is a liar and the father of it" (John 8:44). The truth of the matter is this: people who reject our witness are really rejecting Jesus and the Father who sent Him. We are called to be faithful to the Lord, share the Good News, and let the chips fall where they may.

Don't let the fear of rejection keep you silent. Open your mouth for Jesus and live your life to please Him, regardless of the response of the crowd. Remember, Jesus said, "For whoever is ashamed of Me and My words, of him the Son of Man will be ashamed when He comes in His own glory, and in His Father's, and of the holy angels" (Luke 9:26).

EVENING

Lord, give me boldness and strength to stand for You no matter the obstacles. Help me speak up for Jesus, even if it means others may treat me differently as a result. Help me remember that You have called me to be Your witness. May I be found faithful to You. Thank You that You are always faithful to me—"He who calls you is faithful, who also will do it" (1 Thess. 5:24). In Jesus' name, Amen.

JEFF SCHREVE, TEXARKANA, TX

Week 47, Monday

Good morning, God! Thank You for another day to learn about how awesome You are and what You want to show me this morning. Help me to see what You want me to see and hear what You want me to hear. Help me to join You in where You are working today, and may it change me! You are my God and I love You. In Jesus' name, Amen.

"I will also give You as a light to the Gentiles,
that You should be My salvation to the ends of the earth."
ISAIAH 49:6B

My life was so dark without Jesus! I was stumbling around looking for the light switch in different areas of my life, and then as a seventeen-year-old boy I invited Jesus into my life. The Light came on because the Light came in! Jesus, the Light of the World, came to live inside of me, and my life forever changed. He shows me daily where He wants to make me new as a person, a husband, a dad, a pastor, and a friend. What is your story? Has Jesus turned the light on, or are you stumbling around in the darkness?

Today's verse is not only a promise of what Jesus will do in my life but also a mandate of what I am to do with Jesus. I am to actively pursue getting the name of Jesus to the ends of the earth. Every person deserves to hear the gospel! No other agenda is to be pursued other than getting the name of Jesus to as many people as possible in my lifetime.

Today, Jesus will intersect your life with people walking in darkness, and you have the opportunity to show them where the Light switch is located.

EVENING

Father, help me to rest tonight in the promise that You never slumber or sleep. Thank You for using me today, and I look forward to another adventure with You tomorrow. In Jesus' name, Amen.

MORNING

Good morning, Jesus! Thank You for being my Savior and for being willing to transform my one and only life. I have no idea what I will face today, but You do. I open my hands and my heart to You. Please use me however You see fit today. In Jesus' name, Amen.

"'So which of these three do you think was neighbor to him who fell among the thieves?' And he said, 'He who showed mercy on him.' Then Jesus said to him, 'Go and do likewise.'"

LUKE 10:36, 37

The parable of the Good Samaritan tells the story of what Jesus said matters the most: love. Three different people passed by the injured man, but only one showed real love. Why did the others not stop? Because their agenda and what they thought was important trumped the desperate need of this man. If I'm not careful, this can happen to me.

Today, you and I are faced with a choice. Will I join God in showing radical love, or will I walk on by? What is radical love? It's when I see a need and meet it! I choose to live today with the realization that God is working all around me, and He will place me in the path of desperate needs. Will you walk on by or stop and show real, radical love? Remember, love changes!

EVENING

Jesus, as this day comes to a close, I want to thank You for loving me and not walking past my life. My desperate need sent You to the Cross, and I can never thank You enough for Your sacrifice! Help me to see the needs of those around me and allow You to meet them through me. In Your name I pray, Amen.

Week 47, Wednesday

MORNING

Good morning, heavenly Father! Thank You for another day! You want to show me something this morning that will change today and the rest of my life. I quiet myself and I am listening. I am available to You whenever and however You desire. In Jesus' name I pray, Amen.

"Beloved, you do faithfully whatever you do for the brethren and for strangers, who have borne witness of your love before the church. If you send them forward on their journey in a manner worthy of God, you will do well."

3 JOHN 5, 6

There is a nugget of truth that is consistent in every story of Jesus in the Gospels. Do you know what it is? He never left people the same way He found them! Regardless of their social status, they left the encounter different than when they arrived. Even those who rejected His message left changed. Remember the story of the Roman centurion at the Crucifixion? He encountered Jesus in His lowest moment, but after seeing the skies darkened and rocks split, he said, "Truly this was the Son of God!" (Matt. 27:54). He left different than when he first met Jesus.

So here is the question: does spending time with me change people? Maybe its only a minute or two in the grocery line or longer at a social gathering, but do they leave different? If you need to improve in this area, look at Jesus' example—what does He model? Show respect, listen, look the person in the eye, and leave them with hope! Today is a day of amazing opportunities and chances to interact with friends, family, co-workers, and strangers—help them leave different!

EVENING

Jesus, thank You for showing me how to express Your love to people! Help me learn how to walk slowly through the crowd and display Your care for and interest in people's real needs. In Your name I pray, Amen.

Good morning, God! Thank You for another adventure, another day to spend with You. Thank You that Your promises are just as real for me as anyone else. I surrender in this moment to Your leadership in my life. In Jesus' name, Amen.

"Therefore we also, since we are surrounded by so great a cloud of witnesses, let us lay aside every weight, and the sin which so easily ensnares us, and let us run with endurance the race that is set before us."

HEBREWS 12:1

In 2005 I fulfilled a dream and ran a marathon. It was a test of physical exertion and endurance greater than I could have imagined. Though I finished the race without stopping, I made a crucial error before the race ever began. It was freezing cold outside, and I wore long running pants so my legs would be warm. When I arrived at the starting line, I noticed the seasoned runners weren't wearing them, and this concerned me. As I got four miles into a 26.2-mile race, my legs were so hot, and I was miserable. This affected my endurance and eventually affected how well I finished the race.

I have also made crucial mistakes in the marathon of serving Jesus. I have carried people, fears, expectations, anger, etc. that were not mine to carry, and those burdens have slowed me down in the race of life. Today's verse tells us to throw off every weight and every sin that tries to trip us up—and then hang on to Jesus and run! Do you have things in your life that are weighing you down? What do you need to strip off today?

EVENING

Jesus, thank You for being a finisher! You didn't quit, and You modeled a lean and loving life! You didn't allow sin to weigh you down, and You provided us with the perfect example to follow. Show me what needs to go in my own heart and life, and please help me lay it aside. I don't want to run with it anymore! In Jesus' name, Amen.

Father, thank You for being the perfect Daddy! I don't wear You out, and You believe in me. Thank You! Help me follow Your lead today. Please help me to submit my will to Yours as You guide my desires and decisions in everything I do. In Jesus' name, Amen.

"If you abide in Me, and My words abide in you, you will ask what you desire, and it shall be done for you. By this My Father is glorified, that you bear much fruit; so you will be My disciples."

JOHN 15:7, 8

In my life I have made promises that I didn't keep, and I wish I could go back and ask for a redo so I could fix those mistakes. Have you ever felt that way about decisions you have made in your life? The good news is that Jesus has never felt regret for a promise He didn't keep! When He makes a promise, His character guarantees that He will keep it.

In John 15:7, 8, He makes a promise that is a life source for you and me. If I live with Him and allow Him to change my desires into His desires, He promises to fulfill them. Where we sometimes get confused is when He doesn't give us what we desire. The issue is not the promise—it's what I desire! It's not about Him blessing what I want—it's about me wanting what He's blessing! Where do you need Jesus to change your desires to His today?

EVENING

Jesus, thank You for another day! Help me rest tonight in Your promise that You have it all taken care of! I pray that You will continue molding my will and changing my desires into ones that please You—desires that align with Yours. I love You! In Jesus' name, Amen.

MORNING

Jesus, what a privilege to be able to speak Your name! Thank You for making it possible to know You and to have a relationship with You. Make me more like You today. In Jesus' name I pray, Amen.

"'You are My witnesses,' says the LORD, 'and My servant whom I have chosen, that you may know and believe Me, and understand that I am He. Before Me there was no God formed, nor shall there be after Me.'"
ISAIAH 43:10

My friend, Larry Brown, has a message on this verse entitled "There Ain't Nobody Like Him!" The title may not be perfect grammar, but it is perfect truth! No one can create sunrise but Jesus! No one can make human life except Jesus! No one has been able to completely change a life like Jesus! No one has been able to put a family back together like Jesus! No one has been able to make a drunken daddy sober like Jesus! No one can take a common man or woman and do uncommon things with their lives but Jesus!

In this verse, God reveals His ability to predict the future and show Israel (and us today) that He is truly the only eternal, living God. As His chosen ones, He asks us to be His servants and His witnesses to a watching world. God will enable us to do everything that He has asked of us—to tell others that there is "nobody like Him"!

EVENING

Jesus, You are amazing in every way. Every day that I live I stand more amazed of Your greatness. Help me to never get over being in awe of You and to share that awe with others! In Jesus' name, Amen.

Father, please help me today to serve You with a heart that is filled with joy to over-flowing. You are my Great Shepherd, and You will take care of me because I belong to You. Whatever assignment You have for me today, please help me to meet it with a song in my heart because of Your presence within me. Of all the titles I bear, first and foremost I am Your servant. Give me the power to represent You in the way You desire. Amen.

*"Serve the LORD with gladness; come before His presence with singing.
Know that the LORD, He is God; it is He who has made us,
and not we ourselves; we are His people and the sheep of His pasture."*
PSALM 100:2, 3

We have all had the common experience of someone waiting on us or serving us in a restaurant. Sometimes the experience is good, and sometimes it is not. Both servers may get the food to the table and take care of the essentials—refills, extra napkins, presentation of the check, etc.—but what makes one experience good and the other not? One word: attitude. The attitude of the server can sometimes be the difference between a positive dining experience and a negative one. The server's attitude may be the determining factor about whether or not we return to that place of business.

Do you know that our attitude in serving Christ also leaves either a positive or negative impression on the people we serve in His name? How we serve others, how we treat them in the name of Christ, leaves a lasting impression. Is it any wonder that the psalmist instructs us to serve the Lord with gladness? It is not just the service we render, but the attitude with which we do it that is important to God. Serve the Lord today with a glad and thankful heart. You belong to Him, and you get to represent His kingdom!

EVENING

Lord, thank You for reminding me today through Your Word who You are, who I am, and how You want me to represent You in the world. Help me to see others with Your eyes and serve them as You would. Always help me to remember that this is not about me, but it is about You. Thank You for giving me opportunities to serve You. Amen.

MORNING

Lord, help me to remember today that I am asked to honor You in my work. Remind me when the work gets tedious and I am tempted to do less than my best that You want me to work with all my heart. While I want to do a good job for my employer, the person I want to please the most is You. Thank You for health and the ability to do my job. In Jesus' name, Amen.

"Bondservants, obey in all things your masters according to the flesh, not with eyeservice, as men-pleasers, but in sincerity of heart, fearing God. And whatever you do, do it heartily, as to the Lord and not to men, knowing that from the Lord you will receive the reward of the inheritance; for you serve the Lord Christ."
COLOSSIANS 3:22–24

Compartmentalizing life between the secular and the sacred is a major problem for believers today. Somehow we have come to separate our daily work life and our weekend worship life. Nothing in the Bible, however, suggests we should do such a thing. In fact, Scripture tells us that whatever we do and wherever we do it, we should do it as unto the Lord. Do you ever think about the place where you work as the place that you also serve God? It may not be religious in nature, but God says we are to do all things, including our jobs, as though we are working for Him.

What kind of employee are you? Do you give your best each day because you realize that is what God wants you to do? Just think how God's kingdom could be expanded if every believer gave his or her best in the marketplace of life. What a witness to the watching world! Do your best to lead the way where you work. Remember, it's not just the management you are trying to please, but the King of Glory you want to honor!

EVENING

Father, help me first to remember that ultimately, I work for You. I want my work to reflect the difference You make in my life. At the end of the workday, help me to leave knowing I have done my best and honored You. Always help me remember that I am to serve You every day. In Jesus' name, Amen.

RICK WHITE, FRANKLIN, TN

Week 48, Wednesday

Lord, help me today to remember all of the benefits You bring into my life. Sometimes I get so preoccupied with the concerns of life that I simply fail to pause and remember all You do for me. Because You are the God of my salvation, please save me from my own selfishness. Help me to take the time and really consider all the good things that I receive directly from Your hand. I want to be mindful of all Your benefits. In Jesus' name, Amen.

"Blessed be the LORD, who daily loads us with benefits,
the God of our salvation! Selah."
PSALM 68:19

Years ago, I heard Stewart Briscoe speak about the word *Selah* that appears in the psalms. He equated it to the symbol in music for a rest. He advised that when we see *Selah* in Scripture, we should pause and think about what we have read.

Today, we need to pause and think about the daily benefits God loads into our lives. Benefits are a big attraction in the job market today. In fact, they are essential to life in our economy. Unfortunately some people work in jobs with no benefits, and it complicates life for them. Consider the benefits from the Lord in your life today: health, friendships, peace, power, purpose, love, fellowship, forgiveness, community, etc. Sometimes we forget all the benefits that come as a result of our salvation. Serving Jesus is certainly a joy when you consider eternity, but it is also a joy when you stop and think about the benefits He provides us with today, in the here and now.

He is the God who provides! As you serve Him today, bless His name and forget none of His benefits. He is the God of our salvation!

EVENING

Lord, when I put my head on my pillow tonight, help me look back over this day and consider every benefit that has come from You. The fact that I am able to lie down and go to sleep while You recreate energy within my body is just further proof that You care for me. Please forgive me when I fail to remember that every good gift and every perfect gift comes down from You. Thank You for loving me and being the God of my salvation. In Jesus' name, Amen.

MORNING

Lord, please help me today to remember that the instruments You use for measuring greatness are very different than the ones we use. The way You measure greatness is the only one that really matters. Please help me to make the right decisions today and to seek Your approval. Amen.

"Yet it shall not be so among you; but whoever desires to become great among you, let him be your servant. And whoever desires to be first among you, let him be your slave—just as the Son of Man did not come to be served, but to serve, and to give His life a ransom for many."
MATTHEW 20:26–28

Greatness. Do we really understand what it is all about? We live in a culture that teaches one becomes great through achievement. We are told to get ahead by being first, by being the best, and by pushing our way to the front while pushing others aside. It is rare in our society to celebrate someone for being a servant, and yet that is exactly what Jesus tells us we are to do. Why is it that service industry jobs are usually low paying? It's simple: our society doesn't value serving others. Maybe that is one of the reasons we are told in Scripture not to be too comfortable in this environment. The values of the King and His kingdom are very different from the values of the world we live in.

At one time in my life, all my heroes were well-known individuals—those who had achieved success by worldly standards. Thankfully, that has changed. Most of my heroes today are people who are unknown beyond a small circle of friends and influence. They are truly servants who seem to understand what Jesus meant and live their lives accordingly. Who would have ever thought it? Servants are the greatest.

EVENING

Lord, You are my example in life, and You are the greatest servant in the world. Remind me that serving others is what You came to do, and if I want to be like You, then I must also serve others. Thank You for helping me to see that some of the greatest people in the world are not those who stand on platforms or receive the praise of other men. They are simply servants who go about their daily lives by caring for others. Amen.

RICK WHITE, FRANKLIN, TN

Lord, as I begin this day help me to remember who's in charge. I am here to serve You. I am sure at some point I am going to forget or be tempted to serve another. I am asking the Holy Spirit to keep a check on my loyalty. I don't want to live with a divided heart and mind. Everything I have in my life has come from Your hand of grace. Please don't let me get that confused. In Jesus' name, Amen.

"No one can serve two masters; for either he will hate the one and love the other, or else he will be loyal to the one and despise the other. You cannot serve God and mammon."
MATTHEW 6:24

The sign read "Help Wanted: Part-Time." Easy enough to understand; someone has a job to offer, but it does not require full-time service. Unfortunately, we as Christians sometimes think God has required only part-time service or loyalty from us. Can you imagine part-time loyalty in marriage or friendship? To be loyal on a part-time basis can only mean disloyalty at other times. Jesus says we have to choose which master we are going to serve. Our loyalty cannot be part-time—we have to choose and dedicate ourselves to one master and release the other.

Loyalty is the main ingredient to all healthy relationships. They cannot survive a divided heart. When I married many years ago, I chose to live with my wife for the rest of our years together. But I also chose to sever any other relationships that might try to compete for my loyalty to her. We have to be clear. Jesus does not want part-time loyalty from us. Anything less than a fully devoted life is not what He desires. We make choices every day of life. This is one we have to get right. The stakes are too high to do otherwise.

EVENING

Lord, You say in Your Word that if we lack wisdom, we can ask You for it, so I'm asking. Help me to choose wisely today whom I will serve. I want my heart to be fully devoted to You. Keep me focused on Your purposes so that I am not tempted to follow after my own way. You and You alone are the one true God. In Jesus' name, Amen.

MORNING

Lord, it is much easier to read Scripture than to live Scripture. All week, as I have thought about serving You, the daily challenge to really put it on the line has increased. I cannot do this apart from Your power and strength. My natural desire is for comfort, so I ask You to help me follow You in times of testing. You gave Your life away for me; now teach me how to give my life away for Your kingdom. Amen.

"He who loves his life will lose it, and he who hates his life in this world will keep it for eternal life. If anyone serves Me, let him follow Me; and where I am, there My servant will be also. If anyone serves Me, him My Father will honor."

JOHN 12:25, 26

Did you ever play follow the leader when you were a kid? It was easy, simple, and fun. Following Jesus is not always easy; it is certainly not always simple; and honestly, it is not always fun. But Jesus has called us to follow Him wherever He goes. It means He is the leader. Following Jesus often requires radical changes in life. Goals, desires, and ambitions all have to fall in line with what He desires. What do you do when you want to go one way, but the leader says to go another way? Life is filled with defining moments, and each of us has to make the decision about whom we are going to follow.

When I was a kid I loved being the leader. It meant I could go wherever I wanted to go and everyone else had to follow. Now that I am a Christ follower, it is no longer a game. I cannot always have my way and also follow Him. Who are you going to follow today? Remember, it is really important to follow the One you have called Leader in your life.

EVENING

Lord, I confess my struggle in following You. Something within me wants to believe that I know what is best for my life. Help me to remember all the tools You have given me to be a good follower: Your Word, Your Spirit, and Your church. Lord, forgive me when I stray off the path, and please provide Your light to help me find Your way again. Amen.

RICK WHITE, FRANKLIN, TN

Week 49, Monday

Oh, the wonder and joy that is mine when I hear Your voice, Oh God! I hear You speak through the written words of Your Holy Scripture. I hear You speak through Your Holy Spirit within me. I hear Your gentle whisper, Your still, small voice. Speak, Lord, Your servant is listening. In Jesus' name, Amen.

"But He said, 'More than that, blessed are those who hear the word of God and keep it!'"
LUKE 11:28

The blessings of servanthood begin in the intimacy of a personal relationship with God and the communication intrinsic to it. While God wants us to talk to Him, today's verse says there is a special blessing in learning to listen first while He speaks to us. This blessing is a superior blessing derived from a contrast, a progression, and a choice. It is the contrast between a momentary, mountaintop, spiritual experience and the day-to-day routine of faithful living in the valley of life. It is the progression from good to great and from better to best that reflects the pursuit of excellence and brings the realization of that which is superior. It is the choice between what simply occurs or naturally comes our way and what we purposefully seek with every fiber of our being.

This blessing is also a conditional blessing dependent on what we do once we hear the Word of God. We are to observe it, obey it, keep it, and practice it. We do so by acknowledging that the One who speaks is the One to be obeyed. We do so by yielding, submitting, and humbling ourselves to Him who speaks. We do so by willingly sacrificing our selfish desires for God's perfect plans, purposes, and will. We do so by loving—with all our heart, soul, mind, and strength—the One who loved us first and most. And we do so by making it our goal to please Him who speaks.

To do so is a tribute to God—to who He is and what He's done. To do so is a testimony to God—of our love for Him.

EVENING

Jesus, You are the Living Word of God. As the Shepherd of my soul, I commit to hearing, knowing, and following Your voice. Transform me and bring me into conformity with Your Holy Word and perfect will. Jesus, make me like You. Amen.

MORNING

I can't! Life is hard. Times are tough. Pressures are great. Needs are many. I can't! I am weak. I am weary. I have failed. I can't go on. Did You say, "Take a step"? I can't! Help me, God!

"I can do all things through Christ who strengthens me."
PHILIPPIANS 4:13

The blessings of servanthood continue with a realization of personal dependence on God and an infusion of His strength for any and every situation. The emphasis in today's familiar verse is not on "I can," but on "Christ who." Jesus Christ, God in the flesh, is none other than the Great I AM. He spoke the world into existence. It was His staff that brought plagues upon Egypt and deliverance to Israel. He invaded our earthly existence through His virgin birth in a manger. He changed water to wine, healed infirmities and afflictions, fed thousands, calmed storms, and walked on water. He even raised the dead. Ultimately, He decisively defeated sin and Satan at the Cross and through His resurrection from the dead. He is "Christ who," and He places all that He is and has within us!

As great a truth as that is, it comes with two humbling realizations: we *are* nothing apart from Him, and we *have* nothing apart from Him. The very breath of life is His to impart. Every aspect of our sustenance and provision is from His hand. All our protection and our very survival are from Him. Correspondingly, any activity in which we engage, any endeavor we undertake, and any accomplishment or achievement we realize is, equally, of and from Him. We are totally dependent on Him. We can do nothing apart from Him.

But with Him—in and through His strength that works mightily within us—we can! We can face the challenges of each and every day. We can run the race of life with perseverance and hope. We can live, really live, without the regret of yesterday or a longing for tomorrow, but with contentment—even joy—in whatever circumstances God places us. Truly, through Christ we can do all things!

EVENING

I can! Not in and of myself. But through You I can! Through humble, willing dependence on and confidence in God I can! Because He can. "I can do all things through Christ who strengthens me." Thank You, God!

BOB PERRY, THE VILLAGES, FL

Week 49, Wednesday

Jesus, You have shown me the full extent of Your love. You have washed me—cleansed me—by the sacrifice of Your blood. Moreover, You have filled me with every spiritual blessing. And You have secured my eternal destiny in heaven with You forever. Thank You, Jesus. Now, how shall I live? What can I do in response to all that You have done for me? Show me, O Lord, what is required of me today. Amen.

"For I have given you an example, that you should do as I have done to you. Most assuredly, I say to you, a servant is not greater than his master; nor is he who is sent greater than he who sent him. If you know these things, blessed are you if you do them."

JOHN 13:15–17

The blessing is in the doing! There is a place for contemplation and meditative reflection. There is a time for learning and instruction, training and equipping. But there is also a time and place for going and doing. And the word of Jesus—in this text and for this day—is that the blessing is in the doing! But what is the doing that we are to do? Jesus, the Master Teacher, has trained and taught us well. He has given us mountaintop moments of instruction and insight. But He has also led us into the valley of everyday living and shown us plainly and clearly, by His own example, just what we must do: serve other people.

Serve. Take up the towel and basin. Stoop in humility and lovingly wash the feet of those dirtied by life. See a need. Meet a need.

Serve Others. It's not about us—Jesus has already served us. In this context Jesus does not ask us to serve Him. It's about others—those who are loveable, those who are difficult to love, those who are near to God, and those who are far from Him.

Serve Other People. They matter most to God. And, therefore, they matter most to us. Make people the focus of your service. Serve other people, and you will receive the blessings of servanthood.

EVENING

Jesus, I seek the blessings of servanthood. May Your example sufficiently motivate me to serve other people—in Your name and for Your glory. Amen.

I delight in You, Lord. The thought of You brings a smile to my life. The sight of You smiling at me brings joy to my life. In the morning, I am eager to talk with You. Throughout the day, I choose to walk with You. All through the night, I rest in Your presence. God, You are my delight! Amen.

"Delight yourself also in the LORD, and He shall give you the desires of your heart."
PSALM 37:4

Delight is something we are to do. It is qualified by "also," implying that our delight is to be expanded beyond its present capacity and dimensions to include more than that in which we currently delight. We are to make room for something else, something more, and even something better. Furthermore, our delight is to be "in the LORD." It is to include the Lord and be focused on Him. How do we do that?

We delight ourselves in the Lord by rejoicing in God and the things of God. We don't just long for them and seek after them, but we relish in our experience of them. We see Him at every turn. We hear Him in every thought. We sense His presence and prompting in every circumstance and situation. And we revel in all of it!

Desires are things we want to receive. Desires of the heart are serious, not flippant, substantive, even enduring. The Lord is to grant these desires, so since they are from Him, they are of Him in type and character.

So how do we receive our desires from Him? We recognize and acknowledge the circular or cyclical thought process intrinsic to the psalmist's instruction. Our desires become our delights, and our delights become our desires. In God, what we are to do—delight—and what we are to receive—desires—become one and the same thing. By aligning our delights with God, He willingly grants our desires. Thus, the blessing of God—another blessing of servanthood—is His giving us the desires of our heart.

EVENING

God in whom I delight, You have given me the desires of my heart. You are all that I long for and all that I live for. And You have graciously given Yourself to me—in the person of Your Son and the presence of Your Spirit. Thank You, God. Amen.

Week 49, Friday

O God, I hear there is deliverance in You. I hear there is refuge in You. I hear that grace and mercy are found in You. I hear that kindness and goodness abound in You. May I experience it for myself—taste it and see it—that I, too, might trust in You and be blessed by You. Amen.

"Oh, taste and see that the LORD is good; blessed is the man who trusts in Him!"
PSALM 34:8

There is an invitation extended to each one of us. The psalmist presents it, but God endorses it. It is as if God Himself says, "Taste and see! Try Me out and discover for yourself." If we will accept the invitation, we will personally experience what countless people have already realized. God is good!

While God's goodness is not the sum of His character, it is a realization shared by all who accept His invitation to "taste and see." As we are prone to say, "It is good!" when first tasting a special meal or a delectable dessert, so we are prompted to say, "He is good!" when we "taste" God. As we might say, "It is good!" to describe an enjoyable experience to someone considering sharing in it, so we might describe our experience of God to someone considering sharing in it—"He is good!"

God's goodness stands in contrast to the common misperception that God is not good. Satan has perpetuated the myth that God is mean, vindictive, and out to "get" us. He has further fostered the notion that God does not have our best interest at heart but, rather, capriciously and unlovingly inflicts mere mortals with pain and suffering. Nothing could be further from the truth! When "tasted," God is always found to be good.

What are we to do once we discover God is good? Trust Him. Mentally believe in Him. Emotionally rely on Him. Spiritually take refuge in Him. Physically run to Him. Trust Him and receive His blessing—another of the blessings of servanthood.

EVENING

I praise You, God, for Your goodness! I have experienced it myself and have discovered that You are good—You are good to me! Your goodness prompts me to trust You, fully and completely. And in that I am truly blessed. Thank You, God! Amen.

Gracious and generous heavenly Father, I am rich in You. Whatever measure of earthly wealth I have—great or small, much or little—it is a blessing from Your hand. How should one so blessed live? I ask You to instruct me today. In Jesus' name, Amen.

"Let them do good, that they be rich in good works, ready to give, willing to share, storing up for themselves a good foundation for the time to come, that they may lay hold on eternal life."
1 TIMOTHY 6:18, 19

The blessings of servanthood not only come to us, they also flow through us. God's blessing upon us is never to be an end in itself. We are to serve as a conduit of God's blessings to others. Nowhere is this truer than in regard to material blessings—wealth, riches, and the "stuff" of earthly life.

God, through the apostle Paul, instructs us to "give" and to "share" in order to "do good." The challenge is to be generous and unselfish toward others as God has been generous and unselfish toward us. In doing so, the good that is accomplished is reflective of the goodness of God. In essence, Paul is saying to us, "Be good like God. Be generous toward others, and unselfishly give to and share with others all that God has unselfishly given to and shared with you."

As the blessings of servanthood flow through us, they also accrue to us for all of eternity. The Christlike generosity we exhibit while on earth reinforces the eternal life that awaits us in heaven. By using earthly riches, which are uncertain and insecure, to do the good that God would do for others, we prepare a "good foundation" and "lay hold" of heavenly treasure that is certain and secure for all eternity. Such a promise for the future is the ultimate blessing. Such a life lived right now is the ultimate life.

EVENING

God, here and now, I pledge to live like Zacchaeus, who gave generously to others; like Mary, the sister of Martha, who gave extravagantly; like the famous, unnamed widow, who gave sacrificially; and like Barnabas, who gave encouragingly. May the blessings of servanthood flow through me in this life and to me in eternal life. I pray this in the name of Him who gave His all for me, Jesus Christ. Amen.

BOB PERRY, THE VILLAGES, FL

Week 50, Monday

Father, it's a new day with new opportunities. Thank You for this day that You have set me free to live through Jesus. Thank You for confidence to walk in this freedom today. May I see it and live it—today! Amen.

"Stand fast therefore in the liberty by which Christ has made us free, and do not be entangled again with a yoke of bondage."
GALATIANS 5:1

Freedom . . . what an amazing word, what a beautiful meaning! I'm always reminded of freedom when my kids get helium balloons at restaurants. On our way out to the car, they let them go, and the balloons race to the skies. What picture or illustration or memory comes to your mind when you think about freedom?

At times in our lives we have defined freedom as doing what we want, when we want it, but that's not true freedom—that actually binds us to a cycle of rebellion that will always end in regret. True freedom is found only in surrender. When we surrender our lives to our Creator and heavenly Father through faith in Jesus Christ, we are set free—from our past, present, and future sin, our rebellion, our religion, our "good enough" lists, and our promises to do better next time.

And this is what gives us confidence to "stand fast" in this freedom we have in Christ: He made us free—not our good works, church attendance, or good intentions. And if I didn't earn it, then there is nothing I can do to keep it, so I am no longer bound to live in "bondage" to my own rebellion or my religious performance. I am free!

So where does that leave me? I am free to love, free to give, free to serve. Not because I "have to" but because I am free in Christ. And when you and I realize who we are *in* Christ, it will be the pure motivating factor for what we do *for* Christ.

EVENING

Jesus, You set me free—thank You. Help me to not just realize this freedom, but to rest in it and live in it, as I love, give, and serve those around me. I love You, Jesus! Amen.

MORNING

Heavenly Father, I am weak and You are strong. Today, I surrender my heart, mind, and will to You. It is You who works in me and You who will accomplish Your will in my life. I choose to allow You to work in me today, to make my life pleasing to You. Teach me through this scripture today that it's You who works and You who receives the glory. Anything I try to do on my own will be exactly that—on my own—and all that I allow You to do will bring me rest and true joy. Open my heart and mind today as I hear from You. Amen.

"Now may the God of peace who brought up our Lord Jesus from the dead, that great Shepherd of the sheep, through the blood of the everlasting covenant, make you complete in every good work to do His will, working in you what is well pleasing in His sight, through Jesus Christ, to whom be glory forever and ever. Amen."
HEBREWS 13:20, 21

Take a few moments and break down these verses in sections that you can digest—maybe write each one down. What words or phrases or themes of God's character and promises stand out to you? Maybe it is the truth that God is peace, or that His power raised Jesus from the dead, or that God's covenant cannot be broken, or that He will complete you and that's not your job, or that God is the One who gets the glory. Why was that attribute or promise of God meaningful to you right now? Take a moment and allow that to soak in, and then thank God for the truth of who He is to you—right now.

In what ways can you apply those attributes to fulfill God's promises to someone else today? Find someone to serve, through the promises of who God is making you to be.

EVENING

Father, at the end of this day, I pause to say thank You. Where I missed opportunities, I confess my wrongs and rest in Your grace. Where I yielded to You and You worked through me to serve others, I give You glory. Thank You, Lord. I love You. Amen.

PETE HIXSON, MABLETON, GA

Jesus, thank You for this new day. Today I can choose to allow You to work through me by the power of Your Spirit. I can also choose to retreat back to my flesh. Where my desires are wrong, please change me, and where my flesh is weak, please help me. I love You and thank You for Your grace today—not just in salvation but also in every moment. It's all because of Jesus that I am alive, and it's in Your Spirit that I find true life, so I start my day yielding to You. Amen.

"But the fruit of the Spirit is love, joy, peace, longsuffering, kindness, goodness, faithfulness, gentleness, self-control. Against such there is no law."
GALATIANS 5:22, 23

I was on a mission trip in Honduras, and we were hiking in the mountains for several days. We ate only what we could carry, and most of it was pretty bland and not that good (to this day, I can't stand to even look at Vienna sausages!). We drank only what we were able to filter and fit in our water bottles. But I remember coming upon some trees, and our missionary guide picked some red bananas and we ate them. It was one of the most refreshing and satisfying things I have ever put in my mouth. But why was that? Right now, I can eat bananas all day long if I want to. It was because of the circumstances that we were in that made those bananas so memorable.

We live in a world that is broken, full of unexpected twists, and many times surrounded by days that seem bland, dry, barren, and very difficult. This scripture shows the potential I now have because of my relationship with Jesus—in contrast to my works done on my own in my flesh. It is the overflow of God's Spirit that can bless others. If I will surrender and yield myself to God's Spirit, I can serve others some fresh fruit—these characteristics of God's Spirit—during a time when they so desperately need it!

EVENING

Father, thank You for the opportunity today to give hope and life and enjoyment and truth through the refreshment of Your Spirit in me. May I rest in You and allow You to fill me to be used again. Amen.

MORNING

Lord, today is a new day, and my eyes may be a little sleepy and not quite awake yet physically. However, I ask You to open the eyes of my heart to understand what You are about to tell me regarding who I am in You. Amen.

"The eyes of your understanding being enlightened; that you may know what is the hope of His calling, what are the riches of the glory of His inheritance in the saints."
EPHESIANS 1:18

Have you ever been "enlightened" by something? It may be something you were somewhat familiar with, but then you had that "aha" moment, and it became clear to you. Or maybe it was something you had never even heard of, and you wondered what you ever did before knowing that tidbit of information.

Unfortunately, I believe that many new believers are bombarded with things they are supposed to *do* for Christ before they are ever told who they *are* in Christ. We have such an inheritance in Christ through His forgiveness that covers my past, present, and future. As sons and daughters, we have full access to our heavenly Father in a *relationship* without religion, rules, or bondage. We are completely free and loved and redeemed and justified—and the list could go on and on.

If I don't know what my inheritance is, how will I know how to spend it, how much to spend, or when it will run out? I am convinced that without understanding all that we are in Christ, we will leave so much potential behind because we never understood who we are in Christ. As an overflow of our inheritance in Christ, we live our lives and have the blessing of serving others and pleasing God. I can give away my inheritance because I know that what I am serving out of will never run out!

EVENING

Father in heaven, thank You for this full day, for the opportunities that You presented to me, and for the lessons I learned both through victories and missed opportunities. I rest in Your grace tonight and anticipate another day tomorrow. Thank You that my inheritance in You never runs out! Amen.

PETE HIXSON, MABLETON, GA

Lord, thank You that You are truly Lord over all. You aren't Lord because I say so—You are Lord because You are! You are Lord over creation, time, people, nations, and over my life today. I choose to yield myself to You, and I thank You for who You already are to me today. Amen.

"Both riches and honor come from You, and You reign over all. In Your hand is power and might; in Your hand it is to make great and to give strength to all."

1 CHRONICLES 29:12

I remember watching certain TV shows as a kid such as "Silver Spoons" and looking at what other kids had and wishing I had those things (especially that race car bed that he had!). As an adult I am still drawn to desire certain "things" that appeal to me. We all know that large amounts or even just a little more money or more "things" will not make us any happier. And a good question could be, "What are true riches anyway?" This scripture is very clear that God is in control and that everything comes through His hand.

Take a moment and read this scripture out loud, and when it comes to the word "You" or "Your," give it extra emphasis and say it a little louder and with confidence.

What did that make you aware of, and how did that make you feel? Ask God to reveal to you where you have been placing your trust or your desires for "things" above your desire for Him alone. Thank Him for His grace, and make a conscious decision to trust in His hand, power, and might for your riches, honor, and strength today. Now think about a way you can display God and this truth about Him to others today through serving them.

EVENING

Jesus, I am so grateful for all You have done. I worship You because of who You are and for all You have done, are doing, and will do. You are Lord of all and because of that, I can rest knowing You love me, desire what is best for me, and have a plan for my life. Thank You for the opportunities of this day, and now I rest in Your grace as You bring this day to a close. Amen.

Father, today I rest and trust in the promises of Your patience and love once again. I pray that as I go through this day that I will remember all that You have done for me and blessed me with. And God, give me strength through Your Sprit and allow Your patience to overflow out of me onto the lives of others. Amen.

"For when God made a promise to Abraham, because He could swear by no one greater, He swore by Himself, saying, 'Surely blessing I will bless you, and multiplying I will multiply you.' And so, after he had patiently endured, he obtained the promise."
HEBREWS 6:13–15

My kids crack me up when we are traveling and they say the age-old phrase that we all have probably said at some point in our life: "Are we there yet?" Life is a journey, and I am not so sure that God's desire for us isn't more about the journey than the destination—unless you consider that the destination, heaven, is really an ongoing relationship with our heavenly Father.

Along the way in our earthly journey, we have ups and downs and times where we seem to be able to see more clearly or understand a little better than at other times. It's during the times of waiting that we can easily become distracted and discouraged, and the temptation to give up on certain promises or truths about God seems stronger.

I remember what someone said one time: "Remember in the dark what God told you in the light." What we can know about God is this: He is truth and what He says will come to fruition. When He promised Abraham this blessing, He wasn't thinking "maybe"—God always keeps His word.

What is it in your life today that you have been waiting for that you know God has promised and backs up in His Word, but it has not happened yet? If you need to resurrender to His promise, do that now, talk to Him, trust Him, and then wait for Him to fulfill what He has said to you.

EVENING

Lord Jesus, thank You for this amazing day and week. As I rest physically tonight, may I rest completely in You. Thank You for all the promises You have already fulfilled! Amen.

PETE HIXSON, MABLETON, GA

Lord, as I prepare for the week ahead, I ask that You walk before me and show me the path You have provided for me. Guide me into the situations and circumstances that You want me to experience. And direct me to the people in my life who You want me to reach for Your glory. Through Christ I pray, Amen.

"I will bless the LORD who has given me counsel; my heart also instructs me in the night seasons. I have set the LORD always before me; because He is at my right hand I shall not be moved."

PSALM 16:7, 8

Talk to the president or CEO of any company, and they will tell you that having a dependable and trusted board of directors is vital. Great leaders and decision makers know they don't know everything, so they surround themselves with the right people.

The same is true in our lives. We need to have people around us we can trust to help us make the right decisions. Too many of us, though, have the uncanny ability to ask the wrong people the wrong questions; and as a result we make the wrong decisions and do the wrong things.

Instead of falling into that trap, surround yourself with people who will help you successfully navigate the maze of life. Make sure they have a strong connection with God. And find people who will energize you and motivate you to make the right decisions.

Once you have a strong group around you, don't ignore their advice. Actually use your personal board of directors in your decision-making process. Understand that they are the people God has placed around you to guide you toward the right answers. And listen to the direction they provide to help you experience the most out of life.

EVENING

Dear God, I know that You don't intend for me to go through life flying solo. You have placed people in my life to help me make the most out of every decision. I thank You for bringing people into my life to point me toward You and Your will for my life. Help me continue to keep a strong board of directors. In Jesus' name, Amen.

MORNING

Dear Lord, as I look ahead to today, I thank You for providing me with opportunities to bring hope to the lives of those around me. I pray that You will show me someone who needs to hear Your words of encouragement and hope. And I look forward to all that You are going to do in and through me to reach them for You. Through Jesus Christ I pray, Amen.

"Happy is he who has the God of Jacob for his help, whose hope is in the Lord his God."
PSALM 146:5

As Christians, we have opportunities every day to show the world the hope we have in God. It's a concept that, for many, can be difficult to accept. After all, the argument goes, if God is good, why can life be so difficult at times?

Most of us have faced those tough times in life. Yet, through it all, God remains faithful. And His purpose for our lives always comes through in the end, no matter what we face. We don't usually like to talk about the difficult times in our lives. But they happen. The good news is that God can use those circumstances to produce hope—hope in Him and Him alone. It sounds ironic, but it's true.

You may have faced a dark time in your past. But don't sweep it under the rug. Instead, allow that story to shine light on the fact that God is in control. Allow it to bring encouragement to someone who is facing a difficult situation right now. And show that person that God is the only One who can provide us with hope and ultimately lead us to triumph.

EVENING

Dear Lord, I thank You for bringing me out of my past circumstances and showing me Your faithfulness and unconditional love, no matter what I faced. I ask You to show me someone who needs to hear my story of hope. Please give me the courage to share those difficult moments in my life so that You might bring hope to someone else in crisis. In Christ's name I pray, Amen.

ED YOUNG, GRAPEVINE, TX

Week 51, Wednesday

MORNING

Dear God, I know that You walked through the cosmos to bring me not only a sense of love and security but also a joy that transcends feelings. And I thank You for loving me enough to sacrifice Your only Son so that I can have a relationship with You. Help me today to glorify You through all I do, say, and feel. It is through Jesus I pray, Amen.

"And my soul shall be joyful in the LORD; it shall rejoice in His salvation."
PSALM 35:9

Life is a journey that is full of twists and turns, ups and downs. It's cliché to say that life is a roller coaster. But it's true. And while some of those hills and curves we face are small and insignificant, others have huge implications. And so often, as we face those big moments in life, we can base our actions on the feelings of the moment—anger, hurt, love, fear, anxiety, happiness, jealousy, competitiveness—rather than God's truth and the joy that He provides through His salvation. When we do that, though, we find ourselves drifting from the track God has set before us.

Fortunately, there's another option. Rather than drifting aimlessly through life, we can connect to God through a relationship with Jesus Christ. That doesn't mean we will live free from trouble or difficulty. We will still experience all that life has to offer—good and bad. The good news is that we will experience the peace and joy that only God can provide, rather than riding the ebb and flow of our feelings.

As you face the distractions and decisions in your life, don't place your trust in your feelings. Instead, trust in your relationship with God. Ask Him for guidance and peace. And discover the true protection and guidance that come from a life connected to Him.

EVENING

Heavenly Father, thank You for the opportunity to be connected to You through a relationship with Jesus Christ. Help me to place my trust in You rather than my emotions and feelings. And continue to guide me as I face the obstacles of life. In Jesus' name, Amen.

MORNING

Dear Lord, this morning I thank You for Your presence in my life. I thank You for the fact that You are here with me and that You help guide me every day and in every situation. I ask, God, that You continue to point me down the right path in life and that You allow me the privilege of showing others what it truly means to know You. In Jesus' name I pray, Amen.

"The LORD your God in your midst, the Mighty One, will save; He will rejoice over you with gladness, He will quiet you with His love, He will rejoice over you with singing."
ZEPHANIAH 3:17

Becoming a Christian is the greatest decision anyone can ever make. When we accept Christ, our eternity is secure. That very literally means forever. But forever is a difficult concept to understand. It goes beyond our full comprehension, yet it's a reality.

There's another reality of becoming a Christian that many people have difficulty understanding as well. It's not as vast as forever, not as mind-blowing as eternity. However, it's just as real and just as available.

When we establish a relationship with Christ, He not only secures our forever, but He also provides us with the power and strength to get the most out of today. As today's verse says, He is in our midst. That means in every situation we face, in every victory we have, in every trial we endure, Christ is there with us. And because we have a relationship with Him, we can experience the rejoicing and gladness He provides us through His love—not only in heaven, but also here on earth.

Have faith that God is with you every step of the way through your life. Turn to Him each day. And discover the joy and strength that come with His love.

EVENING

Dear God, as I reflect back on today, I thank You for what You have done through me. I look with anticipation to what You are going to do tomorrow. And I wait expectantly for what You will do in the future. Help me, God, to continue to glorify You and to reflect the true power of Your love in my life so that others may see it and believe. It is through Christ that I pray, Amen.

ED YOUNG, GRAPEVINE, TX

Dear God, I pray that today You would help me to find a way to serve others. So many times it is easy to look at others and assume that they are here to serve me. I ask now that You will open my eyes to the opportunities to put aside that selfish thought and instead begin to look at life through Your perspective. In Christ's name I pray, Amen.

"And He sat down, called the twelve, and said to them,
'If anyone desires to be first, he shall be last of all and servant of all.'"
MARK 9:35

The service industry brings in billions of dollars each year in sales because people love to be waited on hand and foot. But this idea of being served didn't start with the hospitality industry.

Jesus' disciples thought they were going to get a taste of the good life. After all, they were hanging out with the Savior of the world. They kept waiting for Jesus to establish an earthly kingdom, and they tried to position themselves to be His right hand men; but they didn't understand Jesus' purpose on earth.

Jesus came to earth to serve. He traveled from town to town spreading God's life-changing message, healing those in need, confronting the oppressive religious leaders of the day, and ultimately, giving His life as the perfect sacrifice. Jesus showed the disciples what it meant to serve, but they missed it. They were so fixed on their agenda for Jesus that they couldn't see His agenda.

Serving is a litmus test for the Christian life. Do you find yourself in the same boat as the disciples, expecting to be served rather than to serve? If so, you're missing out on all that God has for you. Take your cue from Jesus—serve someone else and discover just what it means to live life to the fullest.

EVENING

Dear God, thank You for leaving Your comfortable place in heaven to serve us here on earth. Because of Your example, I know what it truly means to follow You. I pray that You will continue to teach me how to serve others so that I can experience the full life that You have designed for me. In Jesus' name, Amen.

Dear Lord, every day that I wake up, I know I have a new opportunity to make a difference for You. I ask right now that You provide me with the strength and knowledge to make that difference today. Show me what You want me to learn, and guide me to where You want me to go. It is through Jesus that I pray, Amen.

"For the LORD is righteous, He loves righteousness;
His countenance beholds the upright."

PSALM 11:7

It is amazing how far we can carry a reputation. The girl who dropped her lunch tray in elementary school can carry that reputation through high school. The popular high school jock can carry that notoriety into his career. The overly driven executive can carry that stigma into her relationships. The list goes on and on.

In this verse, God is described as righteous. In other words, He has a perfect reputation. So when we read that He loves righteousness, it may seem like we're up a creek because we don't fit the bill. We've all fallen short of God's standard of perfection. We've all sinned. And it's a reputation that can carry through eternity. But God did something to fix that. And when we welcome Christ into our lives, we gain a new reputation—a reputation of perfection.

What are you known for? Remember, the decisions you make will determine your reputation. And it's a reputation you will carry with you for the rest of your life and beyond. You aren't known for what you would like to have done or how you should have acted. You're known for what you do choose. Don't miss the opportunities to follow Jesus' lead in life and be known as righteous in the eyes of God.

EVENING

Lord, I know that I can be known for so many things. But what I want to be known for is following You. Help me as I go through life to continue turning to Your Son for my direction. Help me to follow Your path for each decision I make and every situation I face, for it is only through You that I can gain a reputation of righteousness and experience the most out of the life You have given to me. In Christ's name I pray, Amen.

Week 52, Monday

God, this morning I begin the last week of this journey. I thank You for all that You have taught me thus far. Thank You for Your patience. I want to know and serve You well. Speak to me through Your Word this week. Give me the courage to face my fears and put Your truths into practice. Open up new doors of opportunity. I don't want to miss out on anything that You have for me. I'm ready to listen, to learn, and to follow You. In Jesus' name, Amen.

"Say to the righteous that it shall be well with them,
for they shall eat the fruit of their doings."
ISAIAH 3:10

You've heard it said, "You reap what you sow." This farming principle means you get out what you put in. The phrase comes from biblical teachings found in both the Old and New Testament writings. It's similar to the popular gym phrase, "No pain, no gain." Whether you devote to the workout plan or choose to cheat, your physical appearance and stamina will reveal your choice. And every time you decide to do the hard thing, you are making an investment that builds toward results.

What's true of physical exercise is also true with spiritual disciplines like serving. More than just an investment in a physical body, sowing good seed in service to others is an investment in eternity. So keep paying the price. Keep doing the right thing, even when the results aren't immediate. Day by day, decision by decision, choose to sow good seed. Stay faithful. Payday is coming when you'll eat the fruit of your labor.

EVENING

Father, open my eyes to opportunities to serve You and to serve others. Help me to focus on Your will and not my own selfishness. I tire easily. I get discouraged when I compare myself to others. I need to look to You as my example and my reward. I need Your grace and strength as I look to serve You in the coming year. I pray my heart will be surrendered to You and Your purpose for me. Give me the courage and strength to stay faithful to Your call. In Jesus' name, Amen.

MORNING

Good morning, Lord! You made this day with all its promise and beauty. I thank You for all of the opportunities before me today, both at home and at work. I know I was created to love You and to serve You. Speak to me this morning as I read Your Word and meditate on Your truth. Grow me to be more like You. May my service be a blessing to You and to those in my sphere of influence. May You find me faithful serving You, my Savior. Amen.

"For you, brethren, have been called to liberty; only do not use liberty as an opportunity for the flesh, but through love serve one another."
GALATIANS 5:13

Everything a servant does is done with someone else in mind. Servanthood is a continual process of laying down one's own agenda. Eventually, selfishness can override the best of the servant's heart and express itself in the most unusual ways. Sometimes selfishness is displayed in pride related to Christian liberty. As a recovering legalist, I'm familiar with judging the freedom of others. But as I've learned the grace of God and the liberty found in Him, I've also had to realize I can be legalistic with my own liberties. Just because we are free to do something does not mean we should do it, and certainly not if it causes another believer to stumble. Any time my liberty in Christ is displayed without the consideration of others, it can be selfishness and sin.

Christian liberty is not a license to act on those liberties to the detriment of weaker believers. In fact, the grace of God demands more, not less. We are not called to defend our liberty; we are to love loudly in service to others.

EVENING

You've set me free from the bondage of sin and legalism. Thank You for the liberty that is found in You. Help me not be legalistic in my liberties. Help me to focus on my relationship with You, not the religion of religious liberty! Forgive me when I've displayed my freedoms in the flesh. Forgive me when my liberty has caused another believer to stumble. Help me to reflect Your grace and Your glory. Teach me to serve with the motivation of love. Thank You for loving me and allowing me to serve You. Amen.

RICHARD MARK LEE, SUGAR HILL, GA

Week 52, Wednesday

Lord, this morning I confess I need You. I can't do this on my own. I need Your strength. There are times I want to quit, give up, or start over with a different environment. Some people call it burnout, but it's just my inclination to run and escape. Thank You for Your faithfulness to me when I want something new. Thank You for Your love for me when I'm not lovely. Thank You for being my Coach and Guide. You are my everything. Today, I open my heart and life to You. Amen.

"My flesh and my heart fail; but God is the strength of my heart and my portion forever."
PSALM 73:26

Serving others can be wearisome. The hurting people you are trying to help often slash out and try to hurt you! People sit on the sidelines and critique and criticize your service. These critics can wear you out with their accusations and suggestions for improvement without ever offering to be a part of the solution.

The Enemy tries to feed us plenty of reasons to give up, to quit trying and stop sacrificing. As a result, servants can sometimes have pity parties. But those moments of pouting come when we are focused on the present instead of the future, when we are focused more on what our critics have to say than what Christ says. We don't answer to our critics, we answer to Christ, our Savior. We all have a date with death in this life. There is more than what this life offers. Eternity is forever. Eternity matters. What we do today impacts eternity.

God is the strength of our heart to help us overcome our own selfishness. His power enables us to impact eternity. He is our Rock when we are unstable. He is our Provider when we have nothing else to give. He is always enough!

EVENING

God, You are my strength and my life. I don't want to be another casualty report for the Enemy to have victory. I long to be used by You for Your glory and Your renown. I'm not giving up. I'm looking ahead because of You. Help me to remember Your sacrificial service and to follow Your example. I lean on You for strength to press on for the fulfillment of Your purposes in my life. In Jesus' name, Amen.

MORNING

Lord, the year is almost over. I've endured some challenges, a few heartaches, and a little grief. I've celebrated some great victories, too. Today, reveal to me what Your goals and dreams are for my life as I look ahead. I need Your help to know the difference between what is good and what is best. Help me to sort it all out. As I consider the days to come, may I walk in step with Your will as a faithful servant. In Christ' name, Amen.

"He has shown you, O man, what is good; and what does the LORD require of you but to do justly, to love mercy, and to walk humbly with your God?"
MICAH 6:8

A servant looks for opportunities to meet a need. A servant does the right thing, regardless of recognition or reward. Consistent acts of love, regardless of the cost, reflect true servanthood. To display such love requires both mercy and humility. Mercy enables us to see needs, to look at others through love's eyes. Seeing others with mercy helps us to see beyond the surface of outward actions or appearances and to the true need lying beneath the surface.

In the biblical text, justice and mercy have the same root effect—seeing the need. Humility is the attitude necessary to meet the need. Humility gives us the grace to lay down our agenda and to give up our own time and resources and plans to reach out to others in love and meet needs.

Good intentions are not enough. Christian service put simply is this: do justice, love mercy, and walk humbly with God! It's love in action—seeing needs and meeting those needs out of the overflow of our relationship with God.

EVENING

God, this may be the hardest lesson for me to learn. I can't do this apart from You. Teach me to be more merciful. I want to see the needs You set before me as opportunities to serve You. Give me the grace to meet those needs as Your servant. I pray I would be more about You than about me. I want my agenda to yield completely to Your agenda. Show me the needs of others, and give me the strength to meet those needs in Your name. Amen.

God, there are times I'm uncertain if I should continue serving in the capacity I am. I need clarity. Grow me through the dry spells. Give me renewed vision for my future. I want to be in the center of Your will. Today, I'm listening to that still, small voice of Your Spirit to lead me. Amen.

"As I was with Moses, so I will be with you. I will not leave you nor forsake you."
JOSHUA 1:5B

L eadership is lonely. Many are surprised to find that serving others can yield times of intense loneliness. But the good news is that God never abandons us. We can serve with greater effectiveness, knowing He is with us.

I work out at a gym twice a week with a trainer. When I began, my intent was to learn from the trainer and later drop him to save some money! I soon learned that when I worked out without the trainer I was not as effective. I performed fewer reps, displayed poor form, and experienced an overall diminished workout. However, I noticed when the trainer is present, my form is better, my reps increase, and the benefit of the exercise is exponential.

My trainer is paid to be present. God, however, stays with us and never leaves us. He doesn't abandon us because He's busy with other things or more important people. He doesn't forget an appointment. He is our Comforter, Teacher, Encourager, and Strength. He is present with us . . . all the time. So when we are serving Him, He notices. He cares and serves as our example. We find renewed strength, knowing He is with us.

When people let you down or take you for granted, remember God has promised to be with you. He is always there cheering for you!

EVENING

Today, I've been reminded of Your constant presence. I confess there are times when I can't feel You, but I walk by faith in the light of Your truth. I need You. I need to know You are there. I need to know You love me and You are cheering for me. Thank You for the fact You are just as available to me as You were to Moses. Thank You for not abandoning me. Thanks for Your guidance, comfort, and strength. I can press on because of You! Amen.

MORNING

Today, I close a chapter of my life as this year comes to a close. You've granted me mercy and strength, for which I thank You. The greatest blessing of my life is You, Lord. To say thank You seems so trite, and yet it is all I have to say and all I have to give. Open my eyes to truth, and give me courage to follow You faithfully. I desperately want Your best and not a cheap substitute. Give me the grace to see You at work today. In Jesus' name, Amen.

"No longer do I call you servants, for a servant does not know what his master is doing; but I have called you friends, for all things that I heard from My Father I have made known to you."

JOHN 15:15

There is a big difference between a servant and a friend. A servant does what the master says when the master says, out of duty. A servant is not entitled to inside information or blessings from the master. Friends, however, share a relationship. Instead of a one-sided interaction of obligation, friendship is based on sharing and blessing. Friendship is founded on love, not duty.

Jesus said we are no longer called servants, but friends! Yes, we are servants of God by choice, but our service to Him is out of an expression of our love for Him. We have a relationship with Him. We are connected to the Father through Jesus. He loves us, listens to us, and knows our needs. Because Jesus is the Master and He has called us friends, we can continue to serve in spite of any obstacle or hindrance. His love and friendship give us all the inspiration we need to willingly serve others in His name.

EVENING

I wrap up this year thanking You, God, for everything You have taught me. This year has been challenging, fun, fearful, and rewarding. Thank You for calling me Your friend. I don't deserve the blessings You've given me, but I gladly receive them. Tonight, I offer them back to You as my service to You. Tomorrow begins a new chapter, a new year, and new opportunities to serve others in Your name as I serve You, my Lord, my Savior, and my God. May You find me faithful as Your servant. Amen.

RICHARD MARK LEE, SUGAR HILL, GA

Bibliography

[1]Aiken, Daniel. *Five Who Changed the World*. Wake Forest, NC: Southeastern Baptist Theological Seminary, 2008.

[2]Dawson, Will. "Josh Hamilton: The Baseball Star's Rise to Recovery." September 19, 2007. http://www.cbn.com/700club/features/amazing/Josh_Hamilton091907.aspx.

[3]Wallington, David. *The Secret Room: The Story of Corrie ten Boom*. http://www.soon.org.uk/true_stories/holocaust.htm

[4]Wirt, Sherwood E., Jesus, *Man of Joy*. Nashville: Thomas Nelson, Inc., 1993.

Contributors

TIM ANDERSON	Clements Baptist; Athens, AL	Week 23
TREVOR BARTON	Hawk Creek Baptist; London, KY	Week 33
KIE BOWMAN	Hyde Park Baptist; Austin, TX	Week 36
MAC BRUNSON	First Baptist Church; Jacksonville, FL	Week 34
EDDIE CARSWELL	New Song Ministries; Woodstock, GA	Week 39
MICHAEL CLOER	Englewood Baptist; Rocky Mount, NC	Week 12
JEFF CROOK	Blackshear Place; Flowery Branch, GA	Week 14
ADAM DOOLEY	Red Bank Baptist; Chattanooga, TN	Week 9
TIM DOWDY	Eagle's Landing Baptist; McDonough, GA	Week 32
GRANT ETHRIDGE	Liberty Baptist Church; Hampton, VA	Week 24
STEVE FLOCKHART	New Season Church; Hiram, GA	Week 16
RONNIE FLOYD	First Baptist Church; Springdale, AR	Week 26
DANNY FORSHEE	First Baptist Church; Lavaca, AR	Week 4
AL GILBERT	Calvary Baptist Church; Winston Salem, NC	Week 6
MIKE HAMLET	First Baptist N. Spartanburg; Spartanburg, SC	Week 20
JUNIOR HILL	Evangelist; Hartselle, AL	Week 15
PETE HIXSON	Vinings Lake Church; Mableton, GA	Week 50
JOHNNY HUNT	First Baptist Church; Woodstock, GA	Week 1
BUCKY KENNEDY	First Baptist Church; Vidalia, GA	Week 30
RICHARD MARK LEE	First Baptist Church; Sugar Hill, GA	Week 52
MICHAEL LEWIS	First Baptist Church; Plant City, FL	Week 7
ED LITTON	First Baptist Church; North Mobile, AL	Week 29
DANNY LOVETT	Temple Baptist Seminary; Chattanooga, TN	Week 3
CHARLES LOWERY	Evangelist; Lindale, TX	Week 5
FRED LOWERY	First Baptist Church; Bossier City, LA	Week 2
DUSTY MCLEMORE	Lindsay Lane Baptist; Athens, AL	Week 25
JAMES MERRITT	Cross Pointe Church; Duluth, GA	Week 21
MIKE ORR	First Baptist Church; Chipley, FL	Week 22
BOB PERRY	First Baptist Church; The Villages, FL	Week 49

BOB PITMAN	Evangelist; Muscle Shoals, AL	Week 28
VANCE PITMAN	Hope Baptist Church; Las Vegas, NV	Week 38
PAUL PURVIS	First Baptist Church; Forsyth, MO	Week 17
PHIL ROBERTS	Midwestern Seminary; Kansas City, MO	Week 8
JEFF SCHREVE	First Baptist Church; Texarkana, TX	Week 46
DAN SPENCER	First Baptist Church; Thomasville, GA	Week 40
ROGER SPRADLIN	Valley Baptist Church; Bakersfield, CA	Week 37
ALLAN TAYLOR	Minister of Education; Woodstock, GA	Week 18
ARDEN TAYLOR	Tri-Cities Baptist; Gray, TN	Week 10
ERIC THOMAS	First Baptist Church; Norfolk, VA	Week 41
KEITH THOMAS	Cottage Hill Baptist; Mobile, AL	Week 31
TED TRAYLOR	Olive Baptist Church; Pensacola, FL	Week 35
BRAD WHITE	LifePoint Church; Tampa, FL	Week 47
RICK WHITE	The People's Church; Franklin, TN	Week 48
MIKE WHITSON	First Baptist Church; Indian Trail, NC	Week 43
KEN WHITTEN	Idlewild Baptist Church; Lutz, FL	Week 27
HAYES WICKER	First Baptist Church; Naples, FL	Week 19
DON WILTON	First Baptist Church; Spartanburg, SC	Week 11
RUSTY WOMACK	Rehoboth Baptist; Tucker, GA	Week 44
LARRY WYNN	Hebron Baptist Church; Dacula, GA	Week 13
SCOTT YIRKA	Hibernia Baptist; Orange Park, FL	Week 42
ED YOUNG	Fellowship Church; Grapevine, TX	Week 51
ROB ZINN	Immanuel; Highland, CA	Week 45

Scripture Index

One Year Devotional Prayer Book

SCRIPTURE	WEEK/DAY	PAGE

Personal Prayer Notes